THE
HARD PARTS

A Memoir of Courage and Triumph

Oksana Masters
with Cassidy Randall

scribner

new york   london   toronto   sydney   new delhi

Scribner
An Imprint of Simon & Schuster, Inc.
1230 Avenue of the Americas
New York, NY 10020

The names of certain persons have been changed.

First Scribner hardcover edition February 2023

SCRIBNER and design are registered trademarks of The Gale Group, Inc., used under license by Simon & Schuster, Inc., the publisher of this work.

For information about special discounts for bulk purchases, please contact Simon & Schuster Special Sales at 1-866-506-1949 or business@simonandschuster.com.

The Simon & Schuster Speakers Bureau can bring authors to your live event. For more information or to book an event, contact the Simon & Schuster Speakers Bureau at 1-866-248-3049 or visit our website at www.simonspeakers.com.

Interior design by Davina Mock-Maniscalco

Manufactured in China

10 9 8 7 6 5 4 3 2 1

Library of Congress Cataloging-in-Publication Data has been applied for.

ISBN 978-1-9821-8550-3
ISBN 978-1-9821-8552-7 (ebook)

For my mom, whose love saved me.
Thank you for sacrificing it all
to give me the world and for opening every door for me.
You are my world and the beat of my heart.

I love you,
Your resilient rascal.

prologue

T his would be a four-to-eight-month recovery. For a *normal* person."

The doctor's proclamation hangs in the air for a silent moment in the harshly lit emergency room. But as I hunch on the hospital bed cradling my newly shattered elbow in my hand, with my two prosthetic legs dangling limp—devices that require two functioning arms to remove and attach to what remains of my real legs (*How am I going to do that with a broken elbow?*)—it's obvious that I'm not a *normal* person.

To my coach, who brought me here from the Bozeman blacktop where I slipped on black ice outside my favorite café, the doctor says:

"She can't race."

The pain in my elbow that's been searing every second with hurt blazes in a white-hot flash—and at the same time my entire body deflates. Something essential and fundamental exits my chest. *I can't race in the Games.* They're only three weeks away. How did this happen? I'm twenty-eight, and my entire life—past and future—hinges on this insane moment. Everything is on the line.

In Pyeongchang in three weeks, I will, for the first time since I discovered what my body could do athletically at thirteen years old, show up as the true athlete I've finally come to believe I am. This time, I won't have to live out of my car like I did before the Games in Sochi, trying to make my mom's finances—borrowed from her retirement fund—last just a little longer. This time, for the first time ever, I have real sponsors, big ones—Nike, Toyota, Visa, Procter & Gamble—who believe in me, too. I can begin to pay back my mother, pay all my debt. Ten years of Paralympic Games, and I've always come in second or third. Never first. But this time. This time I'm favored to sweep gold in every one of my events—to be the *first ever* to bring home a gold medal in cross-country skiing for USA.

Oh, God, I think. *I'll let everyone down. I'm going to lose it all.* I'm eating salt from the tears pouring down my face. Grief already claims my body in waves, filling up the space of what flew from my chest, which I now realize was hope.

Anyone else would have quit by now. This is probably a sign that I should have, too. Every part of my life before this has also been decided for me—why not this? My mind and my body were both already determined by others from the time I was born: what I was capable of doing or what was possible for me in the future. I was told I didn't deserve a mother, didn't deserve a family, didn't belong in this world. I'm just too different.

I've been told I'll never make it as an athlete—that it's an unrealistic, impossible goal, and that I'll only be let down ultimately. I've been shown over and over that I have no voice of my own—have no power.

Except on the start line.

The start line is always a fresh beginning. Nothing has been determined yet. When the clock starts and the red dot turns to green and the high-pitched beep sounds, I begin my new journey. In a race, I'm in control and I *am* control. How I react and adapt and pivot and *move*. That's all me. My strength. My power. My voice for every time I was told no, every time I was weak, every time I was pushed down. Every time I wasn't believed in, every time someone else thought they knew what was best for me.

Turning to me—finally the doctor addresses *me*—he says:

"It's not possible. If you race on that elbow, you'll never be able to use it again. This is where your road stops."

As if he knows anything about my road. Mine has never been a smooth one of clean blacktop and tidy lines. It's crooked gravel cratered in bomb holes and littered with mudslides and twisting U-turns. Was it really going to end here in a colossal explosion that blocks the way forward forever?

Maybe because of the heat consuming my arm, or because I'm hallucinating a little from pain, a vision of dancing flames appears in front of my eyes, superimposed over the doctor's face. I've always loved to get lost in the flames of a fire. At backyard firepits, I stare straight into the core of the blaze, beyond the orange and yellow and the light blue and white and then down past them to the logs, at the layers it takes to *create* that fire.

Before the flame there's wood. Before the wood there are twigs, and before those twigs are even smaller sticks and leaves. You see a huge, roaring, strong fire—but you don't see that it all started from a little tiny twig and a few leaves: things so small, fragile, breakable. And the logs on top of them. When you really look, you see the lines, the age of the tree those logs came from and what that tree must have weathered and been through.

Underneath the flaming vision flashes the trajectory of what I've been through—my experience in Ukraine, coming to America, what I've seen, what I've lost, what I've gained, what I've felt. It all sparked from when I was the weakest. The smallest. The frailest. When I believed I had no value to bring. It sparked from my core, with layer upon layer upon layer creating a fire that grows stronger and stronger while the flame burns longer and higher.

And I think, there on that bed with my broken body and full of my own salt and smoke, *I am so tired of other people determining what I'm capable of.*

I.

I will decide what is possible.

part

one

chapter

one

B^{*link.*} The room is so hot and steamy and close, like a womb. The astringent, cloying smell of heated chlorine hangs in the air. I float in the hot water, blowing bubbles in it, pretending to be a sea animal. The chemicals leave my lips tingly, and I almost forget that my body hurts from whatever the latest surgery was. A woman helps me float, her hand spanning my tiny belly, her short dark hair glowing in the dim room, maybe burnished from candlelight. I can't remember what lit the chamber's darkness, but I see clearly her round face, that hair, her dark features. She's always here in this hot room, in this perfectly square pool, helping me after surgeries. She gently sets warmed glass balls on my back for some kind of therapy. She rubs my small back where the balls heat the skin. In that chlorine-musked sauna, I am happy and loved.

Maybe she's my mother. She's the only one who touches me, offers any affection. She must be. I'm so safe here.

Blink.

Down in the basement, I scrub socks against the washboard and wring them out. After I wash ten socks, the grimy old woman who's one of the laundry ladies produces a sugar cube and places it in my hand. I love sugar. But I'm also so, so hungry, and I'll wash all the socks in the world for another sugar cube. I've learned to make them last for hours. I break off individual sugar crystals with my tongue. That way, by taking so long to eat, I trick my body into feeling full. I reach for more socks and the laundry lady smiles. Maybe this woman is my mom.

Blink.

The woman with the long blond hair is visiting again. I don't know who she is or why she's here. But she's probably the one who is my mother.

Blink.

I come awake. This room is dim. This place is always dark and colorless, and once again I feel the gloom sucking all the vibrancy from everything and swallowing it whole. And it's cold here. I'm always cold, even though at night the old babushkas pile used clothes on us over the scratchy sheet and scratchy thin blanket. They tuck us in so tight, so roughly, without even looking at us, that I sometimes can't move all night from the same position on my back.

From my cot closest to the door, which the babushkas always lock from the outside, I raise my head and look around for Laney. She's in here with me somewhere. There's a row of beds against each wall, and two rows of beds, headboard to headboard, down the center of the room. Most are empty right now—fewer than ten of us are in this big room with thirty beds—but sometimes the room is fuller, with a slowly revolving door of kids coming and going. Laney's been here the whole time I have, though.

She's my best friend in this orphanage. It's the third one I've lived in already. This one doubles as a government-run boarding school serving a different group of kids. We're kept separate from them—the ones who get to go home to their families sometimes. And those in my group are all a little different, physically or mentally. Even though I don't really know that I'm *different*.

I do know sometimes that I don't walk like Laney or most of the other kids. My left leg is shorter than my right by six inches, and it arcs in a C-shape. I have six toes on each foot—a fact that I'm quite proud of—and my feet are different sizes. My hands are different, too, each with five fingers instead of a thumb, and all webbed. I know I've had surgeries. I remember a little bit about them, and I've seen some Ukrainian words on the little cardboard card that comes with me from orphanage to orphanage that lists important things about me.

What I don't realize in my five-year-old awareness is that my legs don't stand straight because I'm missing the weight-bearing bones below my knees, which makes walking awkward and slow on the bones I do have in there. I was also born missing the enamel on my teeth, part of my stomach, my right biceps, and one kidney. The other kidney sits in the wrong spot in my body. At five, I don't grasp that my mother was exposed to the horrific amounts of radiation that settled on this part of Ukraine in the wake of the Chernobyl explosion—that I'm one of the countless children whose inheritance from the disaster is birth defects. Nor do I know the reasons my parents gave me up.

At five, I occasionally brood on looking different—when I can't do things the other kids can. But what weighs most heavily on me is that I don't have a family, and every time a woman is remotely kind to me, I wonder if she is my mother.

———

The old babushkas unlock the door. I sit up, and one takes my head roughly, spits in her hands—I hate this part—and pushes my hair down. My hair has been cut short to make looking for lice easier. I hate that, too. Laney has beautiful long blond hair. I don't know why they let her keep it. With her blue eyes and hair, she's lovely. Like a Ukrainian doll. My hair is black, and crinkly. And now it's covered in old-lady spit.

One of the bigger kids gives me a piggyback ride out of the bedroom—I'm the smallest one and I can't always keep up with the other kids because of my legs, and sometimes they're nice to me like that. I bounce on his back through the weird little sitting room with its old black-and-white TV, silent now, down the bleak long halls lined in radiators, all the way through this huge old building to the dining room. This is the only place we see those other kids. The ones with families. But we sit at our own table by the kitchen, away from them in this cavernous room studded in pillars lined with dark wood halfway up their height, then dusty gray above, like dead trees.

It's always so *loud* in here. There are so many of those other kids, more than a hundred, and there's the constant sound of chairs screeching across the cold off-white floor, which it seems like no one's cleaned in years. We all eat out of metal plates and bowls and drink out of metal cups, and the clanging of them echoes and amplifies. There's talking, whispering, snorts, guffaws, shouts. My body vibrates with all the noise.

My bowl holds a light reddish liquid. We either get bread or broth. Rarely both. Those other kids must have gotten both though, because I see someone chewing across the room, and I know there's nothing in front of me to chew. Maybe there's meat or potatoes in their broth. Or maybe they're just pretending. All I know for sure is that there's never enough for us to eat here in our corner, and I'm always hungry. Sometimes, I can think of nothing else.

After we eat, the caretakers herd us to the toilet room. I hate this part, too. It smells so awful in here, this oppressive little cubicle with makeshift toilets lined against the wall, one right next to the other. We're told to sit, all together where we could turn and look each other in the eyes if we wanted, but instead we just put our heads down while they strap us in. They don't let us up until we've gone, and we won't get another chance until they tell us it's time. And so we all force ourselves to go.

After that, we go to school. We only go for a little while, an hour or two maybe. We troop outside, past the rusting playground, to a smaller fenced-off brick building, where it seems like we spend most of the time being yelled at or having our names written down on the dusty chalkboard. Sometimes we don't go to school at all. Mostly, we just sit in the little room outside the big bedroom and watch the TV that's always tuned to westerns, the French-made ones where the Indians always win, or we roam the echoing halls in packs or pairs while the caretakers ignore us—unless we're bad—and stand around smoking in doorways. I avoid the stairs that lead up from the sitting room though, up through a closed door at the top to the windowless individual rooms on the second floor. I don't even look at those stairs.

Tonight, after the old women have confined us in the too-thin blankets and tossed clothes on us, I struggle free as I do some nights and walk a few steps to the locked bedroom door. It has a skeleton-key hole big enough to look through. I can see a key-shaped view of the common room: the edge of the fringe on the dirty rug, part of the couch, and the arm and big belly of the man who is always out there at night, smoking and watching the TV, which I can't quite see through the hole. He's never there during the day. But he's always there at night.

Even though I'm only five, I know that I don't want to be in that uncomfortable little cot I just escaped from. I want to be watching TV. And this is the only time when *I* get to be in charge of what I do. So I sit down on the cold floor and listen to the show the man is watching, watch its light come through the crack in the door. A few other kids rustle free of their prison covers and come over, too. We sit there shivering, watching the light dancing under the door from scenes changing on the television, shades of gray and flashes of brilliant bright white edging out the heavy night closing in behind us.

———————

Blink.

The woman with light-colored hair—the one who picks me up gently, with care, instead of like I'm an old book or something—gives me a pierogi on a little plate. My belly is already fuller than I can ever remember its being from the real borscht she gave me, but I won't say no to more food. I bite into it. It's filled with sweet cherries and I forget everything else—how sick I am, how sore I am, how hungry I just was (forever), even this amazing room that we're in.

It's dark outside her sheer shades, but it's warm and bright in here. Her TV is in color. It gaily jumps from scene to scene while I finish my pierogi. The space is small and cluttered with so many things, instead of empty like I'm used to.

I think this is her home. I think she brings me here when the others are too aggressive with me, to give me time to get better before I have to go back to the orphanage. But I don't know. I wish I could remember who she is or what she looks like besides her long light hair and her comfortable short body. I think, like always, that she's my mother, and that this is what *home* is and I never want to leave it.

Blink.

The wagon jostles ceaselessly. In the back of it, I'm so nauseous from the bumpy ride that I can't even watch the horses pulling it, so suffocated by feeling sick that it's hard to remember at all how much I like animals. I don't think I've ever ridden in a car or a bus, only these jarring wagons. But we're going to summer camp, a place of light and color, where they take all of us in the boarding school who are orphans while the other kids go *home*. Home. I dream about having one of those.

Blink.

Outside in the lovely afternoon, Laney and I pick daisies that are maybe weeds, but in my head they're enormous sunflowers. She shows me how to weave them together for a crown. I think she's older than me. She must be. She always knows what to say, how to react. Before we finish the crowns, she takes my hand, and we're off running through the yellow light to the fruit trees popping up all over this place where we spend the summer. Plums. Strawberries warm from sun. Laney eats a glowing strawberry first, and I know that it's okay for me to eat one, too. She's always protecting me like that.

She never shows me how to finish the flower crown.

Blink.

I'm bleeding. It won't stop. I can't walk because there's so much blood. I look down at the cage on my left leg, its concentric steel rings that push screws into bone gleaming dully in the gloom. I think they broke the bone first, then put the cage on, but I can't remember. I never look when they tighten the screws. They're trying to make my short leg longer, they told me. But something must have gone wrong this time because the bleeding won't stop.

Blink.

When I wake this morning under my too-tight covers at the boarding school orphanage, it's with the same idea as every other morning: *This is going to be a good day.* It's a new day, after all.

I think this every time.

This morning, things actually *are* different. In the dining hall, it's just us orphans. We get to sit in the center of the room where the other kids usually sit, away from the smelly kitchen. They give us bread *and* soup, with potatoes in it. I've learned by now that this means people are coming to look at us. That's why, instead of my usual ragtag tights and too-small-for-me shirt, I'm wearing one of the dresses that we all share. That's why, instead of just trying to protect my food and eat all of it before the bigger kids grab it, I'm trying to eat properly, like a good girl.

No one actually tells us what these mornings are about. But I've pieced it together, because once the people who come to look at us choose a kid to take into a separate room to go play with them—with the only toys we're allowed to play with; any other toys are kept on high shelves, just to be looked at like decorations—then we won't see that kid again because they've gone *home*, get to be part of a *family*, have a *mother*. I've learned to behave on these days, trying to be quiet and stay out of trouble, and I even try to look cute or adorable or whatever it is we're supposed to do to be chosen.

But I'm usually not picked. Instead, if it's another girl, sometimes the caretakers take my dress off me and put it on the chosen girl right there in the hallway. And then the other kids, some of the older ones who have been here longer, will say:

"How does it feel to be the one who's left?"

"You *still* have no parents."

"No one likes you."

Or sometimes we even hear it from the caretakers—the mean ones—or the other kids at the school.

"Of course no one wants you. *Look* at you."

I think I might have been close to being chosen once, though, in the orphanage before this one. My friend Julia and I were in the room together, I remember. She was younger than me, just a toddler, but I was smaller than she was. I remember us playing, and dancing, and I remember the American couple from a place called Colorado who came to choose her, and how they said, "We will adopt you, too." But when they came to take Julia *home*, they'd changed their minds about me. It was nothing new. I've heard this before. People who say, "We're going to be your new mom and dad." And then they don't come back for you. But this couple said:

"We promise we'll find a home for you. We'll send your picture to people in America who want to adopt, people we know will want a little girl just like you."

This morning I don't get chosen either.

I start to learn that it's easier to cope with anger than sadness and loneliness. I learn to hate the people who come by to choose children. I stop trying to be cute. I make myself stop caring so that I don't get attached to them or to the lie that they might come back for me one day.

Still, each time, through my anger and darkness, Laney finds me and gives me one of her hugs. She's the only one who hugs me, and she has a certain way of doing it. She puts both her hands on my shoulders, arms straight, to look into my face. Then she pulls herself in and wraps her arms around my neck, rests her chin on my shoulder. My whole body relaxes and everything finally stops moving for a moment. I feel so content and happy and calm. I think this must be what it feels like to *come home*.

chapter

two

The year that I was born, 1989, Gay Masters was teaching at the University of Illinois. A speech pathologist with a doctorate, she claims to have made few conscious decisions in her life.

Gay grew up in the far eastern suburbs of Cincinnati in a little town called Milford. But it was less "suburbs" and more "country," a wide-open place where the Masterses never locked their doors and their dog roamed freely. Its remoteness meant that by the time Gay graduated from high school, she'd only been on two dates, her romantic life stifled by protective parents who refused to let their sons drive shoulderless empty roads to pick her up—and those two dates, both at high school dances, were chaperoned by fathers who insisted on doing the driving themselves.

Her own father sold styrofoam, with squeaky foam products left all over the house. But he was unwaveringly honest (maybe a drawback in the cutthroat sales world), and when Gay was in second grade, he quit after his boss asked him to lie to customers. Faced with losing their house, Gay's mother took a job as a legal secretary, a job she kept after her husband reentered the sales business, this time in life insurance.

Gay applied to college—hoping to be a special-education teacher—because it seemed a natural extension of the college prep classes she took in high school. But her mother shot down her first choice, the University of Cincinnati, because of its proximity to home. Gay's mother understood that her daughter was a good girl, a people pleaser to the end, and that her capacity for self-sacrifice, combined with being the youngest sister to a more opinionated older sister and brother, foretold a certain destiny. If the script wasn't rewritten, Gay would be stuck taking care of her parents in their old age, never marrying, never living a life of her own. Gay's mother saw this clearly and vowed to not let it happen.

She worked with two women at the law firm who'd suffered that fate: stayed home, cared for ailing parents, and paid the bills and taxes on the family home. And when their parents died, the other siblings finally deigned to come home and said, "We're selling the house now, so kindly get out. And you won't get any of the money because, after all, you've been living here for free all your life." Those coworkers were the youngest siblings, too, Gay's mother knew, and Gay's siblings had it in them to do that to their little sister.

Gay attended Ohio Wesleyan University, which exactly met her mother's *minimum* distance requirement of two hours from home. It was the same university her brother had graduated from. She took speech-communications classes on his recommendation. Early in the last semester of her senior year, her adviser, whom her brother had also introduced her to, sat her down.

"So, where are you going to grad school?"

"I'm not going to grad school," Gay replied matter-of-factly. "My GMAT scores in psychology were too low."

"I don't mean for psychology. I mean for speech therapy. All the speech-therapy programs are switching to require master's degrees, so you'll need to go to grad school to work in the field."

Just like that, Gay found herself on that career path without remembering when she'd decided to take it.

In her early twenties, between all that schooling, she fell in love with a man from Guyana. They dated for several years before it emerged that he wouldn't be marrying her, let alone having children with her.

"I promised my father that I wouldn't marry a European," he told her on a day that was just like all the others except for this definitive-but-still-confusing declaration.

"But . . . I'm not European."

"You're white. That's a European."

"But . . . your brothers both married white women."

"That's why I promised my father."

She stated the obvious—that he could have told her this at any point in the last eight years—stayed with him another year or two, then gave up. Her mother did get the "never marry" part of the future right, she thought. But, unlike some women, Gay had never lost herself in dreams of marriage—never fantasized about big weddings and exactly how they'd go and what she'd wear. What she dreamed about was children, lots of them, and the question had always been less about marriage and more about whether she'd find a partner who'd entertain the idea of having twelve kids. It was one of the reasons she loved her profession so much: working with so many children. But by the time Gay split from the Guyanese man, she knew that if she wanted to be a mother, she'd likely need to pursue that dream on her own—thanks, again, to the circumstances.

In 1979, Gay's sister died from viral pneumonia. She'd been pregnant with her second child, leaving her first child, only eighteen months old, with the bereaved father. Gay's mother was never the same after. She contracted emphysema, lived on disability, and became so sick she was unable to leave the house for the last years of her life. She passed away in March of 1989, leaving Gay in the depths of grief. Less than three months later, in June, I was born half a world away.

By then Gay had moved, from where she'd finished her doctorate at the University of Buffalo, closer to home to teach at Illinois State University. She found herself locking horns with a chauvinist department chair who threatened, subtly, to thwart her efforts to secure tenure if she didn't perform perfectly and behave herself. He once patted her on the head and said, "Little girl, little girl. You're not in Buffalo anymore."

Gay was then thirty-five years old and considering what options remained for becoming a mother. As she raced against a ticking biological clock on a teacher's less-than-opulent salary, artificial insemination seemed the way to go. She tried calling a sperm bank to see about arrangements.

"Sure, come on in. But we're going to need your husband's permission for you to be inseminated."

She paused. "Let's rewind. I'm single. I don't have a partner. I don't have a husband. That's why I'd like to be inseminated."

"Yes, yes. We just need your husband's permission."

She tried a different sperm bank. But they only let her see the donor's full bio *after* the procedure. Turned out he had a temper, but that was of no consequence because the insemination didn't take. She spoke about her experience to some of her colleagues, including the woman in line to take Gay's classes should she misbehave, who told her:

"It's against the church, you know. It's a sin. If you're a single mom, your child will be a juvenile delinquent."

Gay rolled her eyes. And with that, she went back to Buffalo, where perhaps the world would be a little more progressive regarding aspiring single moms with a professional bent.

And so Gay was led down the next road—to adoption. But she knew that was a much more expensive choice than artificial insemination. To help with the exorbitant cost, Gay approached her father, who'd remarried, to a family friend, shortly after his wife's death. Gay knew her mother would have supported her decision wholeheartedly (albeit with some worry for Gay's inevitably harder path in single parenting). Gay hoped for the same from her father. She called him up.

"I'd like to adopt, Dad, but it's a lot of money. I've been thinking about it. The deal was that when we got married, we'd get ten thousand dollars for our wedding. I'm closer to forty than thirty now, and I don't think I'm ever going to get married. If I do, I won't ask you for anything. I'd like to use that ten thousand dollars to pay for adoption instead."

Without missing a beat he said, "You can't adopt. You can't be a mom. You can't even support yourself."

"I paid for all of my own college and grad school, except for six hundred dollars. I had scholarships and a job. And I've been supporting myself since."

"Don't you have credit card debt?"

Gay dropped the matter, angry and disappointed. She resigned herself to spending the next years saving whatever she could, putting off adoption until she finally had enough money to realize her dream—even if she was fifty by then. She began planning to pick up some private therapy work to augment her salary. Prior to this, she may have made few conscious decisions, but she was damn stubborn about the path she was now on.

One day not too long after, Gay received a letter in the mail. It was from her father. She opened it, and out fell a check, made out to her. The handwritten letter contained only four lines:

Here is the $10,000. I deposited enough to cover it yesterday. Please keep us posted on the progress. I love you.

Gay called her father's house. Her stepmom picked up.

"I told him he was being an ass," she told Gay, who was stunned. "And that if he didn't give you the money, I would. Out of my own savings."

Gay began, in earnest, to explore adoption avenues. She wanted an infant. She knew from her psychology background and her speech-pathology work that a child's first year is critical for emotional stability: developing trust and attachment. Understanding love. But her research made it clear that adopting a baby at birth in the United States wasn't only prohibitively expensive—$20,000 or more, so that even with the money her dad had given her, she'd still need to save for years—but subject to criteria she couldn't meet. The biological mothers of those children nearly exclusively look for two-parent households. Gay's road to motherhood was blocked. Again.

Until she received a call from a woman she'd worked with at an early-childhood-development center. Gay had developed a friendship with the woman, having shown an interest in the woman's own adoptions: she had two little girls, from Russia. And she was also a single mom.

"I have some kids I want you to look at," the friend said.

"You want me to do some work at the center again?"

"No. Just come by. I need you to pick up something."

On a Friday afternoon in mid-June 1995, Gay walked into the early-childhood-development center. The receptionist handed Gay a manila envelope with her name on it. Inside were pictures of two Ukrainian children printed from an adoption newsletter. One was a baby boy, only six months old. The other a little girl. A little girl photographed by a couple from Colorado.

The girl in the photo was far from a baby. She was at least four years old, even though she looked to be impossibly tiny. A small paragraph under the photo mentioned that she'd need surgeries, but was unclear on what or why, and Gay's glance skimmed over it anyway, pulled to the image itself. Pants covered the girl's legs. The too-long shirt buttoned at the throat had short sleeves, but the shape of her hands was lost to overexposure. She played with some sort of toy whose outlines had also blurred in the camera's flare. Even the fullness of her smile was reduced to lines of contrast. The only thing clear in the photo was the girl's eyes, which looked out from under a stark edge of bangs: arresting, dynamic, determined. Hopeful. Those eyes leaped from the page there on the reception desk, reached past Gay's chest, and touched her beating heart with a pure and clarion shock:

That's my daughter.

At that moment Gay Masters did something that, for her, was exceedingly rare: she made a conscious decision and vowed to keep it. She was going to adopt that little girl. Come hell or high water, she'd bring her home.

Over the weekend, as she consulted with friends, they told her to go for the boy. A child past toddler age from a foreign country? "You don't want to deal with that," said one friend. "Go for the boy. Go for the baby."

Gay called the adoption agency on Monday:

"I want Oksana."

The orphanage director approaches us where we sit in front of the TV. He looms over me and barks, "Oksana!"

I'm used to hearing my name called in angry tones. I seem to do something wrong every day. Everyone else is having fun, but I've broken something or crawled up the bookcase or who knows what. Sometimes *I'm* the angry one. Once I broke a window while the caretakers were watching. In that moment I just wanted to have some control.

The director is a big man, and he always brings this weird smell with him. Maybe it's the smell of *old man*. I never know what to expect with him. Sometimes he's kind. Other times he must think that extreme physical force is the only way to get through to me. As I peer up at him from the floor, he says, "Come with me. I want to show you something."

I follow his huge frame into his office, a room I'm in too often for getting in trouble. This room is the only one in this whole place with color: rugs decorating the walls, light pouring through windows. He sits behind his always-messy desk, opens a drawer, and pulls out a tiny square of paper that he places on the wood. He leaves his meaty hand pointedly on top of it.

He looks straight at me. "I have something to tell you. You're going to have a mom. An American woman is going to come and adopt you."

A mom. I almost forget to breathe. I know right then that this time is different. No one came around to look at all the kids first and pick one of us out. I didn't have to wear a dress. This time is so different that I can feel it right in the center of my belly: it must be real. I can't stop looking at his hand. *Well, what's under there? Is it her?*

"She's gonna try and come really, really soon. But you have to be a good girl. If you're bad anymore, I'm going to let her know. She doesn't want a bad girl." I'm nodding, mute, can't say anything, afraid to say anything. I don't smile. I don't want him to know that I'm excited. He could hold that over me somehow, I know.

"Do you want to see a picture of the person who's going to be your mom?"

I nod again, walk around to his side of the desk, where he finally lifts his palm to reveal a tiny image with a face looking out from it. She's wearing glasses above rosy cheeks and a smile, an honest smile, like all the light and color in the world magically captured in this inch-by-inch photo. She's kind. I can tell. It hits me again. This time is real. *That's her. This is going to happen.*

"But you have to be good." He rises from his chair. I'm still looking at the photo when he grabs me, turns me upside down by the legs, and spanks me while my head hangs and bobbles in midair. Just a light punishment, for something I must have done wrong this morning that I can't even remember right now. While he's striking my backside, he says, "If I have to do this one more time, I'll have to tell your mom."

He puts me down, and I hobble out of his office in a daze, barely registering my stinging skin.

The next day, the director finds me again. "Oksana." His tone is kind today. "If you're going to continue to be good, I can let you see your mom's picture each day until she comes. Each day that you're good."

I jump up. I will be so good today. And all the days. I have to be. Or she won't come.

This becomes my ritual: I ask the director, "Can I go look at her picture again? Can I go look at it just one more time?" I begin to forget to hide my excitement from him. Most times, he lets me go to his office, where he pulls out the photo. I study it religiously. It becomes a ceremony, a kind of urgent, necessary rite, to memorize it. I start my eyes at the top, on the deep mahogany waves of her short hair, mapping into my mind its exact shininess and the shape of the curls over her right eyebrow and her smooth forehead on the other side. I travel down to her deep hazel eyes, which look directly at me from a depth of gentleness—and to me, then, through the flat matte of the photo, love. I zoom out to the round shape of her rose-framed glasses, down the curves of her cheeks plump with a smile, through the crease mark on the photo that makes her actual smile appear quirkily crooked, all the way down to where her neck disappears into a pink shirt, so that I can remember the entirety of it. I want this image, her face, to be last thing I see when I close my eyes each night.

Inside the world of that photo, I start to create my life with my *mother.* Some of it is images I've seen on TV, of what a house in America is supposed to look like, what food and meals are supposed to be. Some of it I construct from my own blurred memories of what it feels like when a grown person hugs with affection, treats me like I matter. Most of it is just feelings: warm, full, safe, happy. *Home. Family. Love.*

I'm only five. But I know the rest of my life lives in that tiny square of matte paper.

The adoption agency explained to Gay the disabilities of the girl in the photo. They gave her the number of the couple in Colorado. The man was a physician and had shown the photos to his colleagues. Both legs would need to be amputated. Gay understood. And she didn't care. If anything, it made her move faster.

Gay did everything the adoption agency told her to, with breakneck speed. If she hurried, she could have her daughter home with her in Buffalo for her sixth birthday. By August, she'd finished all the steps, a veritable second dissertation of paperwork, this time on her qualifications to be a mother. She ordered a new birth certificate since her father was unable to produce hers. She compiled various documents on income, completed a home study. She translated, at her own expense, all the papers into Ukrainian, notarized them at the county level, then the state level, then sent the full dossier to Washington, DC, for another set of seals. The agency never helped her. They only told her if her papers were acceptable. Finally, her complete adoption dossier was sent off to the Ukrainian government.

Who said, *No. We're closed.*

Ukraine had placed a moratorium on adoptions of its orphans by foreigners. Gay's adoption agency promised that the moratorium would soon be lifted. *Any day,* they said. But there was also another way, they said. Because of the medical needs of the little girl in question, Gay could bring her daughter to the United States on a medical waiver. The catch, though, was that the girl would have to go back to Ukraine to be formally adopted once the moratorium was lifted—with no guarantee that the Ukrainian government would decide that Gay could have their Ukrainian orphan. Gay decided it was the worth the risk—it was better than this unknowable waiting—and told the agency to move forward with the medical waiver. But the agency dragged its feet, and nothing happened and nothing happened.

While she waited, Gay took language lessons once a week from a Ukrainian woman, Olga, she'd met at the university. Gay brought home tapes and flash cards to practice, to be able to communicate with her daughter. But it's a hard language. Try as she might, she only ever retained a small pool of words, and conjugation was hopeless. She was only able to speak in the infinitive.

In January of 1996, Ukraine finally lifted its moratorium on foreign adoptions. Gay rejoiced. But nothing happened and nothing happened. The Ukrainian government was still writing its rules and regulations for the procedure, resulting in endless bureaucracy and officialism and red tape.

"You know, we can move your paperwork to Russia," the adoption agency told her, a year into the fruitless process. "You could have a baby in two months."

"What about Oksana?"

"Well, you don't *have* to adopt her. She doesn't know about you."

Gay didn't even hesitate. "No. *She's* my daughter. I've decided."

Somewhat surprised—Who wouldn't want a baby? Who wouldn't want to end this heartbreaking waiting?—the agency backed off.

Finally, in October of 1996, Gay got a phone call. Her papers had expired. The seal of the notary on them, one of the first steps in the whole process, had timed out. She'd have to compile and complete and translate and notarize everything. All over again.

Thank God they're not allowed to tell her I'm coming, Gay thought. *She'd never survive this.*

———

Blink.

It's black in the upstairs room. Laney is in here with me. I can't see anything. Footsteps sound. I taste the bitter choke of my fear. She tells me to get under the bed. I wiggle under just before the door opens. Leave her up there. Alone.

Blink.

He hits me so hard. It's always a man who does the hitting to punish us, maybe because they're so much bigger. But I can't cry. If I do, it will be the bigger kids hitting me. Because if one of us cries—after what happens at night, or if you're sore or in pain—then all of us are punished for it. They'll take us upstairs and lock us up alone in dark rooms where we don't know when we'll be let out. And so the bigger kids will hit me if I cry.

But Laney always protects me. She puts me behind her and makes the kids hit her instead. And I let her. God help me, I always let her.

Blink.

"Your American mom is going to take care of that little leg," the director tells me, watching me move across the hallway after the other kids. I step on my arcing short leg with its floating knee, quickly, and swing my long leg out and around, weight it quickly. "She's going to give you a new leg. A brand-new one. When you get to America. But you have to be good. Do you hear me, Oksana?"

Blink.

Ice streams down my small body. I can't escape it. It screams from hoses or maybe it's just a faucet, but it hits nonstop with violent, heavy pressure. I'm wearing all my clothes and I can't move from this shower area of the horrible dark toilet room where there's never anything but the sound of water: dropping, leaking, spraying, encasing. If I move, a woman behind me sprays me hard with another hose of ice. It's always women in here, holding me in the freeze. For this, I must have been bad again. I'm forced to just stand there for who knows how long. *Long.* And only the sound of water. Soon the excruciating pain eases, it ebbs, and it's replaced by a soothing calm. I feel as though I'm no longer in my body. I love this feeling, until I find myself again back in bed, tucked in too hard, and still in my wet clothes. They always make you wear them to bed. It's part of the punishment in this place where it's always cold and I can see my breath and the pipes are covered in ice.

Blink.

My mother does not come today, either.

"It's because you're a bad girl, Oksana. Your mom is not coming. I told her that you're bad and she's not going to come for you. She's not going to be your mom anymore."

The words still sound in my head as the metal of the chair freezes my skin, even through the weird foam pieces that cover parts of it. I can't remember how I got here. I feel like I was just walking down the hall and one of the men snatched me and carried me here and set me down. Another man moves into my view. He carries pliers. He reaches toward me with them. I panic. Scream. Try to get up and run. Other men come and hold me down. It takes four of them to immobilize my little body. The man brings the pliers toward my face. I can't even shake my head—someone is holding it with a vise grip.

This room is dark, just like everywhere else. The single window looks like it's been covered in spiderwebs from the inside. Like a haunted house. Then I feel my jaw being forced open and I taste the rust of old blood and terrible steel and there is only *pain pain pain*.

I'm in what they call the recovery room, with its big hospital bed with a little metal ledge on it—the only thing in the lonely room. My entire face hurts. My mouth fills with blood. I spit it into an old tin bucket. It feels like I fill the bucket over and over. I can't understand how I could even have any blood left inside me. I don't know if this was punishment for something I did or if my tooth actually needed to be pulled.

I start to believe the director that maybe my mother isn't coming. Maybe she can see everything I do. Then I start to think that she can see what happens at night. *Of course she doesn't want me.* I start to believe in my mind that she's not coming. But in my heart, every time I look at her picture, I believe that she *is*. I don't have the words and can't name the feelings, but when I look at her image, I feel solid. Connected. Tied to something.

The nights here are the longest. They go on forever. Days go by in seconds, short windows, and quick bursts. But the dark lasts for ages.

Over the nights, over the months, through the years that blend and move and morph like dreams, the feeling transmitted through the picture of the woman who'll be my mother becomes the only thing that gets me through. It's the thin thread of possibility I hold on to, to get me through this hell.

Gay received her expired papers back in the mail—although it turned out to be only a letter of her rejection, accompanied by the papers of a California couple who'd already successfully adopted, somehow mixed up. It didn't matter. She had to start from scratch anyway. She performed all the steps again, without question. She didn't flag and she didn't despair—instead, she threw herself into executing everything that was asked of her.

And she never stopped preparing for her daughter's coming. She joined an Eastern European adoption forum, receiving tips, support, and hope from people midprocess or who'd successfully adopted. She bought a child's bed and collected clothes from friends who were parents. She asked her artist aunt to paint a mural on her soon-to-be-daughter's bedroom wall. She bought a trundle bed for little-girl sleepovers. She nested. She paid off bills.

This time, at the last step, instead of a foreign moratorium, the obstacle became a looming US government shutdown. Gay called the State Department one morning, hoping to get her sealed new dossier sent out to Ukraine before it was locked up in a mail room and languished for an untold length of time while politicians bickered and her daughter aged and wondered and mourned.

"Yes, everything's going to be closed," the woman on the phone told her. "But if you get me a FedEx number, I'll get your documents shipped as soon as I can."

Gay read her a number through the line. The government shut down at noon that day.

The dossier made it out.

chapter

three

We're only doing this because I told Laney I was so hungry. My insides are always so cavernously hollow, but now it's a sharp, sharp pain, like a knife slicing from my throat all the way down the emptiness. I was the one who said we should go find food, that even though we're not allowed out of our rooms, we could do it. We're smart girls, and we could do this and be back before anyone noticed we'd left. I'm always the opinionated one—the one to push us to get into trouble. And she's always the one who protects me when we do.

We steal out of the upstairs room. Laney opens the door so slowly it doesn't make a sound. It's the middle of the night, coal dark in the hallways. I follow her as we creep over the cold floor that's like bare cement. She tells me when to move, when to stay still. Because I'm never quiet or sneaky. I'm always so clumsy, and she knows that about me. She's my best friend, after all. We inch down a black stairway toward the smell of potatoes. Potatoes cooking in sewer water. Even though I'm starving, my stomach turns a little from chewing on the stench of it.

The pillars are ominous towers in the smelly gloom, backlit faintly by some slim light coming from under a door somewhere ahead. All the chairs are stacked on top of the tables in the shadowy dining room. Except at one table, the chairs are still down, pulled up, as if someone had just been sitting there. Laney is whispering that she knows where to find bread. Good. Neither of us wants sewer potatoes. I imagine the taste of bread, the crumbly swallow of it, the feel of actual food filling up the space in my body. We're crawling, quiet, urgently quiet, across the dingy floor toward the weak light, the terrible smell, the idea of a bite of something real in our mouths.

My leg slips out from under me. The right one, the longer one. It hits the ground with a thump, then strikes one of the chairs at that table. The chair leg shrieks on the floor, a short scream in the dark. In the echoing stillness of the empty chamber, the shriek radiates, expands, then dies suddenly into enormous silence.

"What was that?" a voice says, menace in it, from not so far away. We freeze, look at each other.

The voices approach. Women, men. It's hard to tell how many. They come closer. I'm terrified. My fear paralyzes me. Laney whispers, "Be quiet," and pushes me under the far end of the table. She's crawling after me. The footsteps are here.

Something grabs her. I see her small hand hit the floor. It makes a quick sweaty screech as it drags across this horrible floor away from me. Then it's gone. I see nothing. I'm frozen but for my whole body shaking.

There's a noise. A thud. Three of them. Loud, but faint, something hard striking something soft. My brain recognizes it. But I've never heard it like this. Someone being hit so hard. I can't breathe. I can't move. How could they hit her so hard?

Laney never makes a sound.

Three sets of footsteps move away. They leave her, lying there on the cruel floor in the dark. They're done with her. She doesn't move. She's silent. I can't— I don't— I—

I hear the footsteps begin to return.

"I thought I saw two of them."

They're going to kill me. I run. Past her tiny body all alone there.

It's the last time I see her.

I wish they'd killed me, too.

Finally, in December of 1996, nineteen months after she saw the grainy photo of the little girl, Gay got the news that it was time: she could arrive in Ukraine January 13, adopt her daughter no later than January 15, and process her visa out of Warsaw no later than January 20. Gay decided to buy a fake Christmas tree that wouldn't shed needles while she was gone and stock presents under it. It didn't matter to her that Christmas in America and Christmas by the Orthodox calendar in Ukraine would already have passed; she'd already missed two Christmases with her daughter thanks to moratoriums and delays. That artificial tree with its presents would complete the anticipated life with her daughter. *Her daughter.* What an incredible phrase that was. She put the tree together, placed presents under it, and prepared to head overseas.

She'd never traveled internationally before. But now she'd fly to Warsaw, and from there to Lviv, Ukraine, and take a night train the eight hours to Kyiv to formalize paperwork—she'd been told not to fly directly into Kyiv, where people were stopping taxis and stealing from passengers—and then drive five hours to the tiny village of Izyaslav, where the combination boarding school and orphanage stood. Then she'd have to do it all in reverse, newly adopted daughter in tow. She prepared to navigate it all, alone. At least, though, she'd been told by her friends on the Eastern European Adoption Coalition Listserv who'd completed adoptions (mostly in Russia), there'd be facilitators and translators and drivers and homestays and meals. She had her notebook and flash cards from her Ukrainian lessons and a Ukrainian dictionary.

It was still intimidating as hell.

One afternoon, her phone rang. On the other end, out of the blue, was her artist aunt.

"Can I come with you?"

Sherry was the wife of her uncle, her father's youngest brother. Maybe this was why Gay had always wanted children: her father was one of eight. One girl came first, then out popped her father, the first in a string of seven boys. Aunt Sherry and the uncle had moved to Cincinnati when Gay was eleven or twelve. Gay was always at their house, playing and helping with their three younger children. Sherry was the fun one, the adventurous one, the world traveler. She didn't seem to have the capacity for negativity, regularly telling her children, "You can't make me sad or upset. Mom's blowing up her bubble and staying in here."

"*Can* you come?" Gay said to her aunt through sudden waves of relief. "*Please* come. Only I don't have enough to pay for your airfare."

"I'll pay for both of our flights. You just cover everything else."

Gay checked her budget. She had enough for expenses for seven days for the two of them. On the long-awaited medical waiver that Gay's agency had finally filed, a judge in Ukraine had waived the ten-day rule that dictated the length of time adoptive parents had to wait in the country with their adopted children before processing them out. *Seven days should be more than enough,* she thought. *Thank God.*

They put me up here almost every night now. I'm so rarely allowed to sleep downstairs. I'm alone. Laney is gone, no longer here to protect me. They must have known I was down there, too, that night. They're punishing me. I deserve it. For what happened to her. It was my fault we were down there. It was my fault. And I let her protect me. Oh, God, I always let her. I want to ask about her. *Where's Laney?* Some deep-down part of me knows that she's gone forever, some deep part of me understands what I heard and saw. But I can't acknowledge it, I have to believe that maybe she's okay somewhere. But I know better than to ask about her. I can imagine all too well what will happen to me if I ask.

The door opens. A triangle of light. A pair of ugly shoes steps one, two, three toward the bed.

Please. Please. Get me out of here. Please.

———————

They've said that my *mother* is on her way. Actually on her way now, to me, here. They give me the picture of her to keep. I've never had something of my own. I keep it in my nightstand, the tiny table that separates our cots in the big sleeping room downstairs. I can look at it whenever I want now. And I look at it as much as I can. It's my lifeline.

———————

I'm lying in the horrid hospital bed in the medical room. There's so much pain across my belly, it scorches my abdomen down low in slicing pulses. I look down. Black stitches crisscross a long wound carved across my skin like a brand. If I try, I can remember how it happened, but I'm already burying it somewhere deep—deep with Laney, nearly out of sight. Maybe it never happened. Never happened at all.

———————

Gay and Sherry arrived in Kyiv at eight in the morning, exhausted and grimed with travel. They walked into the adoption agency at nine, right when it opened, to see the officials, who knew they were coming. But, oh, there was a meeting of some sort, could they wait awhile? Gay and Sherry waited. At ten thirty, they were invited upstairs.

———————

They tell me she is coming *today*. My *mother* is coming. She is coming to take me *home*.

"She'll be here before you go to bed," the director says.

By now, it's hard to believe him about anything, but I decide I want to believe him about this.

"Your paperwork is no good," the official told Gay. Through a translator, of course.

No, she thought. *This can't be happening.*

"You must rewrite your request without naming the child specifically." No reason for this bizarre requirement was offered.

"You've *got* to be kidding me," Gay said—under her breath, though, for fear of upsetting these all-powerful officials standing in her way to her daughter.

"And all paperwork must be retranslated."

Gay grit her teeth.

This day is endless. The afternoon drags on. I don't care about the western on the TV. The shadows lengthen outside, reach inside to cover us, and she's not here and she's not here. I don't trust these people, these "caretakers," anymore, they never keep their word. Maybe she's not coming after all. But I refuse to go to bed, because what if she *is* coming? And if I just don't go to sleep, at all, anymore, if I don't shut my eyes, maybe she'll come. Maybe all I've had to do this whole time is stay awake through the forever nights.

I refuse to go to bed. I yell. I pitch a fit. One of my best ones.

But they pick me up and bundle me into bed anyway, downstairs with all the other kids this time, and tuck me in so I can't move. They tell me they'll wake me up when she comes. If she comes. I stare into the dark, willing my eyes to stay open. They're so heavy, though, and I can't manage it for long.

After paying bribes and shuttling around Kyiv for paperwork and translating, and haggling and convincing and driving through the dark that comes early on Ukrainian winter nights, Gay and Sherry walked into the orphanage just before midnight. *It's so cold in here,* Gay thought. *There must not be any heat.* The director, the caretakers, the translators, everyone wore coats, and so she didn't take hers off, either. They walked down the dark, deathly quiet hall. She'd been told all the boarding school kids had gone home for winter break. Only six children, orphans, were left here. Gay's excitement should have been out of place in that cavernous building, but she couldn't feel anything except the rising thrill of anticipation, made deliriously sweet with the hard passage of so much time.

She followed them through a door and into a room that felt far too big for six children, the meager light from the hallway barely illuminating rows of beds and landing on the slow breathing of small bodies.

I hear voices in my dream, from far away. They get louder. I feel a little nudge on my shoulder.

"Oksana." The director's baritone.

I open my eyes slowly. I can't rouse myself from this dream. In front of me are several shadowy figures. One, who stands a little aside from the others, wears a velvety coat, its fur hood lying down on her back below dark hair floating around her shoulders—everything is dark, I can't see with the light from the door in my eyes.

"Oksana. Do you know who this is?"

In the chill of the hushed room, Gay watched the director move to a cot, say something in a low voice, and nudge the pile there. The pile sat up, blearily it seemed, and turned into a girl wearing a full sweater. *Not because she's waiting for me*, Gay thought. *Because it's so cold in here.* The director said something in Ukrainian Gay couldn't quite catch. The girl turned to look at her. Gay felt suddenly at a loss, afraid of scaring the girl. Gay was a perfect stranger, after all, and it was the middle of the night, and a small child had just woken up to find several people standing over her. Gay had no idea what to do.

My world crystallizes to the figure with the fur hood. Everyone else fades away: the director, whoever these other people are, every other orphan in the room with me. It's only me and her.

Because I'm so worried this is still a dream and fear that she'll turn and walk away and leave me here alone, without her, forever, I grab the tiny photo from my nightstand and hold it out to her, this solid piece of evidence the only thing that can make this moment real.

"I know you. I have your picture. You're my mom."

Gay's heart filled impossibly. The small voice, the little hand clutching Gay's crinkled passport photo, broke her paralysis. She found herself next to the cot without remembering taking the steps and knelt down. From her coat, she pulled a stuffed elephant. She'd had one of her own just like this when she was little. Her mother had sewn it, one for each of her children. She'd sewn one for each of her grandchildren, too, before she died, including one for Gay's still-imagined child. She must have known Gay would need it one day. Now, from the cold floor beside the little cot, Gay offered it into the hands of the suddenly not-sleepy girl and said:

"I know you, too. You're my daughter."

I ask them to let me go with her, right then and there. It doesn't matter that it's the middle of the night. She's my *mother*. And this is the first time I've gotten to say that to a human being—not just to a picture. Of course they don't let me, though, or let her stay in this room with me. They reassure me that she'll be back in the morning. And even though I don't believe anything they say anymore, I believe this. Because my mother's eyes tell me she will.

As they all file out, I can't stop thinking, *I have a family.* Everything I dreamed, everything I made up in my mind, is going to come true. The last waking thought I remember is *I must have done something good. What did I do? And how do I do it again so that good things keep happening?*

For the first time in my life, I fall asleep with a smile on my face. For the first time in my life, I'm not afraid to show it. No one can use my feelings against me anymore. No one will hurt me anymore. Because I have a *mother*.

This is the beginning.

Of course, that wasn't the end of the story of how my mother came to save me from the bleak life I was facing. The full story contains more hurdles, more twists and U-turns, and nothing simple. Simple, apparently, is for people *other* than my mother and me.

After having to leave me there at the orphanage that first night we met, Gay and Aunt Sherry wandered the streets of Izyaslav (on foot; their driver had abandoned them at the orphanage) in search of food. They hadn't eaten all day—Ukrainians, they'd joke later, apparently don't eat or pee. They knew there wouldn't be much, if anything, in the quiet village of only ten thousand people. But eventually they found a store that was still open. Inside, a skeleton of aisles sat empty but for two Coca-Cola bottles gathering dust, a barrel of dried fish, and one bag of mandarin oranges. They opted for the oranges. In their tiny rented apartment in town, the hot water was off. It only came on for two hours in the morning and two hours at night, and they'd long missed the window. The electricity was off, too, shut down hours before.

But that was just the beginning of their rough road.

After my adoption was completed on January 15 and the judge in town waived the ten-day wait, my mother's facilitator discovered that my original birth certificate and relinquishment papers—mandatory documents Gay would need to process me out of Europe—weren't in the records in town, but all the way in Khmelnytskyi. The facilitator drove the two hours to retrieve them, only to have a vindictive official there threaten to arrest us all for illegal activity. When the facilitator returned to Izyaslav to fetch my mother and bring her before the Khmelnytskyi official to convince him everything was aboveboard and to pay the requisite bribe, I believed my mother would get in that car and never come back to the orphanage for me. She didn't want me after all, I thought, and I refused to be consoled. The facilitator finally told my mother to leave something with me so that I'd know she planned to come back. Lacking anything of value, Gay left Aunt Sherry, who spent the day painting the dead-tree pillars in the orphanage cafeteria with cheerful Winnie-the-Pooh scenes, delighting the orphans despite the fact that that none of us knew who the bear and his diverse array of animal friends were.

Untangling the red tape exhausted another week, creating for my mother and Sherry a ritual of each day making the long walk from town to the orphanage. There, the caretakers showed Gay the medical room where the men with pliers had inflicted such pain, with its single cot and its cupboard empty except for a roll of gauze. "We have a great need for medicine," the staff told Gay, and in response she handed over the generic Tylenol she'd brought with her. She also learned that the teachers in the boarding school hadn't been paid since August. People here are dying in droves, she was told—destitute and sick and hungry with no one to help them.

When Gay brought me to her apartment she'd rented in town before we finally left, she changed me into the clothes she'd brought for me—shirts and pants made for a much younger girl to fit my undersized body. When she returned the clothes I'd been wearing to the orphanage, they counted each item, meticulously, to be sure it was all there.

Those first days, I refused to learn English—despite everything, I loved my home country. It was all I knew. I told my mother I'd solve the problem. "I'm a smart girl. I'll teach you Ukrainian." I didn't know that she'd already tried to learn the language. But in a rare lucky turn of events for us, the high school kids in town, who'd heard two Americans were visiting for an extended period, came to practice their English and relieve my poor mother of our halting communication. I'd been trying to tell her my head hurt—a lingering reminder of the pliers incident—to which, not comprehending, she'd reply in her stilted Ukrainian, "Good, good." When the students finally told her what I'd been saying, she sprang, horrified, into action to care for me.

One of those last days in Izyaslav, I asked her to find Laney and adopt her, too. But when my mother approached the director and the caretakers about her, they were elusive, unsettled, disturbingly closemouthed. Also on one of those last days, I finally pulled the last gruesome black stitch from the furrowed scar on my lower belly, the one that had been stuck there when they removed all the others. When I showed it to my mother, exclaiming, "I got it!," she went pale. When I refused to talk about how I'd received the wound, and the caretakers were equally closemouthed about it, Gay hurried as best she could to get me out of there—that town, that country.

There are other details of those days before my new life really began—many of them sad. All that matters now is the big picture: My mother had come for me. And she was taking me home.

part
two

chapter

four

We land in Buffalo at nine o'clock at night, after twenty-six hours of traveling. My mom's next-door neighbor collects us from the airport and excitedly insists I open the Christmas presents waiting for me under the tree (good thing it was artificial—that poor tree would have dropped all of its needles to the floor waiting for us to finally come back from Ukraine). But it's late, and I don't understand what the neighbor's saying.

Mom puts the brakes on that idea: "Tomorrow. Now, we need to sleep."

I'm too tired to notice the house, too tired to notice much about my new room. My mother puts me in the bed, she pulls out the trundle beside me, and we crash into sleep.

My eyes pop open and it's still dark. It's not even 5:00 a.m. in Buffalo, but it's morning to our bodies, still on Ukrainian time, and we're wide-awake. And *hungry*. My mother discovers that, despite all that her friends and neighbors have done for her in the past months and weeks, no one has thought to stock her fridge for our arrival. She doesn't even have bread for a piece of toast. It's too early for stores to be open. Except one, my mother says. Walmart.

I'm still dazed and sleepy when we walk into the blazing lights of the box store, past the improbable sliding doors that open without either of us touching them. I'm stopped dead by the scene before me, staring open-mouthed, when Mom scoops me up and settles me into the front of a blue cart, my legs dangling down. She rolls me through endless rows of perfectly organized *things*: toys, stuffed animals, books, clothes, food. So much food. Everything is brand-new. And clean. I try to touch every single thing that we pass.

I'm amazed. It's the most beautiful thing I've ever seen.

In one of the food aisles, we pass something I recognize. The box looks different, and I can't read the words on it, but I know that illustration. I would know it anywhere. Sugar cubes. I gasp.

"I know this!" I say in Ukrainian, pointing to it.

She doesn't understand the words, but she reads my expression. She smiles and drops a box into the blue cart.

When we pull up to the house after Walmart, I truly see it for the first time. It doesn't have a classic white picket fence like in the movies I've seen, but to me it looks like the American dream. A perfectly symmetrical, faded green two-story with gabled windows and steps leading to a front door right in the middle. Inside, all the doors are wooden, with crystal doorknobs. I learn right away to open them with my thumbless hands. I spend the morning turning on every light—the light switches are so different here, I'm obsessed with them—and opening every drawer. I pick up every single thing in each drawer one by one and ask my mother in Ukrainian, "Yours?"—and sometimes, "Mine?" Mom entertains this patiently, even when I can tell she's getting a little exhausted from the thorough inventorying.

Upstairs in my own room, I can't believe so *many* things are mine. It seems like there are thousands of stuffed animals. Aunt Sherry had painted a mural on the wall of my bedroom (*my* bedroom, I can barely understand that), and I recognize the bear and his friends that she painted on the dead-tree pillars at the orphanage. Winnie-the-Pooh, Piglet, Eeyore, grass and sky and white fluffy clouds. Mom and Aunt Sherry had read me books about them while we waited back in Ukraine, and now I think that all animals must talk to one another and to their human best friends. I line all my stuffed animals and dolls in a circle around me on the bed, the elephant my mother gave me in the center. I don't know what to do with them since I've never had stuffed animals. So I just talk to them, as if they could talk back to me.

I name every doll Laney.

Associations with the place where I spent the last seven years of my life—even though parts of that span were horrible—make me happy, put me at ease. I still don't fully comprehend that *this* is my home. That I'm never going back there. That I won't have to face hunger like that ever again.

I start hoarding sugar cubes under my bed, though, just in case.

My mother sleeps right next to me every night. I hate sleep, I'm not good at it. It's so quiet here, and the silence leaves space for all the things I've been trying to forget to creep back in. I ask my mother—in our evolving language of Ukrainian, English, and charades—for a crib, even though I'm almost eight years old. I need more walls to protect me. She hauls an armchair up and faces it toward the wall so that it feels like a cocoon and positions the trundle bed on the other side of it. It helps. I hold tight to the elephant she gives me each night. I keep waiting. For the door to open. For someone else to come in.

When no one else comes, I start to realize that what happened to me in Ukraine wasn't normal. I begin to feel ashamed. And I don't even know why.

Mom takes me to a doctor, a pediatrician, a few days after we get home. She makes sure there's a translator there who can read Ukrainian and speaks English. She brings the medical card, the single document she has of my fraught medical history, to try to figure out what vaccinations I've had and what I need. The doctor brings out a needle. And I *panic*. I identify needles with intense pain.

My mother had a feeling about this; she'd discovered back in Izyaslav that in the worn-out medical room in the boarding school, they used the same needle for hundreds of kids, a single enormous one blunted by dozens and dozens of tiny arms until it felt like a wolf incisor. On the inside of my arm is an angry red scar just under my elbow from when I had to be in the medical room for something—I can't remember what, maybe don't want to remember—when they left the needle in too long for an IV and had to cut it out of my skin.

I pitch a fit, and the man translating tells my mother, "Just try it again later, she's too out of control."

"I can't back down just because she's throwing a fit," Mom replies calmly. "It needs to be done."

They manage to give me the shot. I just start laughing. Because the needle is so small and sharp that I barely even feel it.

After that it's the orthopedic surgeon, the same one Mom showed my pictures to years ago at the start of her adoption journey. She brings the translator again, who carries me to the examining table while the surgeon looks at my legs. The translator carries me to the X-ray room. And he carries me back to the examining table. My feet never touch the ground. I feel like a princess in the picture books Mom reads me.

The surgeon returns and places the X-rays on a lit wall. "Do you see these little white flecks in the left leg that look like salt from a shaker?" he asks my mother. She nods. "That's her tibia. Or what tried to be her tibia. And on the right, do you see these bones? Those are fibulas, but they're overgrown. They're trying to be weight-bearing bones, but they're not and never can be. If she'd been born here in the US, both of her legs would have been amputated above the knee at birth."

My mother examines the X-rays, but not with surprise—she'd already heard this from the Colorado doctor who took my photo.

"So when do you want to schedule surgery?"

My mother whips her attention to the surgeon, caught off guard. "As in, both legs?"

"Yes, you need to amputate right away."

Now she's horrified. And getting angry. In a transformation I'll come to know well, my mother turns into a bear. With a cub to protect.

"She doesn't even speak English! Sure, I've got a translator here, but she doesn't understand me, or you. And she most certainly doesn't *understand* what taking a leg means. She has no one she trusts, she barely even knows *me* yet. And you want me to do that to her? No. We won't be amputating until she's ready."

"It has to be done." The surgeon, apparently not really listening, moves to leave the room.

"Wait, I have more questions," Mom says. "Should I make her stop jumping off my porch in the meantime, then? It's about three feet to the ground. Now I'm worried she might break what bones *are* in there."

The surgeon turns back. "What are you talking about? She can't even *walk*."

"You're right, she can't walk." My mother smiles. "She runs."

The translator lifts me onto the floor. He tells me to run around the room a bit. I obey.

"Oh," the surgeon says somewhat weakly. Mom looks at him expectantly. But not smugly. I would come to know this about her, too, that even when she was right, she was too busy advocating for me to rub anyone's face in it.

Eventually, my mother gets me to the right doctors and specialists to fashion a brace for my long right leg and a prosthetic for my left one, so that for the first time in my life my legs are the same length.

She never makes me stop jumping off the porch.

Olga, who tried to teach Mom Ukrainian, and her husband have come over to meet me. They're drinking tea with my mom at the kitchen table and speaking to me in my own language. I'm telling them about the impossible number of stuffed animals in my room, and I run up to grab the elephant to bring it back down to show them. I'm wearing tights without shoes, running on the hardwood floor in the kitchen with elephant in hand. I skid across the floor, miss the stop—I've never been good at stopping quickly on the best of days with my legs the way they are—and smack into the table with my head, hard. I bounce back like a cartoon character from the force of it and land on my butt.

The adults are all looking at me open-mouthed. They're waiting for me to melt down. But I jump to my feet and laugh hysterically, laugh really loud, to show them that I'm not going to cry. *Don't worry, no one needs to hit me, I'm not going to cry.*

Olga asks me why I'm laughing. I stop, look around this house, where I think maybe I might finally be safe. In this *home*, with my mom right next to me, I feel the safest I've ever felt before in my short life. So I tell Olga about the caretakers and the big kids. She relays this to my confused mother in English. Mom looks at me from a bottomless well of something I've almost never seen—maybe it's compassion—and then she just nods. As if this explains a lot.

Mom wakes and hears me crying in the night. She's a deep sleeper, like she's underwater or on another planet, even when she's in the trundle

44

bed right next to me. I've cried every night, but this is the first time she's woken to it. I tell her it's because my legs hurt. They always do, after a day of using them to be a normal kid. But sometimes the tears aren't just for the pain in my legs. Sometimes all those memories that I stuffed down so deep won't stay down. They claw to the surface, horrifying shapes and sounds and feelings made more terrifying by their vagueness. But I can't tell Mom. I don't want her to think something's wrong with me. I don't want her to give me back.

A few days after being *home*, I ask Mom in our mix of languages and sign, "When do I get to go to school?"

She looks surprised. "In a couple of weeks."

She'd thought I'd want time to adjust to our life. She still has another month and a half of leave left from the university, set up so that I have time to adjust to our life here before we're separated for hours at a time by school and work.

"No, I go now, Mom."

I liked school in Ukraine. I was the best student in my class. They made me the class monitor—if the teacher ever left the room, I got to be in charge. I'd write down the names of the kids who were bad in a little book, since it seemed like that was the only thing the teacher did, anyway. And I'm confident I'll like school here.

"Oh, kiddo." Mom has reservations. But she already knows I'm strong-willed and won't back down. Or maybe it's just stubbornness. Either way, she recognizes the trait in me because we share it. She also knows that I'm such a confident kid—a weird anomaly considering the environment I came from—that I'll likely be fine. The next morning, she gets me ready for my first day at school.

Mom had already let the elementary school in our neighborhood know that I'd be coming, and that I'd have some special needs, and she ensured that I'd have a translator with me for the first months. When we get to the school this morning though, she still has to register me—and it quickly becomes clear that the school administrators have misread the "special needs" heads-up and intend to put me in a special education class.

"What?" Mom says with no small amount of incredulity and heat. "Of course not. She's very smart."

"Well. We've done some research. It seems that children born after Chernobyl have cognitive disabilities." The administrator is getting defensive.

"Your research wasn't comprehensive, then. This child doesn't need to be in special ed. No," Mom says. Definitively.

They begin debating what grade I should be in, then. Maybe kindergarten, the administrators think. Mom says I was in second grade in Ukraine. But I can't read English yet, so maybe first grade to let me catch up. The administrators repeat that it should be kindergarten because I'm small and they're still not convinced I have normal intelligence.

I've gotten bored while they talk, and someone handed me a crayon and paper to entertain myself. I draw a bit. Then, since I'm in school after all, I do a little math practice next to my drawing. I write out a couple of numbers, three digits each, and add them.

One of the administrators notices. "Oh. Whoa. First grade it is."

School in America is *not* like school back in Ukraine. It's so *long*. How do these kids sit through six and a half hours?! And it's all in English. (The translator is only with me a couple hours of the day, and she speaks Russian, not Ukrainian, despite what Mom specified to the school.) *And* they give you work to take home with you, so it's like you're *always* in class, no matter where you are. I'm so exhausted after my first day that I refuse to go back. I don't want to go to school after all.

But Mom's already told the university she's returning to work, so she can't stay home with me. She takes to bribing me to go to school in the mornings. She says, *"Khlib"*—in Ukrainian, the word for "sweet bread." After Walmart on my first day here, Mom took me to Burger King and ordered me French toast sticks. Now I can't get enough of those things. So I agree to get in the car, where we go through the Burger King drive-through. Then, while I'm too blissed-out on fast-food sweet bread to argue, Mom drives to the school.

I fall for it every time.

Mom is taking me to the ice-skating rink today. In Buffalo, this is apparently what people do in winter. It's the general pastime to be out on the ice skating or playing hockey. Mom found an adaptive program that pairs kids with special needs with a volunteer who teaches them to skate, one-on-one. She thinks it will help me make friends—or at least learn how to. From day one of meeting Mom, I've been connected to her and trusted her unconditionally. But I have trouble creating bonds with other people. I don't even understand what a "friend" is. She says my English will also get better without my even realizing it. And—the selling point—it's *fun*, she tells me.

We get to the rink, and all kinds of kids are there. Some are using walkers. Some are missing limbs. Some have cognitive disabilities. I feel a little confused because even though I've got braces on my legs now, I still don't think of myself as being like . . . them. I've figured out how to do pretty much everything I want to do, so I'm not really *disabled*.

It's like when I tried the swing set.

A few months ago, when it was still warm, I watched another kid from our neighborhood who'd come over to play hang from the metal frame of the swing set in our backyard. He traversed across the bar with his hands, his legs dangling in midair. He reached the other side, dropped to the ground, smiled at me triumphantly, and ran home.

47

"Mom! I want to do that!"

I ran to the swing set, but I couldn't shimmy up the A-frame to the top bar. My five-fingered, webbed hands just wouldn't do what I needed them to do.

"Lift me up!" I demanded. Mom hoisted me up to the bar, even though I'd grown eight inches in six months and was no longer so light—real food at regular intervals had been good to me.

But my hands couldn't grasp the metal, and I fell back into her arms.

"Again!" I told her. She gamely helped me try, at least twenty times, with the same result. Finally, exhausted, she put me down on the ground.

"Oh, Oksana. I'm so sorry, honey. This is one of the things you need thumbs for. You just can't do that."

The next day, I asked the babysitter—one of Mom's graduate students—to take me out to the swing set. She babysat me for two weeks, and I asked her that every day.

"Come watch," I said to Mom, dragging her outside. I climbed the metal frame and traversed the bar. By myself. She watched, beaming.

It was the last time my mother ever said, "You can't do that."

Now at the ice rink, Mom can tell I'm holding back a little. She kneels down to me. "You know, it never hurts anything to just try. Let's just try it."

I take her hand and walk toward the ice.

The volunteer I get paired with is named Angela. She's sixteen or seventeen. She's been skating for years and tells me she also loves dancing and acrobatics—she wants to be a performer one day—and that she'll teach me how to do jumps on skates when I'm ready. "If you want," she adds quickly.

I like her.

Angela helps Mom and me put my skates on. Mom had to buy two pairs, because my feet are different sizes. The prosthetic foot on my short left leg is smaller than my real right foot, which has extra bones in it. I show Angela my six toes through my sock. She's suitably impressed. She takes my arms and helps me out onto the ice, leaving Mom on the bench to watch.

By the end of the hour, I can move on the ice without Angela's help. She's gentle, encouraging, and so fun that I forget that everyone in this program is supposed to be *disabled*. Every time my skate glides on the ice, for however short of a step, every time Angela cheers and we laugh, I fall in love with skating a little more.

Over the next few months, Angela becomes like a big sister to me. I look forward to going to the rink. I'm enthralled with the feel of gliding on ice that's been freshly polished by the Zamboni. Over the winter, I get to learn a routine that all the kids perform at the end of the year. I love figuring out how to get my body to do the moves for it on the ice.

Mom and I bond even more, if that's possible, over skating. It turns out her mom, whom I never got to meet, loved it, too. The two of them would watch ice-skating together for hours. Mom and I start watching all the world championships, following Kristi Yamaguchi and Tara Lipinski. Mom already knows the names of all the jumps and stunts. I learn them, too. We'll be watching a competition on TV and I'm making up my own routine on the living room floor while Mom praises how well I always seem to know where my body is in space.

That, I think but don't tell her, is a survival skill where I came from.

chapter

five

Mom's big, old-fashioned secretary desk, with three skinny drawers, a hutch with glass over it, and a piece of wood that pulls out to write on, slides into my vision as I walk past the living room. I've passed that desk countless times, and I riffled through it plenty when Mom first brought me home. But I definitely haven't looked in there since I could speak English. And I suddenly, badly, want to.

Mom's outside talking to the neighbor. I can tell by the sound of her voice that she's deep in conversation. I pull out the bottom drawer. It's a mishmash of junk. I paw through it, find nothing interesting, and move on to the second drawer. Pictures. The ones of me are on top, including those that the adoption agency sent Mom. I should want to flip through the whole stack, but something pulls me to the top drawer. I open that one.

It's papers. Documents. I've never seen them before, Mom must have put them here sometime recently. I pull them out, spread them on the floor. A few have a seal: interlocking yellow lines on a blue field. I recognize it. The Ukrainian seal. Happiness floods me. I'm so proud of where I come from. Even though bad things happened to me there, I'm still so proud.

There's an old cardboard square—thick, worn-out cardboard paper—with my name, *Oksana Alexandrovna Bondarchuck*, typewritten across the top. Below is a list of dates and medical procedures, all the times I was in the hospital. Parts of my body shudder as if electrocuted—my left leg, my hands, scars on my arms. I put the cardboard down.

A lot of the papers have Mom's name on them, in English and Ukrainian. A lot seem like government papers, and I don't know what they mean. And then I see a different paper. No seal. It's handwritten. At the bottom are signed names. Oksana Bondarchuck. And Alexander Bondarchuck.

My birth parents. My breath gets stuck in my throat. My hands shake as I lift the paper up.

The writing says they relinquish me to the government. It says they give me up.

"Oksana?"

I didn't hear Mom come in. I whirl, clutching the letter. I forget that I've been bad and gone through her things.

"They signed me away?" I'm stricken. Then the anger starts to rise, surprising me, mingled with a cruel hurt. "They threw me away!"

Mom kneels down. She peels the paper out of my hand before I can shred it, like I want to. She puts her hands on my shoulders—*just like Laney*—and looks into my eyes. "Oksana, I think your parents were very young when they had you. And I think they didn't have much money." Mom knows so much about the state of Ukraine at my birth—she did so much research—and she saw things in that rural place when she came to adopt me that I would never have seen with such young eyes. While she's had me in therapy pretty much from day one of bringing me home, the therapists have never talked about *this* with me.

Mom explains to me in a way I can understand. She's always honest with me. "They thought that the government could take better care of you than they could. They didn't *want* to give you away. They were probably told they *couldn't* keep you."

I'm sniffling, but I'm doing a good job of holding back the tears. I have to be good so Mom doesn't want to sign me away, too. But then, as if she's read my mind, she says:

"And I will *never* give you away. I'm your mother for life. And I'm so *proud* to be your mom. I'm so lucky that you're my daughter. I knew that from the first moment I saw your face in a picture. That you were special. And you are—you're worth everything to me."

I see in her eyes that she means it. I let her lead me away from the mess I've made on the floor, leaning into her comfortable and safe body. But I don't forget those papers are there.

After I've been in America almost a year, Mom tells me that I get to pick out a kitten. One of her cats—she had two—had died of old age a few months before. Mom decides it's my turn to have a cat of my own. We go to the Humane Society. She tells me I can choose whichever one I want. We walk through the long hall with its wide cages. There are adult cats, kittens, teenager cats, endless rows of felines. I don't see any that catch my attention. Then, at the end of the row, there's a sad-looking dark tabby kitten. He's listless. It's hard to tell whether he's alive.

"I want this one," I tell Mom decisively.

"Are you sure?" She eyes the kitten. "Don't you want one that's more . . . playful?"

"I want him."

Mom goes to tell the guy at the front desk that we'd like to adopt this kitten.

"Yeaaahhh, you might want to tell her to pick out a different cat. This one is likely to die. He's already on the list to be put down for his medical issues."

That cinches it. Mom's on board now, too. We adopt him on the spot.

I name him Buddy.

Buddy almost doesn't make it. The first night we bring him home, he vomits and spews diarrhea all over the floor. Mom has a great vet though, and the woman saves him. I think he might have died a couple of times in her care, but she pulls him through. That kitten is a force. I love him from the first moment.

There's just one small problem. He's got deadly claws.

It might be my fault. I put him through hell trying to give him make-overs, painting his nails, dressing him up. And I didn't know how to cuddle him. I'd hug him so hard I nearly suffocated him, and his claws would pop out in an effort to save himself. Soon it just became habit for him. I take to wearing three sweaters at a time so I can play with him. He also likes to go for my ankles. It's a game for him. Whenever I walk near him, he chases after me to catch my feet and claws at them. I wear socks, and in my mind, the issue's resolved.

But Mom has a longer view of this. She knows I'm going to need my short leg amputated soon. I'm likely to be on crutches after, and then try-ing to learn how to walk again. A cat attacking my ankles might not be the best recovery therapy. She starts thinking about whether Buddy might need to be declawed.

Around the same time, I'm set to have my own hand surgery.

Now that my English has become better, Mom makes sure I'm part of this process, that I understand everything. I'm there when the surgeons explain to Mom that in addition to the obvious issue of my webbed fin-gers, there are other anomalies. The X-rays reveal that I have duplicate sets of bones. It's the reason my fingers are so thick and why I have nail beds in two different spots on each finger. And, of course, I have no thumbs. They tell Mom that they'll do their best to remove bones, unite the nail beds, and, the big undertaking, move one of my fingers on each hand into a thumb position. It won't actually *be* a thumb because I won't have those muscles or the big pad on my palm that attaches to a real thumb. But it will be the next best thing. They'll do a skin graft for the thumb procedure. Mom doesn't think to ask where from my body they'll get the skin.

They'll do one hand at a time. They'll start with the left, they say, because my right hand is dominant.

"Actually," Mom tries to tell them, "it depends on the task. She's figured out how to do everything from cutting to turning on faucets, but it depends which hand she uses."

They say they'll start with the left anyway. And it will be outpatient surgery; Mom can take me home that day.

"Really?" my mom says. "Huh. Seems like that should be worth a night or two in the hospital."

Don't worry, they reassure her. Also, this will be only one of many hand surgeries. We can only work on them a little bit at a time, the doctors say, because of the extensive healing required with so many nerves.

Mom explains things to me even more clearly. "They're going to make your hands better. You'll be able to do more." I trust her. "And Buddy's going to have hand surgery, too. You'll get to heal up together."

I like this idea. I take Buddy in my sweater-padded arms and talk to him about our upcoming operations. He doesn't seem scared, so I'm not either.

The night before surgery, Mom gets the sofa in the living room set up as a bed with all my favorite stuffed animals lining the cushions. She rents movies for me to watch. And she makes a feast of Ukrainian food that I still weirdly identify as comfort food, even though I never remember eating much in Ukraine.

I don't remember much from the hospital, or Mom walking me to the red line where she has to give my hand to a nurse, terrified I'll think she's abandoning me. I don't remember struggling against the nurses who try to get a needle in me for an IV. I just black out and leave my body, as I've trained myself to.

When Mom is allowed into the recovery room to see me and help me get ready to leave, she understands how much the doctors failed to prepare her for how to care for me. My hand is bound into an enormous bundle that winds all the way up my arm. It looks like a giant turkey leg. The dressing won't fit through the sleeve of the T-shirt she brought for me. She can't get my underpants or shorts on either, because the skin graft came from high up on my inner thigh. And it's so sore there that I can't let anyone close to it. The nurses let Mom take me home in my operating gown. She'll go to Goodwill later to get T-shirts big enough for my gauze-wrapped hand to fit through.

I don't remember much from the recovery, either, except that the doctors put pins through each of my fingers to keep them together, and the pins have to come out after the swelling goes down. The doctors had told Mom they'd give her a sedative for me before I came to the hospital for that procedure. But they never did. When we get to the hospital and Mom asks about it, the nurse says, "Well, do you have any Benadryl on you? That should work."

"Benadryl?" Mom is furious.

I scream through the whole process.

I come home from school with an assignment to make a family tree. I've noticed that in school in the United States everything always seems to come back to family. Family history. Family genes. But I can't ask Mom, "Who do I look like? Where do I come from?" I start to understand that my past is hidden by an impenetrable curtain, and that makes me different.

When I look in the mirror, I begin to have a disjointed, lonely association with my own image. I have no idea who I look like. I am only me. And I'm such a visual person that I begin to see, really *see*, my friends with their families. My best friend, Jessica, who lives in the house across the block, smiles just like her mom. I notice it in other kids around the neighborhood, and at ice-skating. *She has the same hair as her dad. His brother moves the exact same way he does.* My desire for that same connection grows, balloons, metastasizes. Staring in the mirror, I start to hate my reflection.

Who am I, even? No one knows that I'm alive.

I start to create an image of my birth mom. What her hair must look like. How she talks. How she moves. The image is a little like the blond woman from my hazy memories who used to visit the orphanage, and a little like the other woman with the soft body who took me to her home sometimes to nurse me back to some semblance of health. And it's also a little like me.

At the same time, without my knowing or understanding it, my angst and confusion and anger at feeling so lost and different begin to wind around this image of my birth mom. Become part of it. Become part of me and my reflection in the mirror.

"So I'll get a brand-new one, right?" I ask Mom.

I'm currently stalling before bed, showing off my trick of swinging my short left leg up behind my head. I can pull my hair back behind my ear with my toes. I'm ridiculously flexible, double-jointed, and missing a quadriceps muscle, which makes for easy contortions. I love this little leg. I love all the parts of my body.

My friends in the United States, which I've slowly made—especially

Jessica—must have had incredible parents who taught them to treat me like a normal person, who embrace the way I am. I still don't think of myself as being any different from them.

Even though, two months after my hand surgeries, Mom and I are sitting here talking about how it's time to remove my beloved, but not very functional, left leg.

"A brand-new what, Oksana?"

"They said my American mom would get me a brand-new leg."

"Who told you that, honey?"

"At the orphanage."

She explains to me, again, that *amputation* means that my leg will be removed for good above the knee, so that only my thigh will remain. "You *will* get a kind of new leg, though, remember how we talked about it? It's called a prosthetic. We'll learn together how to walk on it. And you'll run and jump and ride your bike, just like before. Only better, with less pain now."

I hear her talking. But I don't really listen. I'm too busy imagining what my perfect new leg will look like when I wake up from surgery, how amazing it will be not to wear the fake foot. My two real legs will finally be the same size. I can't wait.

———

Mom schedules my amputation for May. She prepares for me to miss the last month of school, scheduling home services for studying and my care, and she preps a bag for me for my stay in the hospital for the five days after the surgery, like the doctors advise her. She schedules therapy sessions for me, so I can understand what it means to lose my leg, since she's pretty sure I don't. She even, through her Listserv of parents who've adopted Eastern European children, sets up a visit to a neighboring city so I can meet another girl who's had her leg amputated, from cancer. We stay in a hotel with a pool, and I watch as the girl removes her prosthetic to swim, as she puts it back on after she dries off to walk around again. This doesn't apply to me, though, so I'm not sure why Mom went to the trouble.

The night before my operation, Mom makes me a feast of Ukrainian food, just like she did before my hand surgeries. It's becoming a tradition.

"This is your last night with Little Leg," Mom said. We'd taken to calling it that, a nickname for my beloved short limb. She sets me up on the sofa bed in the living room, where she's piled all my stuffed animals and the requisite stack of videos, and we have a ceremony for my doomed leg.

It's like saying goodbye to a friend. I pull it to me and kiss it. She kisses it and caresses it. We whisper kind words to it to send it on its way.

"I love you," I say to it. I'll miss my Little Leg. But I'm so excited to see the new one that I grieve less than I probably should. We eat some cake that Mom made, then we head upstairs and she turns out the light in our bedroom.

"Wait, Mom? Can you just tell it you love it, one more time?"

My mother, she always obliges the weird wishes of a neurotic nine-year-old.

Where is my leg?!

"Mom, when are they putting it on?" I've finally woken up enough from surgery to see that the doctors didn't attach a new leg. There's just a *stump*, without a knee or a shin or a foot. I don't know what I'm supposed to do with that. *It's gone. There's nothing there.* I'm confused, a little frantic, and desperate for her to understand.

Mom hugs me, stays with me, explains over and over about the prosthetic and what it means. This time, I try to listen. But I'm still in pain and so nauseous from the anesthetic that it's hard to understand anything.

The doctors told Mom I'd be in the hospital for five days. They try to send me home after two.

"You've got to be kidding," Mom says to the surgeon, disgusted. "She's still vomiting and you haven't even taken her off the morphine yet."

They let me stay. One more day.

―――――――――

At home, after I've been laid out on the couch for a few days, I think I finally understand that there was never any magic new leg waiting in the wings to replace my short leg. It's just . . . gone. But my brain and my nerves are slow to catch up to that fact. They don't register that a limb isn't there anymore. They keep sending phantom feelings down through the ghost of a limb, relaying signals to stretch or itch and then, maybe in all-out panic, sending signals to feel pain in a leg that's not even there to feel it. The sensation starts as a deep fire within my not-there Little Leg that grows and radiates until I'm convinced I'm in physical pain that I can't do anything about.

Just as strange are the itches. Those appear just behind my missing knee, right below the phantom joint. I reach down to scratch air. And the feeling disappears. It becomes a game, feeling the sensations move around my phantom leg to try to find the imagined different parts of it.

Mom has trouble keeping me on the couch. I keep getting up to go retrieve something or run outside to see a friend or grab a snack or do any of the things kids want to do besides lie on a sofa. And I fall, because I keep forgetting my leg isn't there. Every time. Mom jokes that she's going to put a leash on me.

―――――――――

When we see the prosthetist a month after my surgery, he doesn't bring me a normal leg like I've envisioned. He brings me a piece of plastic and metal. I look at this bizarre thing that's supposed to be part of me now, and despite that Mom and my prosthetist will see my tears, I start crying. I can't stop myself. My cherished short leg is lost forever. And I will never be getting a beautiful, functional, same-length-as-my-other *real* leg.

The prosthetist is kind. He's probably used to dealing with bereft, befuddled little kids. He explains how this fake leg works and how I'll attach it to my "residual leg." Pediatric prosthetics aren't just plain metal, they have different colors, and I get to pick out the colors of the socket and the straps—hot pink. He teaches me how to use the hinged knee: put pressure on the prosthetic toe to release the hinge. Then the hinge swings freely until I swing the leg around with my hip to lock the mechanism so it won't bend.

I have the impression that the doctors have said to Mom that this is it. We've dealt with the problem leg. I can keep my other leg.

Relieved, I cling to this reality as a foundational part of me.

———————

Somewhere in the healing, while my stump is getting used to the prosthetic, an abscess develops on the stump's surface, becomes infected, painful. Mom takes me to the hospital to get it taken care of.

I'm lying on my back on the exam table. The doctor says he'll need to give me a shot of antibiotics.

"She's afraid of needles," Mom warns him. "Make sure you just talk her through it. And I'll be right here, honey," Mom says to me, her hand on my shoulder.

The doctor leaves, returns with a kit of needles and gauze and vials, and two male nurses in tow. I feel the nerves rising through my belly like a swarm of bees, up through my chest into my throat. I tense. Mom leans down and talks to me. I don't hear what she says. As the doctor approaches with the needle, I can't control myself. I try to jump off the table. The two nurses spring into motion, one on either side.

The moment their hands touch my body, I freeze. Mom watches my body go deathly still, the blood leave my skin, the life leave my eyes. I'm there, but I'm not. At the sight of me, Mom stops breathing for a moment.

Later, at home, Mom settles me on the couch. She waits until I'm comfortable, surrounded by my stuffed animals, the video player ready to go.

"Oksana," she says gently. "Did something happen to you? In Ukraine?"

I don't look at her.

"You know you can tell me anything. You're safe with me. I'll keep you safe, always."

"Nothing happened. I was always good." I hit PLAY on the remote.

I can't tell Mom. Any of it. I don't want her to think that she adopted a bad girl who deserved all those punishments. She won't love me anymore.

I can't let her send me back there.

Mom needs to know, now, about my past as much as I want to know whom I come from, but for more tangible reasons. Every time a doctor asks about family medical history, about how I might react to medications, what might be predicted about my future health, she comes up short. And it kills her a little more each time.

She has the names of my birth parents from my relinquishment papers, and she finally asks Olga to help her find them. Olga's sister, who still lives in Ukraine, scours the internet for those names and finds a matching couple living in Khmelnytskyi. She passes on the phone number. Olga calls it for my mom, who could never hope to speak sufficiently fluent Ukrainian for this conversation.

Across the ocean, a woman picks up the phone. Olga explains that she's looking for the mother of a girl born in 1989 with several birth defects—that she's hoping for any family medical history that might be helpful.

There's a silence. The woman on the other end of the line starts to say something, hesitates. Then she tells Olga she has the wrong number and hangs up.

By then, even though I've never told her anything and deny everything, Mom understands enough to know that things had been dark for me in Ukraine. She stops trying to find my birth family. She becomes angry, too, in her own way. She decides they don't deserve to know where I am or how I'm doing—that if they want to know, they can come find me themselves. In the meantime, she'll protect me with everything she has.

I get back to ice-skating as soon as I can. Angela's not sure I can jump with my prosthetic leg, but she's game to try it. Some of the other volunteers are outright incredulous. "It won't work," I hear them say. "She won't be able to do it."

This only makes me more determined. Angela and I practice executing a single lutz. It's the classic figure-skating move, where a skater glides backward in a beautiful curve before taking off and spinning once. In pushing off the serrated edges of the skate to launch myself airborne, I feel powerful. Capable. I forget that I even have a fake leg. It's just along for the ride. My right, real leg is doing all the work.

In my mind I'm sailing through the air, twirling three times, and landing with a perfect flourish. In reality I'm an inch off the ice and barely making a ninety-degree turn. But I want to work toward a full spin. I want to nail it, like Kristi Yamaguchi. I want to practice and practice until I get it, no matter what it takes. It's the first goal I've ever set for myself.

Before I can accomplish it, Mom tells me we're leaving Buffalo.

chapter

six

Sometime in the middle of my school year in fifth grade, Mom's new department chair at the university tells her they won't be renewing her speech-language pathology position next year. With her PhD, Mom's an expensive faculty member to keep on board. The chair wants that money for research. Mom could go into the K–12 public school system—but she's spent the last few years working with the law clinic at the university to advocate *against* the district, on behalf of kids with speech and language-based learning issues who are being mistreated in classes. And she needs a university position, where the benefits are better. She can't care for me and my jumble of medical needs without those. She finds a new position at the University of Louisville in Kentucky, starting at the beginning of the next school year.

The biggest task for Mom, though, is telling me that we have to leave the only place I've ever associated with *home.*

"What am I going to *do?*" I fume. I am so *angry.* "I won't be able to skate there. I won't have any friends. I won't be able to do *anything.*" She's taking me away from everything I know. Everything that makes me happy.

"Well, you know the rule when you move to Kentucky," she says.

Obviously I don't. I don't know anything about Kentucky. I don't want to know, either. I already hate Kentucky. But I have to admit that, despite myself, I'm curious about what she's going to say next.

"Every person has to go horseback riding."

I stare at her. I hadn't expected her to say *that*. It reaches down through my funk and lifts me up just the slightest. "Really?"

She nods. Mom knows I love animals. She also knows that I'm one of the most gullible people on the planet. And of course I choose to believe her.

It's not enough, though. I'm so sad at the idea of leaving here that it hangs over all my days, all the time. I don't know anything in America but this house that is *home*. And if we leave it, what does that mean? What are we going to? The only other reality I know is a murky series of orphanages.

Around the same time, the fact of my fake leg, the understanding that I actually *am* different, finally sinks in. I begin to feel it in the way the other kids look at me. In the way I look at myself. I'm still not overly self-conscious about my legs, though. People might see my legs and think (or even say out loud), *Oh. You're disabled.* But they see my hands, and they think, *What the hell is wrong with that girl's hands?*

It's my hands that I hate.

All the surgeries haven't made them look normal. Far from it. My fingers are still a little webbed. My weird thumb-finger looks nothing like a thumb. The pins and staples left horrible scars. I still don't have normal nails, and I'll never be able to paint them like other girls—I don't want to draw more attention to them than they already get.

It's impossible to forget about my legs since I deal with the prosthetic constantly. But I still forget about my hands being different. Until I see myself in the mirror, trying to brush my hair or button a blouse. I stop still, staring at them, thinking, *My God, what* are *those?* At a time when girls start to care what they look like, begin comparing themselves to other girls, and become deep wells of self-consciousness, I take to wearing long sleeves to try to cover my telltale hands, sweating determinedly through the summer in the name of concealment.

I begin to learn what *ugly* is.

Some friends stand up for me in school when other kids make comments about my hands. I stand up for myself, too. I start cursing and yelling. More than once, I'm sent to the principal's office for screaming "Fuck you!" at another kid to stop the relentless teasing.

I start to think that no one likes me. I'm *so* different, people must all hate me. So I start to hate myself. After all, I'm such a freak show that my birth mother gave me up.

Maybe I should never have come here. Only when I came to America did I start hating myself—did I understand what *disabled* means and how it marks you. Limits you.

I begin to get sick all the time. All the frustration I'm holding in starts poisoning me from the inside. I start saying, "I don't want to live anymore." It becomes a refrain.

In March, as winter lets up in the north and our time in Buffalo ticks toward its end, Mom takes me to another therapist. It's just a thirty-minute assessment, Mom says. I head into the therapy room with the woman, leaving Mom in the waiting room.

I don't talk. I don't talk much anyway to anyone but Mom, let alone to strangers. The therapist gives me sheets of paper, colored pencils, markers, invites me to draw if I want. I look at the blank pages with blank eyes. I pick up a pencil, slowly draw the clumsy outlines of a horse.

"Do you like animals?"

I nod shyly.

"Does your mom have any pets?"

She's found the chink in my armor. I hear myself start talking about Buddy. I tell her stories about my stuffed animals, about watching

Scooby-Doo and how I still like to watch *Barney* even though I'm way too old for it.

Under my hands, without my realizing it, as if the white page has turned into a Ouija board of drawing, shapes start to form while my mind is occupied talking to the woman about safe things.

An hour later, the therapist goes out to find Mom. She doesn't give Mom an update. She just asks, "Can I give her some hot chocolate?"

"Of course," Mom says, curious but patient and nonintrusive. Like always. "If she'll drink it. Is she okay?"

The therapist nods and returns to me.

The drawings keep coming. One image repeats itself among the others. A set of stairs. Two beds in a room. One on this side, one on that side. No windows. And a huge figure, always dark, looming into, over, encompassing the scene.

Another hour passes. The therapist again leaves me in the room with my drawings and pencils and markers to go talk to Mom.

My mother drops a magazine into her lap to look into the therapist's face, which has gone dead serious.

"This is going to be a long process. There's a lot there. She's likely to need therapy the rest of her life."

Mom closes her eyes, nods, as the weight of all the unnamable things she's been unable to protect me from rises in her chest like a dense fog.

"And I think we need to put her on an antidepressant. She has severe depression and anxiety, and she's dealing with PTSD as well."

Mom regards the therapist, trying to take this all in without breaking down right there in the chair. She knew the frustration that consumed me. She knew the anxiety, the hypervigilance. Other therapists have told her all that. But Mom has never fully processed the relentless diagnoses the therapist uses now because I'm also always smiling, laughing, bubbly, a master at hiding behind an "everything's fine" mask. The shapes of some things click into place in Mom's head, pulled into focus from the blurry whole of her daughter's youth, increasingly revealed as sinister.

"Can you tell me anything about what you learned?" she asks the therapist, even knowing, with her psychology background, that the woman won't, can't, not really.

"I can tell you that it will be hard for her to experience good things as truly good. She may never be able to be in a healthy romantic relationship. Unless we can keep her in therapy, and on some meds to help her manage." The therapist pauses for a moment, considering. Then she shakes her head.

"It's her story to tell you when she's ready."

———————

"*Mom*, I'll work on it when I get back! Let's *go*," I say in my best convincing voice, which unfortunately sounds more like a whine. We're going to miss the school concert if we don't go, and I'm in the chorus.

Mom relents. "Okay, but you do have to finish this project for tomorrow. And you know it will be late when we get back, past your normal bedtime."

I have an art project due. It was a partner project, and it would have been done this afternoon in class, but the other girl changed it and ruined everything. It looks horrible. I was mad, but I didn't do any of the things I normally would—crumple papers, throw pencils across the room, yell. I've been on a low dose of medication for a couple of weeks now, and maybe that's helping. Instead, I just refused to turn it in and have the other kids—or my teacher—think that this mess was my work. I need to redo the whole thing. But first, I want to sing with the other kids. And Mom lets me.

It's already past my bedtime when we get back. But I sit down at the kitchen table and get to work with the scissors and glue and construction paper. By the time it looks good enough for my standards, it's after ten. I look down at my lovely art project. And I have this bizarre feeling that I can't figure out.

"Mom"—she's been reading at the table to keep me company—"I feel really weird."

"Are you hungry?" Mom knows I'm so used to hunger that I often won't eat unless she hands me something.

"No, it's not that. I don't know what it is, I've never felt like this."

"Does something hurt?"

"No."

"Are you sad? Or mad at the girl in your class?"

"No. It's good, it's like . . . I just feel warm all over. From the inside out."

Mom sits back and looks at me, a smile breaking across her face like a wave. "Oksana, you're *happy*."

The feeling is so unfamiliar that I can't get used to it. Everything feels so comfortable and safe and secure. I find myself needing to replicate what my body knows is normal, because it's not this. Especially at night. My body inexplicably reacts negatively to the not-normal of feeling safe, and I'm confused and scared, and the only thing that makes me calm down is the familiar feel of pain. I smuggle the scissors from downstairs up to my room. Under the covers, I drag the blade across my skin in places no one will see. Not even Mom.

It releases the confusing pressure building up in my chest, my throat, and behind my mouth in a sickness that wants to choke me.

This is the only outlet I know right now.

A couple weeks before the end of the school year in Buffalo, Mom gets a call from my school nurse. "Mrs. Masters?"

"It's Ms.," Mom says almost absently, tired by now of making this distinction for people.

"Are you available to come and pick up Oksana?"

"Why? Is she okay?"

"She's . . . Well. No. She's not okay. We have her on suicide watch."

I'd finally expressed a plan, out loud, to fulfill those thoughts I'd been having. Not to Mom. To Jessica. The medication makes me dull, but it doesn't chase away what's happened, and I don't know how to escape. I'm too young, too confused, too far under the drowning water to think there might be a subtle but crucial addition to that phrase *I don't want to live anymore*—that the solution lies in thinking, *I don't want to live* like this *anymore*. I tell Jessica I have these pills now, that I can take a bunch of them at once and solve everything: my hands, my legs, my lost image in the mirror, having to leave Buffalo, everything from before that I've buried down deep and can't talk about. Jessica, totally freaked-out, tells the nurse.

Mom, palm now perpetually to her chest like someone's knifed her there, drops her last projects at the university and takes the remainder of her vacation days. She stays with me twenty-four hours, seven days a week, only leaving me with Jessica's parents to get groceries or fill prescriptions. She grieves, alone, that this is all her fault for triggering it, for making us leave the only place I've felt safe enough to call *home*.

———

Mom directs the movers as they pack up our furniture and other stuff into a big orange van. When it drives away, I feel nothing. Not until Mom and I are packing up the car with our personal necessities and our two cats do I feel my chest start to cave in. Soon there's nothing else to do, and we're standing in the driveway looking back at our empty house. I take it in for the last time: The symmetrical gabled windows, one of which looks out from my bedroom, with Aunt Sherry's mural painted on the wall in there.

The front porch I used to jump off of with my two real legs. Mom puts her arm around me.

Jessica and her parents have come to say goodbye. When the tears come, I blame it on something else. I still can't stand to cry in front of anyone.

"I'm not crying. It's these stupid allergies. I can't wait to get out of here and not worry about these allergies anymore."

But Jessica can see right through me, and she's crying, too, hugging me. Her parents are crying. We're all bawling.

Except Mom. She still doesn't allow herself to cry in front of me. She knows it makes me scared that I've done something wrong and she'll send me back to Ukraine. I know that many times she's left the room or held her emotions on a tight leash to make sure I feel safe. She's doing it now. Even though she must be feeling just as much sadness, leaving the house she brought her daughter *home* to.

We get in the car. I twist my neck to stare at the house until it slides out of view, and I keep looking even after. It's a long time before I face forward, to watch the yellow lines lying on the road carrying us into the unknown.

chapter

seven

I walk with a throng of kids through the double doors of my new middle school. Then I freeze, just inside by the glass window of an office, with people streaming by me like a rock in a river. The three-story building appeared massive from the outside. In here, though, the ceilings are low-slung, pushing the crowds close and trapping the roar of sound from thousands of sixth, seventh, and eighth graders greeting one another, gossiping, shouting. Whispers magnify. Bursts of laughter thunder. Lockers slam. Zippers zip up and down on backpacks. The packed hallway is in constant movement.

Every face is new. Unfamiliar.

Standing there, my body vibrates with the hypervigilance that defines my physical existence: knowing what's around me, who's behind me, what each sound means and where it's coming from and how I navigate it or defend from it or hide from it. In here, I might explode. *This is not okay. This is not okay.*

I close my eyes. Take a deep breath. Open them. At the end of the hallway through the teeming mass of students sits the elevator, next to the set of stairs that kids hop and skip effortlessly up and down. I finger the elevator key in my pocket that the staff gave my mom for me to use. I zero in on the dull silver doors. I force myself to move, take a few steps.

"You walk weird. What's wrong with you?"

Oh my God. I snap my head up, but the boy who said it is already walking away, just a quick pass-and-jab job. Other kids stare. I look down at the jeans covering my legs. Of course no one here would know what I'm working with. But I'd planned it that way so that I'd appear more normal. To myself and to everyone else. I'd had a good hair day this morning (thank God), and my face is miraculously free from any zits. My outfit is on point (which I know because I spent forty-five minutes picking it out last night). But *of course* I still look weird.

I clench my teeth and keep moving through the turbulence. *Just try to walk normal.* People watch, knots of kids part before me, but I make it to the elevator without further comment. I take out the key, and as I fit it into the lock to open the doors:

"What makes *you* so special?"

My body flashes hot. I don't even turn to look at the mob to identify the source. I try to shrink into my backpack. I can't handle this kind of ridicule every time I wait for the elevator, the only one riding it while literally everyone else takes the stairs like normal people. I pocket the key again and resolutely turn toward the looming flight.

I grab hold of the railing and step up on my real leg. Then my prosthetic. I put pressure on the fake toe to release the hinged knee and get it to bend and lift, then swing it to get it to lock, praying it won't land in that limbo where it swings wildly back and forth and I have no control over it. In the rush to get to class, people push past and pile up behind me. I close my ears to the murmurs and the not-so-whispered taunts— "Freak"—and tune out everything, intent on making it to the top, to the classroom, where I can sit down somewhere in the back and just take a moment to exhale and relax without people staring at me.

My first class is history. I walk into the half-full room, students rustling around in their backpacks and shifting in chairs under the indifferent reign of a teacher my schedule card names Mr. Rathbun. Standing at the front of the classroom, he's a short, skinny old man wound up like a too-tight spring. He sees me move through the door, nods, and points.

"Hi, yes, I've heard about you. We've set you up over here."

I look where his bony finger directs. So does every other kid in the room. A phone book sits on the floor at the foot of one of the desk/chair combos in the center of the class, a conspicuous prop so that my prosthetic can reach the ground instead of dangling and creating uncomfortable pressure on the rest of my lower body. *Yep, that will* really *help me fit in,* I think. *I hate school. I hate this city.*

I wish I were back home.

———————————

I walk in the front door of our new house, drained from my body's overdrive all day in hypervigilance mode, and from being so aware of people's reactions to me even while I spent so much energy trying to look like everyone else. I'm still reeling from trying to get around the three-story school with all its stupid flights of stairs. I go straight to my room, slinging my backpack on the floor. I unbutton the jeans that hid my legs and slide them down, twisting to sit on the bed. Above the foam padding that I insisted the doctors install around the calf so the prosthetic looks more like a real leg when under pants, and above that traitorous hinge that serves as a knee, I undo the pink straps I used to think were so cool. I hook my fingers inside the plastic socket that goes all the way up to my hip and makes sitting for long periods so uncomfortable—*Thank you, phone book, even though I hate you*—and push it off, exposing the sleeve that's supposed to protect my thigh from rubbing. I slide that off, too, like a nylon only way less sexy. Air flow caresses my skin for the first time in hours. It feels like I just dumped a ton of bricks. I stand, pull my jeans back up, and hop toward my bedroom door, heading for the kitchen to raid the fridge.

This is always the first thing I do whenever I get home from anywhere, my walk-in-the-door routine. At home, where no one can see me, I feel so much more mobile relying on just my real leg.

It's a weird juxtaposition. With my prosthetic on, I have two legs. I sometimes even forget that I'm missing one. Sometimes, at the prosthetist's office, when he leaves the socket on but takes off the knee or foot to work on them, I suddenly think, *Oh yeah, I'm an amputee.* With both legs, I feel as normal as I possibly can. But without my fake leg, I'm free.

There's a difference.

Blink.

I'm crying. Everything hurts so much. I can't escape the weight. An instant need to survive, to free myself from this, eclipses everything, and for the first time, I struggle. Hard. There's a metallic flick. Something small flashes in the thin light from under the closed door—

Blink.

I wake. Gasping, horrified. I don't want to know what that was playing out in my dream. It didn't happen. It didn't happen.

I won't fall asleep again.

I try to keep my eyes open while Mr. Rathbun drones on from his static post in front of the whiteboard. In the last couple weeks, I've learned that he is the kind of teacher who doesn't, well . . . *teach.* He assigns chapters to read and what seems like busywork to go with it, and if anyone doesn't get a concept, he calls them out for their lack of understanding in front of the entire class. He's the total opposite of my science teacher, Mrs. Adams.

Far younger and with a thick fall of dark red hair, she speaks to us—me—in direct tones that make us feel like adults. She always wants to ensure her students understand, asking straightforwardly and somehow nonmortifyingly "Are you getting this?" in a way that leaves the student feeling both confident and attended to. And to me, she's always asking, "Are you getting around okay? What do you need?" She senses my stubbornness, that I'll never actually ask for help, and so she asks me instead.

"Now, if you could all pull out your assignments from last night," Mr. Rathbun says in his reedy voice, turning away from us to riffle through his desk before he even finishes the sentence.

In the shuffling and murmuring, I hear the girl next to me mutter under her breath, "I hate how he just talks *at* us. Like we're not even people."

I look over at her. A beauty with blond hair and bright blue eyes, she always sits at the desk next to me. But it's the first time I've heard her say anything except when Mr. Rathbun has called on her. More than just quiet, like me, she seems incredibly shy, retreating into consistently hunched shoulders to hide her slightly heavier frame that's already much more developed than the rest of ours. The both of us are so uncomfortable in our appearance, I think. She glances up and catches my eye.

"I know," I say, equally conspiratorial. "Like he'd rather be anywhere else."

She smiles, a little hesitantly. We put our heads back down as Mr. Rathbun starts in again. I replay my words in my head, proud of myself for making her smile, for talking at all. I might be opinionated, but that's only once I feel comfortable. I'm not a raging extrovert. No one would ever find me at the center of a crowd leading the conversation. I'm the one in the corner of the room.

The girl doodles something on a piece of paper, folds it, and passes it to me, low down by our hips. I open it quietly in my lap. A doodle of Mr. Rathbun with a wide-open mouth, a few stick-figure kids snoozing z's. I stifle a giggle. Mr. Rathbun pauses and glares at me. I straighten my face and duck my head, embarrassed at the gazes turning my way. I'm still the troublemaker, apparently, always the one getting caught.

At the end of class, as people pack up and shoot out of their chairs, the blond girl turns to me.

"I'm Summer. What's your next class?"

I pause a second, surprised that anyone is speaking to me. *Don't be weird, just respond.* "I'm Oksana. I'm going to math, down the other end."

"Want to walk with me?" She seems just as surprised with herself. She has that look of being hopeful without wanting to seem like it, not wanting to overplay her hand, not wanting to seem too invested. I know that look well.

"Yeah. That'd be great."

Inside my chest, something loosens. As we walk into the hall side by side, some pressure gives, just a little bit, and for the space of that walk down the hall, everything feels easy and safe.

———

"I think I want to try out for the dance team," I say to Mrs. Adams. Everyone else has already filed out after class. I often stay a few minutes longer to talk to her. She's become my favorite teacher. She's in charge of the dance team, which my friend Hannah is trying out for next week.

Hannah was thrilled when I told her I wanted to try out, too. "Yesss!" she squealed. "We can practice together, perform at all the basketball and football games, ride the bus together to away games. And we'd get to wear those cute outfits. It would be so fun!"

It *would* be fun. I've made a few more friends by now, but I'm still trying to fit in here.

Mrs. Adams turns from wiping the board, her cloud of hair floating in sync. "Really? That's great! We're teaching the routine after school tomorrow, then you'll have a few days to practice it before tryouts. Can you make it?"

"Yes! I'll come with Hannah. We'll practice together."

I head to my next class. This is what I love about Mrs. Adams. Even though she checks in on me sometimes to see if I need some physical assistance, I trust her to treat me like everyone else: like there's nothing *wrong* with me.

———————

Hannah comes down off her turn and stops, stumped. Again. "What's the next move, Oksana?" she asks for the umpteenth time as I sit leaning against her bedroom wall.

"It's the grapevine step, you know, where you clap after?" I half mime it from my sitting position.

In my head, the routine Mrs. Adams and a few of the dance team girls showed us for tryouts plays like a film. I can *see* every step. I just can't *do* them. Not yet, anyway. I need a lot more practice to get good enough on my hinged prosthetic knee. I imagine that once I figure it out, I'll be able to spin *forever* on my fake leg. Like the lutz in ice-skating, only better. But I'm not sure I want Hannah to watch me learn how to dance just yet. She's *good.* She just can't remember all the steps in order. But she has the moves, and she has the bubbly personality. She'll make the team for sure.

I think I have a real chance, too. I want it bad enough. I want to be part of a team. I'm so exhausted from standing out.

"Like this, right?" Hannah steps and grins while I clap in time with her from the floor.

———————

"Oksana, um, can I talk to you for a moment?" Mrs. Adams says.

Hannah and I are sitting in the bleachers of the gym. It's the afternoon of tryouts, and it's almost time. I've been jittery with excitement all day, and the two of us are joking back and forth, barely able to contain our nerves.

Hannah and I look up at Mrs. Adams, our giggles toning down a notch to expectant smiles. My favorite teacher stops in front of us, frowns at Hannah (who, confused, fails to take the hint to leave), then focuses on me.

"So. Actually . . . I don't think I can let you try out."

My stomach drops. I hear Hannah gasp beside me. "What?" I say.

"Your prosthetic is going to pose a danger to the other girls. I know it can be hard for you to control. It might hurt someone. I'm so sorry, Oksana, I just can't let you participate. I hope you can understand."

I sit speechless, staring at her. Hannah is silent beside me. Mrs. Adams moves as if to hug me, and that breaks my paralysis. I rush for the girls' bathroom, praying neither of them follow. I slam inside the empty bathroom just before the tears let loose. I cry in disbelief. Flooded with shame and embarrassment, I look up and catch my reflection in the murky mirror.

Disabled. The word flashes behind my eyes. I've never thought of myself like that before. But now I'm unequivocally the freak show with the capacity to hurt other people with my fake leg. *Disabled.*

I scrub away the tears, splash cold water on my face. Then I walk out of the bathroom, on my abominable fake leg, to go and support Hannah, who needs help remembering the steps. I go sit on the bleachers to watch the *able*-bodied girls compete for a spot on a team I'll never even be allowed to try to make.

My mother walks purposefully into the gym and makes a beeline for Mrs. Adams, standing in front of the dance team with its new recruits. I've stayed after school to hang out with Hannah—who of course made the team yesterday—before her very first practice, and Mom's come to pick me up. The dance team is sharing the floor with the boys' basketball team, and Mrs. Adams's voice competes with shouts from the coach, the screech of shoes across the shiny floor, and the constant thunk of basketballs.

"I need to speak to you," Mom says, interrupting Mrs. Adams's instructions to the girls.

Mrs. Adams looks pointedly at the team arrayed in front of her, and back at Mom.

"Now." Mom leads Mrs. Adams a few feet away.

Oh my God. I want to sink into the bleachers and disappear. This is going to be mortifying.

"I was *there* at the practices," Mom says to Mrs. Adams. "Oksana was the only one who knew the routine. And she's one of the only girls who doesn't make the team? What is that about?" My mother rarely gets angry. She's kind and gentle. When she does get angry, you just hope the fierceness is on your behalf instead of directed at you.

"She couldn't *execute* all the steps, though," Mrs. Adams says, somewhat unprepared for the force that is my mother in protective mode.

"She might not have been able to do all the steps exactly the way you wanted, but there are ways around that. She's the only one who can do the splits. Have her do the splits in front of the team while they do a different move. I've watched enough cheerleading to know that's a common setup—one or two people are adding different moves to spice up the monotony of twelve girls doing the exact same thing."

"I just—I don't have the time to adapt every routine."

"You don't have time? Or you just don't want to?"

Mrs. Adams bristles. "I have to get back to my team now, we're performing at halftime in a few days. We need to practice."

Mom blocks her way. "It's a school sport! It's supposed to be for *every*body."

"We're not going to be able to win any medals if she's on the team!" Mrs. Adams finally says. "That's not fair to the other girls."

"She was the *only* girl who knew the routine, and you know that." Mom's voice rises above the gym noise to match Mrs. Adams's. They're shouting at each other now. "You're discriminating against her because of a physical difference. I could sue the pants off of you."

The color drains from Mrs. Adams's face. She knows my mother's right. Point: Mom. But I'm too busy dying of embarrassment to appreciate the win. Plus, despite everything, I still like Mrs. Adams. I need to get us out of here.

My mother is not a fighter. Despite her mama bear moments, I've never seen her get violent. But as I walk up to the two of them, I'm sure she might slap Mrs. Adams right there in the gym in front of fifty people.

"It's okay." I keep my head down. "I didn't really want to do it anyway. Let's just go." I pull Mom away.

On the ride home, I don't say anything. I have nothing to say.

Maybe volleyball will be different.

Summer's playing on the school's intramural team. She tells me how fun it is, how noncompetitive—there are no tryouts, anyone can be on the team—and that I should come play, too. Her mom's one of the coaches. Which is the likely reason I'm allowed to play at all.

At least they make me feel like I'm part of the team. Now, with practices after school, I have something else on my schedule to look forward to. I get to know the other girls, have a great time learning how the game works, and how to bump and pass the ball. In sharing this sport with Summer, we make new friends together, become part of a *group* of friends. And I just love the appearance of volleyball with its no-nonsense athletic clothing.

Except on my body.

Because my amputation is above the knee, my prosthetic socket goes all the way to my hip. With those tiny volleyball shorts, my fake leg is on full display to the world. So I make sure everything on the prosthetic matches: the plastic, the foam, the straps. But no matter how cute and put-together it looks, the shorts don't care. They ride up and get stuck in the socket. It's so painful we have to stop scrimmage games so I can sort it out.

That makes people mad. Most of the girls don't care, they're just on the court to have a good time. But their competitive parents—they care. They think I'm inhibiting the team.

So it starts to happen that when the games against other teams begin, the coaches never call me in. I sit on the sidelines.

I'm not stupid. I know exactly what's going on. I stay on the team anyway because practicing and then cheering from the sidelines is better than nothing. I make sure I never let on that it bothers me. Because that would be even more embarrassing than this already is.

Blink.

I'm starving. The old feeling of hunger is a pain that goes straight through me. The gloom of the cavernous room reeks of potatoes cooking in swamp water, the darkness weakly lit by a sterile light coming from under a door somewhere.

Laney's whispered voice: "Get under there. Don't move."

The screech of her hand on the cold floor as it's dragged into the dark.

Blink.

I yank myself awake, my throat constricting my voice. I can't breathe. I'm soaked in sweat. The sheets are wet with my terror. I drag air into my lungs. When I can finally feel my voice again, I scream at the top of my lungs, "Mom! Mom!"

She's right next to me in an instant. She's never far away. She gathers me in. "It was just a dream. Just a nightmare. Do you want to tell me about it?"

"No." I'm shaking. "It's nothing. It was nothing. I just wanted to make sure you're still here."

I can't go back to sleep. I picture picked flowers for crowns that hang limp. I think of the sugar cubes I still hoard under the bed.

Night after night, the dreams keep coming, the memories I've buried so deep scream to the surface and soak me in their sweaty fear.

After they wake me, I spend the rest of the night burying them again so I don't remember them in the morning. Then each night when they return, I'm shocked and horrified and confused.

I don't understand what's happening to me.

––––––––––

I yank the prosthetic socket over my leg, panting from the effort. *It shouldn't be this hard,* I think. It's almost uncomfortably tight. Did the plastic shrink with the weather, or something? Is that even a thing? I pull my jeans over my hips. I have to suck in my stomach to button them. What is *happening*?

I stop eating as much. I don't want to gain weight. Most of the other girls at school are so skinny. Besides, I *have* to be able to fit into my prosthetic.

Within a couple of weeks, I've gained twenty pounds. While barely eating. Mom, alarmed at my sudden drop in food consumption, takes me to our new psychiatrist in Louisville.

"I think it's those new meds you put her on," Mom says to him. Psychiatrists here seem to operate differently from the ones we had in Buffalo. They ask one or two questions, that's it, then add meds or adjust a dose. It seems a little abrupt for playing God with my head.

"Yes, weight gain is certainly a side effect," he says, unconcerned. "But they're much better for anxiety. Besides, she was underweight before. What are you worried about? That you're passing on your weight issues to her?"

Mom's not skinny. She never has been. It's never bothered her that I know of, and she doesn't have any "issues" that I know of either. But now she gets angry.

"First of all, she's not my biological daughter, remember? I'm not worried about passing on any genetic 'weight issues.' Second, her prosthetic doesn't fit! That's not a minor concern. It's too tight, it's causing her pain."

"Well, just get a new socket."

Mom snorts. "Sockets cost thousands of dollars. And they take *weeks* to construct and fit. That's not the solution. There have to be some medications with less side effects that will help her anxiety without creating more of it in a different form."

He puts me on something else. There's always something else. I don't even know what my real emotions are anymore, what I'd be like without pills clouding my brain.

It's always someone else deciding what's good for me.

Some days, I fake being sick so I can stay home from school. Mom suspects occasionally—she even caught me once with the thermometer against my bedside lamp—but I've also legitimately been sick so many times that she doesn't call me out on it.

Part of it is that I've never liked school. But the other part is those papers in the top drawer of Mom's secretary desk that we hauled from Buffalo. Once she goes to work, I creep out of my bed.

At thirteen, I can't really speak Ukrainian anymore. I can still read Ukrainian letters, but it's fading fast. I know the handwritten paper with my birth parents' names on it, though. I take it to the computer, and I google their names and, even though I've done it a dozen times before, I hope something new will pop up in the search. As if I'll find my birth family that easily. But it turns out that Oksana and Alexander Bondarchuck are the Ukrainian equivalent of Jane and John Smith.

I'm intrigued by the idea of my family. But the rage has built, too. Because even if I can't read much Ukrainian anymore, I know exactly what that first sentence says. It's seared into my brain. *We relinquish our daughter.* How can someone write a sentence like that? And just *give up* a living child?

Spent by now, I put all the papers back in the order I found them. I'm careful about this every time. I don't want Mom thinking that I'm snooping through these documents because I want to leave her for my birth family. I'd never leave her.

Plus, she gets mad when I'm in her stuff. I shut the drawer quietly and head back upstairs.

"Mom, stop *asking*! I don't want to do it."

"It might be a good way to meet people. And you might love it." Mom is persistent. And stubborn. Just like me, to the endless frustration of both of us. "Why don't you just try it once?"

Since spring started, Mom has been trying to convince me to go rowing on the Ohio River. Ever since Randy Mills decided that it would be good for me. Randy is the adaptive resource teacher at school—basically, heading up assistance for students with special needs. Such as me. He was the phone-book architect. Randy—that's how he introduces himself to students, I can't imagine calling him Mr. Mills—has his own special need: a hearing aid for one of his ears. His lack of hearing means he's always talking loudly and standing too close to you, which left me unsure if I liked him the first few times I met him. Then he brought up this adaptive rowing program he manages on Saturday mornings on the Ohio, which snakes somewhere through Louisville. I've never even seen the river, let alone given a thought to rowing on it. But Randy won't let it go, and hence Mom won't let it go, like a telephone game of nagging me, asking over and over, "Why don't you just give it a try?"

"Because it's *adaptive* rowing, Mom, that's why," I say, her face hopeful but sort of exhausted from my refusals. "For *disabled* people." I most definitely don't want to be associated with a parasport because that will mean I'm one of those people, too. I have one real leg. I'm not para. Plus, losing out on the dance team and sitting on the sidelines in volleyball games is excruciating enough. I don't need to try this thing that will only prove that I *am* disabled. I'd rather do something with Hannah or Summer to deepen those friendships I'm forming and start to feel more like a part of what *they're* doing. And they certainly can't try rowing with me because it's only for people like . . . me.

Then Mrs. Adams tells me that Kevin Smith, the cutest guy in the seventh grade, the one I've had a crush on for weeks, is also rowing with Randy. Turns out the adaptive part is for people with cognitive needs, too, and Kevin apparently has a touch of ADHD.

Which is how I find myself saying to my mom one Saturday morning at an ungodly early hour, in an indifferent tone of voice to show that I don't care *that* much and she most certainly isn't right and hasn't by any means won this argument, "*Okay*. I'll try rowing. Can you take me down there?"

We show up late. The program started at 7:00 a.m.—when any self-respecting teenager is still in bed on a weekend morning and dreaming about lounging on the couch all day—and it had already been past seven when I told Mom that I wanted to go. Then we got lost on our way to the waterfront because Mom and I are both navigationally challenged.

When we finally find it, neither of us can believe we've never seen the river before. The Ohio is huge, a wide brown ribbon of flat rushing water. Waterfront Park, where the program is held, is a strip of public beach with a big square dock located down the bank from a squat redbrick building that's seen better days. The University of Louisville rowing club is housed here, but the scene on the dock is pretty much the opposite of a gathering of scholarship-awarded college athletes.

A wide range of bodies crowds the floating platform and spills onto shore, from teenagers with Down's syndrome to a man in his forties in a wheelchair missing both legs. Parents and volunteers hover over participants sitting, standing, staggering on the floating dock, or struggling into boats. I spot Randy, kneeling down on the dock to adjust something for a girl a little older than me who's floating in a boat and holding on to the bobbing platform—for dear life, it looks to me. As Mom and I make our way out of the car, Randy stands his tall, thin frame upright, his approaching-middle-age slight belly outlined against his T-shirt as he jogs over to a pile of paddles, life vests, and other unfamiliar gear, selects some kind of strap, and jogs back to the dock.

There's no sign of Kevin Smith. And thank God for that. I don't want to be lumped into this group. This is not going to be for me at *all*. I turn to Mom to suggest that we can still leave. We hadn't told Randy we were coming, and we were late anyway. No one would even know I'd showed up.

But then Randy looks up and sees us. He raises his hand in surprised welcome. *Great. Now we're stuck.* He waves us down, characteristically excited. This whole program is Randy's baby, from creation to execution, a passion project to get people on the water to experience what he saw as the sport's therapeutic miracles. He directs it in his free time, aided by a few consistent volunteers. It seems like a pretty expansive program for someone's free time. Despite myself, I'm impressed.

We make our way down the steep wooden ramp on the bank to the edge of the dock. I stop at its edge and eye the thing: a sketchy-looking massive platform of weathered, settled wood and rusty metal. Worse than its peeling appearance, it's a floating dock. It rolls and vibrates with the movement of water and people. It's terrifying, a nightmare for my free-swinging hinge of a mechanical knee. *How the hell am I even supposed to walk on this?*

Randy catches my expression. "Oksana, I'm so glad you're here!" He moves toward me as the girl he'd been helping pushes away from the dock. "We'll get you warmed up on a rower so you can get a feel for it. Come on over here."

He steps off the dock and steers me away from it—*Thank God*—toward a contraption on the grass.

"You'll hop on this with your prosthetic on, but then we'll take it off for getting in the boat, so we can fit the seat to you well and you can feel the push of the stroke. This is sort of like a dry practice run."

What? I am *not* taking my leg off in front of people. With my prosthetic on, I have two legs. I'm normal. Even though everyone here has to take some sort of adaptive measure to get in a boat—remove something, rejigger something, have help—I am, above all else, a thirteen-year-old girl very conscious of my body and how I appear. Taking off my leg in front of these people would be an admission that I'm in the same category. That I'm *para*.

But for now I say nothing. I settle myself onto the rower, and Randy adjusts some things, shows me how to use it, then leaves me there to "get warmed up." He steers Mom away, saying something about tasks needing to be done. I know she'd be happy to be put to work away from the waterline—she has hated water ever since a long unintentional swim on the Snake River during a rafting trip when she was younger. In their absence, I wrestle with the old machine to the rhythm of a mantra playing in my head: *I shouldn't be here. I shouldn't be doing this. I am not part of this.*

Randy returns shortly. "Okay, I'm ready for you!" He's toting an ugly orange life jacket. I sigh and clip it around my torso, then follow him nervously down to the dock.

The chaos has settled a bit now that people are out in boats on the water, and so has the bucking platform, thankfully. I make it to the edge without embarrassing myself. I look down at the boat. It's as well-worn as the dock, long, and maybe once was beige sometime before I was born. Its narrow, flat-covered decks open to a small cockpit with a front seat and a back seat, all of it just a few inches above the water. I survey the river. The dock sits on a slow channel separated from the enormous current of water by a treed island. It's calm here. But what about out there?

"Okay, let's sit down and get the prosthetic off."

"No," I say, more harshly than I mean to. "I'll leave it on."

Randy considers me. Then he just nods. "Well, let's sit down and put both feet in the boat, and I'll help you into it. Then I'll get in and take you out to explain some things."

I lower myself onto the splintered wood. It's covered in duck-poop stains, mossy and disgustingly soft and saturated with a cloying mildewy smell from people constantly brushing and splashing the poop off into the water.

This is gross. I hate rowing.

Randy hands me down onto the front seat, then bends to adjust some things by my feet. Suddenly, as I feel the boat bob under my hips, I forget about wanting to hate this. I forget all about Kevin Smith.

I am on water. I'm floating on water.

Randy settles himself into the back seat. "Okay, now push the blade against the dock, and that will move us out."

I pick up the oar handles. I nudge out the oar closest to the dock, feel resistance against the moldy wood, lean into it, and push harder. Both oars fall into the water with a precise, quiet plunk as we drift away.

I feel that sound in my chest, like a calm touch. On the surface of the water, the oars create tiny circles on either side of the boat, circles that get bigger and bigger, and the farther we drift, the bigger the circles become, chasing our boat and encompassing it. I can't take my eyes off them.

I exhale. I didn't even know I'd been holding my breath.

Randy breaks my spell. Gently, like he knows what I'm experiencing.

He probably does. He explains the mechanics of the oars to me: *feather*, where the blades are parallel to the water as you swing them away from you. *Square*, where the blades cut the water to push it away as you pull the oars toward you. He demonstrates. Then he tells me it's my turn.

I face forward again, pick up the oars, hover them. I push them out like birds winging over the water. Then I turn them—square them—drop them into the water, and push.

The water pushes back.

I didn't expect that. I don't know what I expected, though. Maybe for the boat to be more wobbly, or for the motion to be one-sided, but definitely not for the water to be a partner in this.

I stroke again. The boat skims across the river's surface.

I can be in control here. Of the movement, the direction, the speed.

All of the storm that's been raging inside my head, inside my body, I push into the water. Then the oars emerge so gracefully under my power, like a release. I release it all under my hands.

I stroke again. And again. I forget anyone else is in the boat with me.

I fall into the rhythm of it, I live inside the sound of that rhythm: *dunk-duh-dunk*. The feeling of moving my arms forward, of the oars in my hands, the split-second pause while I turn the blade, the drop, the *push*, the *resistance*, the release. The quick burst of power that becomes quietly smooth.

My body is good at this. It knows this. It knows water.

Suddenly I'm back in a hot dark room with a square little pool and the sounds of water, the smell of water. The feel of the memory floods me. My body remembers. It relaxes. Even as all five of my senses wake up, my constant bodily hypervigilance that has told me since I can remember, *Be aware of this noise, of this person behind you, of where your body is and what could happen to it,* leaks away. Because I'm not afraid. I'm comfortable here. I'm safe. I feel something inside me open up and let go, just like the oar letting go of the water under my hands to take the next stroke.

For a moment, I can't identify the release I'm feeling, I've felt it so rarely. Then I think, *Oh.*

This is happiness.

———

All week, I think about rowing. I can't wait to get back on the water. I haven't looked forward to something like this since . . . I don't know if I *ever* have.

The second Saturday morning, Randy says to me, "Do you want to try taking off your leg this time? You'll have more control of the boat, be directly connected."

He offers it gently, such a central characteristic of his. I don't like many men. Even Kevin Smith—I think he's cute, but I don't want to actually *talk* to him. But Randy's kindness, his being something of a dreamer, those glasses he's always pushing up the bridge of his nose, the way he listens with full concentration to whoever is speaking to him—it all adds up to a benign demeanor that lets me trust him. After last week I feel like I've known him my whole life.

On the dock in the early-morning light, I look around. I realize that everyone else is so focused on dealing with their own adaptions, and so expectant that everyone else getting into a boat has something of their own to deal with, that I'm being dramatic and a little silly to hide mine. And if Randy says that I'll be even more connected to the water without it . . .

I sit down on the dock. I take off my leg.

Randy helps me into the boat. My stump is strapped in above where my knee would have been. My other foot, flush against the pedal, feels so far away from where my stump ends. I look back up at my prosthetic on the dock. For the umpteenth time since I was nine years old—somehow these moments still hit with surprising frequency—I think, *This is my life. I have a fake leg. I have NO LEG.*

But added to that old thought is a new feeling. A freeing sensation, similar to taking off my leg at home. Because this is the first time I've ever taken it off in front of anyone who isn't my mom or my doctor.

I push away from the dock, Randy in the seat behind me. Plunk. That sound. Those ripples. I push the water, and with it all the conflicting and maddening thoughts I have about my body. My fake leg recedes as I row away from it. The pink straps, the foam padding, the shoe—*How funny that someone will stumble on it and freak out about a lonely disembodied leg wearing a shoe*—shrink and disappear from view as I escape into the rhythm of push, resistance, and release, thinking after a few minutes, *I love this.*

I love it.

Then suddenly the revelation: *I'm here* because *of that thing on the dock.* If not for my fake leg, if not for my amputation, if not for my weird body and all its problems that have caused me so much pain . . . I would never have tried this sport. I would never have experienced this thing that is opening me up like this. I've never felt this way about my body before.

And my last thought, before I disappear into the strokes:

It's going to be okay.

I still hate school. But I begin looking forward to rowing as the thing I get to do after I make it through the week. I want to improve, be stronger, faster, more fluid. I begin venturing beyond the slow channel into the current, stroking through a body of water bigger and more powerful than I ever imagined. The city rises beyond it, as if I'm outside it looking in.

I come to understand that rowing is a sport that's exactly the same for able-bodied people. We all propel ourselves the same way with our arms and torso. Perhaps they can reach a little farther in bending their knees or have more power in pushing off with their legs. But that just means I speed up my stroke to keep pace.

I get to know Bobby, Randy's partner in crime, whose specialty is coaching on the water while Randy sets up the equipment for rowers. It's Bobby who, when he watches my stroke and the force I use in the push and resistance, says to me in his calm Southern accent, "Don't fight the release."

Rowing becomes my lighthouse through the violent storms, signaling the way to survival. Every time I feel myself getting lost, it flashes again to bring me back. Over the next weeks, I work my way closer and closer to that beacon.

Then the doctors say:

"Tell us when you're ready for that second amputation."

chapter

eight

It starts with crazy pain in my foot, in the fall of my seventh-grade year. Not phantom pain in my ghost foot. In the real foot I have left. Every time I take a step, pain shoots up my foot into my leg. Over the years, all the doctors have assured me that I'll be able to keep my real leg. Maybe that impression is just the determined blinders of a thirteen-year-old. Maybe no doctors ever actually said that. But it's the belief I've clung to. I don't know what this pain means, but I can't lose my last real leg.

Mom does some research and takes me to the best pediatric orthopedic surgeon in Louisville.

The surgeon spends a lot of time with us. After she's looked at my X-rays, she explains that I have multiple stress fractures. The way my leg works, the foot more or less points straight down, as if I'm unintentionally pointing my toes all the time, which means all of my weight (all whopping eighty-five pounds of it without my prosthetic on the other side) is absorbed by the ball of my foot rather than the whole foot. There are also duplicate bones in my foot—and not just from my sixth toe, which I used to be so proud of, which was surgically removed long ago—causing some issues, and my ankle anatomy is off from taking the weight an intact tibia is supposed to bear. On top of all that, my knee has a deformity that angles the joint outward.

The surgeon lays out a schedule of about five to ten surgeries, all told, to address the pain. Then she hits us with the kicker.

"But these are Band-Aid solutions that will let her keep her leg until she's about twenty-five," the surgeon says, mostly to Mom. As if I can't understand. "But then she's likely to need the leg amputated after that. So I think it's really just a question of *when* the amputation will happen. I'll give you some time to think about all this and we'll schedule a follow-up."

I don't know if even *devastated* is a strong enough word. Or maybe it's not the right word at all because I'm not conceding the amputation. I'm only deigning to consider it. Not even that actually. I'm deigning to *think* about considering it. And the only way I will think about considering it is if it's a below-the-knee amputation.

I know exactly what it means to live without a knee. I've already had years of experience with it on my left side. Because here's what so many people don't understand: for every joint you're missing, it's an exponential loss of ability. Missing my feet would be like having a paper cut. Having one full prosthetic leg, and one fully functioning real leg, is more annoying, like an ingrown hair. Missing both feet *and* both knees?

I would never be able to run. Or jump. Stand up from the ground. Sit up without leverage. Ride a bike. Or—as ridiculous as it sounds— I'd never have that perfect romantic knee-pop pose when a boy gives me the best kiss in the world. But even the smallest thing like that *matters.* Like the fact that having two above-the-knee prosthetics with sockets all the way to the hip would not only mean I'd never be able to sit comfortably for the rest of my life; it would affect the way I could dress. I already have to buy jeans two sizes too big just to fit one prosthetic hip socket. What would I wear with two?

I think of my current prosthetic knee like an old-school storm door, the kind with a thick rusty spring that locks out if you push the door wide enough. My fake knee sounds just like that. I carry WD-40 in my backpack and purses just so people won't turn and stare at whatever made that horror-movie noise. I refuse to carry more WD-40 in my purse.

And then I realize . . . *rowing*. How will I row? My real leg stabilizes me in the boat. It's what I push off of in the stroke to pull the oars through the water, what makes the seat slide so satisfyingly in an endless fluid motion. I'll have to relearn how to row. It might not feel like the same sport for me, I might not love it in the same way anymore. I'm not even sure it's possible without legs.

What if I lose it entirely?

Blink.

The door opens, cutting the blackness of the second-floor room. The shadow moves in. It grows, monstrous, in the eerie slip of sickly light. A pair of ugly shoes takes one step. Stops. Two steps. Silence. The door creaks shut. An eternity of blackness. Then there's a hot weight, rusty bedsprings cut into my back—

Blink.

I yank myself awake, soaked in sweat yet again, heaving silently. I'm never screaming.

I have no voice.

I'm still afraid of my own bedroom at night. I've plotted out the likelihood of someone being able to approach the back of our house unnoticed, vault fifteen feet to my second-floor window, and get inside. Where they'd wait for me.

My abandonment issues pick up, too, if that's even possible. In my thirteen-year-old brain, I don't realize that's the term for what I'm dealing with. I do know that when my key sticks in the lock to our front door, I panic that Mom's changed the locks or moved altogether without me. When she's sad, I think it's my fault and that she'll leave me behind somewhere. When she's angry, I think it's directed at me and that she'll ship me back to Ukraine—that she's not going to keep me.

On top of all that drama, I have the typical teenage relationship with Mom: *Nurture me and love me, but let me push you away while I gain independence.*

"I just want to fit *in*, Mom." I've said this so many times to her—every time I'm depressed about my prosthetics, when my jeans won't fit right over them, when they don't look like real legs under my pants, when my gait is off, when I've fallen *again*, when I can't bear my hands, when I just want to wear a pair of cute shoes for once—I've lost count.

"Fitting in is boring. What you want is to stand *out*. Standing out is cool!"

She always responds this way. Something about hearing your mom say "cool" in her mom voice sets every teenager on edge. It ticks me off. I yell about being tired of standing out, hating all these things that were done to me, the unfairness of being born this way, of being so ugly. Mom counters every complaint, until we've gotten nowhere and we're both spent and mad.

"My dream is that we survive your adolescence without killing each other," Mom says dryly to me at the end of it.

"Well, maybe something's wrong," I say, suddenly panicked. "We shouldn't be fighting so much!"

She just laughs. "My mom and my sister fought like cats and dogs. That's why I think you must be one of them reincarnated. Or maybe both, actually, since they were both such strong—headstrong—independent women." She considers me. "Yep, definitely both."

She's a superhero for taking care of me through all this.

Up until now, I've been pretty good at keeping my body and my mind separate, dissociating the memories from the marks on my skin. But in trying to make this decision about my real leg, I'm having trouble maintaining the separation. It's the scars. The scars on my arms. The scars on my legs. And the scar on my stomach. The ugliest one. The one I hate the most. I want to wear bikinis, I want to get a belly-button ring (Mom will *never* let me), I want to just be a normal teenage girl. But that scar. I've always told my mom that I don't know how I got it. It's not exactly a lie. I can't access that memory anymore, except in nightmares. I've entombed it.

I decide that all of this must be the fault of my horrible hands, which bear the most scars, from multiple surgeries. People are constantly staring at them. Part of the problem is that I talk with my hands all the time. I lose focus if they're just sitting in my lap. I can't tell a story without wild gestures. But then I'll notice that people are staring at my hands instead of paying attention to what I'm saying.

Maybe . . . Maybe, if I didn't have these hands. Maybe all of this would just go away.

After school while Mom is still at work, I look for a pair of scissors. I will take care of this. I'll start with my right hand. I lay it out on the dining room table, scissors in my left hand. If I just cut straight across the knuckles . . . I place the scissors there. And I squeeze the handles together.

I don't feel pain. I'm an expert at dissociating. Thanks to all my experiences, I'm like a mystic, able to float above my body to escape hurt. As the blades slice skin and constrict my bones, I feel pressure, I feel wetness as the blood spurts, and that's all. But my fingers remain firmly attached to my hand.

I snap out of it. Coming back to myself, I open the scissors. I remove them from my skin. I put them down. I think more than anything else, I wanted the control of this exact moment: of *stopping*. I look down at my bloody hand. *What the hell was I aiming for here? Where was I going to go with this?* All at once, the pain rushes in. Even still, I feel distant from it. More of an *Oh, there it is* feeling than anything panic inducing. I jam paper towels around my fingers to stop the blood, try to clean it up one-handed from the floor and table. I run the scissors under the kitchen faucet.

Mom comes home. She sees me holding the paper towels, sees the blood splotches. She probably sees the scissors still sitting there in the sink. But she doesn't question me right then. It's not her priority to know why, only to make me safe and well and free from immediate hurt. She bundles me into the car and rushes me to the emergency room.

The pain in my foot and leg has become unmanageable. The brace the surgeon gave me as a last-ditch attempt to save the leg, that's supposed to push my knee in the right direction, isn't working. Plus, it's ugly as hell. I can't wear cute jeans with it, let alone cute shoes (*of course* the girl without a foot is obsessed with shoes). With a brace, you have to get wide shoes, and the only shoes wide enough are Skechers. *No one* wants to wear Skechers in middle school.

But—the important point of appearance and fashion aside—the pain has gotten so bad that I can't even do the things I want to do. I can't go to the mall with my friends, I can't play volleyball. I can't even walk without excruciating pain.

I come to the understanding that, like this, my life won't go where I want it to. And that's my breaking point.

This has to change. Even though my emotions are nowhere near under control, I think I'm finally ready.

"Mom," I say one afternoon. "I think I'm okay with them taking my leg."

In January, we're back at the orthopedic surgeon's office for our follow-up appointment. We've been waiting in the consultation room for nearly two hours when an assistant walks in to clean it. She's clearly shocked to find us there and scurries to get the surgeon. We should have taken that as a sign that today wouldn't go well.

The surgeon walks in and doesn't apologize for making us wait. She just sits down, looks at us, and says, "What can I do for you today?"

We're a little confused. She doesn't seem to remember that this is a big moment, when we're reporting our agonized decision. Shouldn't she tee it up better? But Mom looks at me reassuringly, allowing me to make the pronouncement of my own fate.

I take a deep breath. "I'm ready for the amputation." I'm proud of the steadiness in my voice.

Horror flashes across the surgeon's face. "Oh my *God*. I would never amputate the leg of a thirteen-year-old!" She turns to Mom in disbelief. "She won't even be able to get up to go to the bathroom at night!"

Of all the hardships to point out, this seems like an odd one for her to pick. But Mom and I are so shocked that we don't register the oddity. We're just staring at her.

Mom scrambles back on point before I do. "If you remember," she says, admirably calm considering how much I know she'd like to punch this woman, "you gave us a choice between an impossible scenario of multiple surgeries that would involve tons of recovery time and pain, and who knows what kind of leg function in between—or amputation. We made this appointment last time to come back to you with our decision. Do you not write down your notes or something?"

The surgeon refuses to budge. I'm trying hard not to let her see me cry. Mom sends me out to the front waiting room, and halfway down the hall, I hear her begin to ream the woman in a voice barely below a shout. I can't hear the exact words, but I know I'm glad I'm not that surgeon.

For a second opinion (or "a sane one," Mom says), Mom takes me an hour and a half away to Shriners Hospitals for Children in Lexington.

When this surgeon returns from examining the X-rays they've just taken, he looks from the sheets in his hand to me several times, in something like bewilderment.

"Can you just walk down this hallway?" he asks me.

He watches carefully.

"Walk down again?"

I do.

"And a couple more times?"

He tells me to hold tight for a minute and strides away. He comes back with a couple other doctors in tow.

"Look at this," he tells them, like I'm not even there. "I've never seen anything like it. She doesn't even have a true knee or any weight-bearing bones, and she's *walking*." He gestures for me to walk again to illustrate the improbability of it.

This is an old routine for me. It's the same thing surgeons would do with my hands. "Just draw something with this pencil?" "Just turn the doorknob one more time?" I'm a medical mystery, either a miracle or an aberration—hard to say which, although I get the sense it's the latter since there doesn't seem to be a normal bone or muscle in my whole body. I shouldn't be able to physiologically write or hold coffee mugs or walk down hallways.

The surgeon and his team film me walking. They review the home videos Mom brought with her, at their request, of me walking and running and jumping. They consult.

Finally, the doctor comes back with his decision. "The leg can't be saved. As you grow into an adult, the weight will be too much for the anatomy to support."

I've already come to terms with losing the leg. Now I'm on the edge of my seat for whether I can keep my knee. My freedom. My future.

"But, we can save the joint and do a below-the-knee amputation."

I'm so relieved I don't even have the words for it.

Then he says, "Just let us know when you're ready."

I stare at him. He'd said it as if this were just a casual thing, like a hair appointment or a date to go for a cup of coffee. As if I'd just call them up and say, "Hey, how's Thursday for you, maybe around three, to take off my leg and change the course of my life forever?" *How many body parts do they take off every day,* I'm thinking, *that this is how nonchalantly they phrase it?!*

We make the appointment for late March.

"Mom, I'm just gonna pee real quick," I say as the two of us head out of Taco Bell. We're on our way home from Wisconsin, where we went to the wedding of one of Mom's good friends. Taco Bell is always our go-to pit stop on road trips—I've loved fast food since I landed in America, and I *really* love Taco Bell.

"Me, too, we still have a lot of driving." Mom follows me. I walk down the short hallway and head right, pushing open the door.

"Oksana, what are you doing? That's the men's!"

I look up. "Oh." I back out. "I didn't know where I was."

The thing is, for a minute, I had *no idea* where I was, and I didn't realize it until I heard Mom's voice. I slipped away and blacked out, and that door was a different door. I shake it off. I'm just tired.

In the car, I take the back seat so I can sleep while Mom drives. We've been on the road maybe ten minutes, are just back on the highway, when my throat constricts. My body goes hot. My hypervigilance kicks in hard, and I'm overwhelmed with dread, a need to get out of this car *now*, and it's so strong I think my heart might beat right out of my chest. But I'm suffocating, I can't do anything. I kick Mom's seat as hard as I can, over and over, to get her attention, gasping, "I can't breathe, I can't breathe."

Mom slams on the brakes, pulls to the shoulder, and flies out of the driver's seat. She opens my door and pulls me into the air, into her arms, at light speed. Cars zoom by, the roar of each like a bed of nails dragged across my skin. Mom tells me I'm safe, talks softly, slowly, inhales with me, exhales with me, until I can breathe again and my heart slows.

Mom puts me in the front seat. She keeps a close eye on me. I seem to be fine, though. I'm still freaked-out, but the sense of foreboding dread is gone from my chest.

A couple hours later, a song comes on the car radio that I love, and I can't remember the name of it. "Mom, who is this? I want the CD! We need to figure out who it's by."

It's dark by now. We're driving through a construction zone. Reflective orange barriers whiz by on either side, taking up the whole of the shoulder.

"Oh, it's Jimmy Eat World," Mom says. I'm a little embarrassed that she knows and I don't. "We can pick it up next time we're out."

"Okay."

The overhead light comes on in the car. I've opened the passenger door. I'm about to get out at the Target parking lot, where we always go shopping. But we're going so fast the door nearly closes on my foot, which I've moved to set it on the pavement and climb out of the car.

"Whoa!" Mom yells.

I snap my eyes to her, panicked. She pulls over as soon as she can.

"I thought we were at Target," I tell her, scared.

"Thank God you had your seat belt on."

I look down. "Mom."

My seat belt is unfastened.

I don't remember touching it.

It's a holiday weekend, so we can't get to my regular psychiatrist when we get home. Mom takes me to the emergency room instead. She tells the doctor there, when it's finally our turn to be seen, that my psychiatrist put me on a new medication, and that perhaps that's the problem.

"Here's what you should do. I'm going to write a prescription for"— he ticks off three major drugs that I can't hold on to the names of, that I've never been on—"that you'll want to have her take together, and then you can call her psychiatrist tomorrow." Behind him, out of his sight, the horrified nurse is mouthing to Mom, *Don't give her those.*

Mom agrees. But she doesn't know what else to do. She's terrified I'm going to hurt myself (I'm terrified I'm going to hurt *her*, somehow). She takes me to the Louisville psych hospital instead, hoping for a better prescription. One of the doctors there asks me some questions, privately, and is apparently alarmed enough at the answers that he goes out and tells Mom, "We're going to have to admit her."

"I can't do that!" Mom replies, desperate but, as ever, my strongest advocate and the only one who knows that I would incorrectly interpret her abandoning me in this place as the ultimate betrayal. "I can't just leave her here."

The doctor suggests day treatment as an alternative. Mom can pick me up every night. Neither of us can believe we're even talking about this, but we're both scared. Even though Mom would never show it.

Before the end of my first day in that place, Mom gets a call.

"She's had seventeen panic attacks in the last hour," the nurse says. "We're going to take her off the Paxil and put her on Wellbutrin."

Three days later, Mom gets another call, this time from the doctor: "We don't think she belongs here."

I've already told Mom about the thirteen-year-old in my day group that has two kids, the sixteen-year-old who's attempted suicide seven times. "She just needs therapy. And the right meds."

Mom couldn't agree more. *And school, and her friends,* she thinks, but doesn't see the point in telling the doctor that. She comes to get me immediately.

———

A couple nights before we leave for Shriners for my second amputation, I have a sleepover with a few of my friends. One of the dads who's come to drop off his daughter chats with Mom about my situation in the front room.

"Oh, you must be amputating the left leg," he says, watching me walk with his daughter into the living room.

"That one's already been amputated. It's the right this time."

"No, no, it's the *left* leg," he tells her—as if my own mother doesn't know. I'm so used to this that I barely register the conversation. Since my right leg operates so weirdly, and I religiously wear jeans to hide both legs, kids are always telling me that my prosthetic is clearly my real leg. By this point, I just think it's funny. But Mom pushes the man toward the door and then politely shuts it on him.

———

The surgeon finds Mom in my pre-op room and ushers her out into the hallway. I'm already gowned and capped and lying on the bed they'll wheel into the operating room, floating on the happy juice the doctors gave me as a presurgical sedative. Mom has authorized them to give me an epidural in addition to putting me under and for pain management postsurgery; the surgeon says that research indicates that approach results in little to no phantom pain after the surgery. But right now I'm not thinking about after. I'm not thinking about anything. Thanks to the happy juice, I'm pretty loopy.

"So," the surgeon says to Mom, "the team and I have been back there reviewing the videos. We need to amputate above the knee. The joint won't handle a below-the-knee prosthetic."

"*What?*" Mom is thunderstruck. This changes everything. "You promised her a functioning *knee*. Now she's going to wake up from surgery and realize you took it anyway? You can't do that to her. We have to cancel. We can't go through with this right now."

"Well, let's go ask her." At Shriners, I'm considered an adult who must give consent to procedures. The team isn't supposed to change the plan without my agreement.

"You already gave her the happy juice," Mom protests. "She's cognitively impaired right now."

"Oh, it will be fine. Let's go in and ask."

Apparently, the surgeon comes in to ask me. Apparently, I say, "Okay." The surgeon takes it as informed consent.

I have no memory of that interaction.

———

When I wake from surgery, I'm disoriented, as I always am, in and out and struggling to come to. No one is around. I can hear the beeps of machines. I'm lying on my back. I can't stand this position. I never sleep on my back. My body gets a weird feeling sort of like nausea with the shaking and quivering. It's too vulnerable.

I try to sit up. The first thing that registers is that I can't feel my *left* leg. At all. I can't feel the stump or even the phantom leg. I can't lift it. *Did they mess up? Did they take off the rest of my left leg instead of my right leg?* But I look down to see my right leg encased in a thick bright orange cast. It's huge. But it's short. With a clean straight line at the bottom. *Huh. Was my leg below the knee really that long? Where is my knee supposed to bend in this thing?*

Then the pain comes screaming in. My right leg is consumed with it. I moan, then I shout. Mom's there immediately. The epidural needle shifted, apparently, and it numbed my left leg instead of my right. I can't think, I can't even breathe.

Mom navigates the nursing team. "The epidural isn't working. She needs morphine. Can you get an IV in there quickly?"

"Oh, she probably just has weak pain tolerance," the nurse says.

Mom's eyebrows shoot up under her bangs; I have a sadistically high pain tolerance. She doesn't know how good I am at dissociating pain, though. Sometimes—not right now—instead of distracting myself from pain, I'll remain in the moment of it. I visualize the pain and try to see what's happening inside. I know the different types of hurt: weird, satisfying, nagging, painful, horrific. It's the reason I know my body so well. I'm a connoisseur of pain. This pain right now is so intense that I'm having mini-seizures in my leg and I'm still so out of it that I can't dissociate.

The nurse continues, "She just needs to lie on her other side and we'll hope the epidural needle shifts. She just needs to give the medicine a chance."

"*Hope it shifts?* Are you crazy? She just had her leg *amputated* and she has no pain meds. Get my daughter some morphine *now.*"

When the agony finally abates, that's when I can feel that my legs are exactly the same.

There's no knee. On either side.

I don't say anything. I just roll over and stare at the wall. When the tears come, I'm so far gone that I don't even care who sees them.

———

The pain in my stump is all-consuming. Instead of an Ace bandage, which Mom and I had expected after surgery, my stump has a cast on it that conceals what's happening under there. But I tell Mom that the pain isn't normal. It's *weird*. And it's mostly concentrated on the back of my leg, not the end.

They let me go home a few days after surgery. I'm in a rented wheelchair. A friend of Mom's built a ramp up to our front door, but it's pretty steep. I think in my foggy state as Mom huffs me up it that it definitely wouldn't pass any inspections. Mom sets me up, as usual, on the sofa bed.

The weird, intense pain on the back of my leg doesn't let up. Mom drives me to Shriners so they can remove the cast, which reveals a huge open wound down low where the sutures are supposed to be. It's like someone forgot to suture that part—which is essentially what happened. In changing the plan on the fly to steal my knee, the surgical team didn't leave enough skin to close the incision. The wound is probably the size of a silver dollar, but it feels like it's the size of Texas.

The team demonstrates wound care and sends us home. Mom changes my dressings every day, but still has to drive me the hour and a half to Shriners three times over the next two weeks to have it cleaned. It's so enormous and festering that the fourth time, on Easter Sunday, the medical team says I need to be admitted for vacuum-assisted closure, called a wound VAC. They attach a machine to the skin to pull fluid, reduce air pressure, and help keep the area clean so it can finally heal.

They tell me I can't leave this hospital bed for three weeks.

———

Without rowing, there's no release from my thoughts or emotions. I'm captive to them in the blank hospital room. Over and over I think, *Now I'm not just ugly. I have nothing left physically. I'm done.* I've taken a thousand steps backward from where I was just a couple weeks ago, stroking across the Ohio River under my own full power.

The dreams continue to rage. I can't stop them. I have no control over them. I wake sweating and silently screaming in the night, memories boiling and accumulating with no way to unchain them from me.

I'm at war with my body and I'm losing, and my mind is a hurricane that wants to tear me apart.

Three weeks turn into five. Mom sleeps in the window seat in my hospital room, a tiny alcove that was never meant to be a bed. She only leaves for work, driving the seventy-five miles to Louisville, and then she comes right back. I stop speaking to anyone except her. She becomes my voice. When the wound VAC machine comes off twice a week for a few minutes for a change of my dressings, Mom helps me take a bath, washes my hair.

A social worker comes by. I hear her talking to Mom outside my room.

"We think she's severely depressed."

"You *think*? She's a teenage girl who just lost her *second* leg—way above what she was told—and she's been stuck in here for over a month. She hasn't gotten to see her friends, and her life as she knew it was ripped from her without her knowledge or consent. Of *course* she's depressed. We just need to get her out of here."

At seven weeks, the doctors say it should be good to go—in just six more weeks. Mom goes to cry in her car (not for the first time) so that I don't see her tears. She keeps herself together for me so she can be my rock.

I stop eating. The nurses view it as anorexia and suggest Mom is partly the cause.

"Do you think," one nurse says hesitatingly to Mom, "that you might be putting your weight issues on her? Maybe that's where this is coming from—she's worried about obesity running in the family?"

Mom is fierce. Her fury is all the more terrifying for her smooth expression. "She's not my biological child. Have you not even *read* her chart? Second, you don't know her history. She's so used to being starved that she never eats unless she smells food or I hand her something. She's not anorexic. She's depressed. And we just need to *get her out of here*."

One morning, a big man with a healthy belly strolls into my room, wearing striped pants and an apron. He introduces himself as the head chef at Shriners. It's clear he's worked with kids for a long time. He chats with me for a bit, then says, "I know you're having some trouble in here. I want to be able to make it better, not worse. What are some of the foods that you really like, that I could pick up for you on my way into the hospital?"

It's the first time anyone in here has *seen* me, has asked me what *I* want, instead of making decisions based on what they think is best for me. (How about "We're changing our minds, let's get her out of pre-op and make sure she really knows what she's agreeing to before just going through with it.")

I smile for the first time in what feels like years. "Strawberries. I really like strawberries."

The next morning, and every morning after, he trundles into my room toting ripe red fruit. "These are just for you." He hands them to me. Happy to make me happy, even for only a moment.

One Saturday afternoon, a few girls from my volleyball team visit. It makes me realize how isolated I've felt here. No friends have come to see me; Shriners is a long way from Louisville. The feeling of joy that floods me when those girls walk into my horrid hospital room is so foreign that for a moment I'm speechless. I've missed several volleyball games, and they tell me they've missed *me*. They present me with a volleyball. On each of its lines, the team has written messages: encouragement, love, inspiration.

I look out my window from this prison bed, but in my mind I'm rowing. I move through each stroke, leaning forward smoothly from my head and hips, reaching, the extra bit of reach where it feels like I've almost dislocated my shoulder. That moment when I let go of my grip on the oars so my palms are just resting on them until I feel that *catch* of the water—my favorite part, always—and then I pull into my ribs as hard as I can.

The minute I can get out of here, I'm going to row. Every single day, every time I can get out on the river.

Outside my window is a tree, a beautiful strong one with broad leaves. I spend a lot of time watching it. Even though it's rooted to the earth, it's always moving. Rain, sun, storm, wind: some part of it is always in motion.

When I get out of here, I'll be like that tree. I'll do anything and everything I can with my body. I don't know exactly what I want, but I know I don't want this: lying down while someone else makes decisions for me. And I know with some elemental certainty that there will come a day when I'm back in this situation, the remaining parts of my legs and the rest of my mangled body have given up for good.

Until then, I will move.

Finally, I get my appointment with the prosthetist, and I receive my new matching legs. On my first session with them, the physical therapist tells me the plan is to wear them for half an hour twice during the day. Not walk on them or anything. Just wear them. It's painful and uncomfortable on my new amputation—the back of my leg looks like a clumsily darned sock—but I will endure anything just to get out of here.

During our second session, the PT says, the plan is to stand up on my new legs. Just stand.

I stand. I walk all over the hospital's physical therapy room.

"Okay, great job! That's enough for today."

But I see the set of PT stairs, a little stairway to nowhere in the corner. "Oh, can I try those?"

"Maybe tomorrow, or in a couple of days."

"No. Today."

I walk up the PT steps and back down them. I walk down a full flight of regular stairs. I walk outside, onto the grass. I don't stop walking until they threaten to tackle me.

Finally, a week before eighth grade starts, I'm allowed to go home. The medical team gives me forearm crutches (these slip under the wrists rather than the armpits—they tell me that many amputees use them to walk without falling) and a wheelchair that I'm supposed to use for the first three months at school. I don't want to use a wheelchair. I can't propel a wheelchair with my hands the way they are. But more than that, I don't want my body to exist in that way: sitting still.

I work hard with the crutches at home. I use them at school for one day. Then I walk. Freely.

It's not that easy, though. I *hate* this second prosthetic. I never wanted this, not to this extent—needing an assistive device just to walk with. What grates just as much, I'm taking a cornucopia of medications just to be "normal"—because I'm apparently not normal without them? What is so wrong with my real self? What I hate the most, though, is that someone else knows the exact dose of a pill to *make* me normal. How does someone else know what's going to make me happy?

But without the medications, my mind is a series of dark tunnels. For the short term, I'm stuck with them.

nine

I'm just going to try it with both prosthetics on," I tell Randy, finally, blessedly, back at the dock for the first time since surgery. I feel like I just got comfortable with taking one leg off to get in the boat, and I can't imagine taking off two.

Randy doesn't argue. I'm only a teenager, but he lets me come to this on my own terms. He offers help where he sees I need it in struggling to step down into the boat. But I can't get myself in the seat well enough, can't strap my legs in because I don't have control of the knees. I won't be able to manipulate them to push off of. I look up at Randy hopelessly.

He just smiles. "Don't worry. Here, come on out. I'm gonna fix some things while you take your legs off."

He leans over the dock with his torso half in the boat. When I'm ready, he asks, "Do you want me to lift you in?" I hesitate. I'm not great at walking on both my stumps yet. But it's important to me to figure this out for myself. I half stagger, half crawl my way over, take his arms as I lower myself down. I hold on to the dock with one hand for dear life while Randy straps my quads in.

"Okay, read to push off?"

I'm not, but I nod anyway. I give the slightest of pushes. And I feel *so* unstable. I can feel every tiny movement of the boat. Like I'm trying to balance on three giant exercise balls stacked on top of each other and the slightest shift means toppling.

I drop the oars into the water. I feel that lovely plink the same way, in my chest, and it makes me exhale the breath I didn't know I was holding. I gingerly reach forward. The seat goes nowhere, which is bizarre. That's what Randy was doing: securing it in place. I dip the oars and pull back. With nothing to push off of, I have only my trunk to power the stroke. I can feel my right quad flexing as I try to push against what's not there—feel my abs taking up the slack of my absent leg. This will take some getting used to, no question. It's not the movement I envisioned from my hospital bed all those interminable days. It's shifting and finding control and searching for the balance points under my hips, which sense everything now.

But the feel of pulling the oars to my ribs is the same. The sensation of the *release* is the same.

Then I notice something else. I'm flying on the water. I've dropped an instant ten or twelve pounds in losing the leg, and I'm *fast*. Maybe I could get used to this.

I *will* get used to it. Because I can't imagine stopping.

"Oh, man, Oksana, we gotta row again."

Kimberly's in the boat with me this morning. We never row the whole time when we're together. We just stroke far enough out so that it looks like we're talking shop, and we giggle and gossip until the current brings us back toward the dock. Then we repeat. Kimberly was a new volunteer when I came back to the rowing program after the hospital. She's supposed to be my able-bodied partner or guide or whatever Randy calls it, but we're basically the same age, so we're just a pair of teenagers instead.

She's a good rower, though. We start going with the rowing club to head races—time trials—usually just five-kilometer races. We pile into the hot van, which I hate. I always take the back, battling savage car sickness in favor of a bench seat so that I can take off my legs. The club's old yellow Penske truck follows behind with all our boats. We tend to look like a traveling circus when we show up at races. Kimberly and I do pretty well, though. I like the competition. I like the focus in my head when everything else inside it goes quiet.

———

"You have the most amazing sense of where your body is in space," Mom says to me—she seems to repeat this yearly—as she watches me step down from the curb to get in the car for school. "And how to make it so that you're okay in that space."

Yep, lots *of practice with that,* I think.

But it's not easy. Far from it. The higher an amputation is, the less sensation you have to feel where you are and to leverage the ground. I'm sixteen by now and pretty comfortable on my prosthetics. But it's still terrifying to swing a free-dangling hinge of a knee and not be entirely sure where your foot might land.

We're running late by the time Mom drops me off. I didn't leave enough time to get my legs on this morning. They're like elaborate pieces of weird art now: foam carefully cut and shaped into an outline of calves and thighs with nylon pulled over to secure it in place. Under my pants— also carefully chosen to hang right to hide the bulge of liner squeezed by the socket that looks like an extra butt—I'm so desperate for them to look like real legs. I never wear shorts or skirts.

When I step out of the car, I hear the first bell ring to signal everyone to get to homeroom. As I rush inside—no one's around, all have scurried to class with the first bell—I can tell that something is loose in my right leg. There's foreign movement somewhere down there. *Oh my God, this is not good.* I step onto the ramp by the drama room.

My right leg collapses and I fall hard on my face, backpack flying up to hit me in the head. It's not zipped. Pens and my lunch and lip gloss go flying.

The second bell rings. Homeroom is starting.

Under my jeans, my knee has come apart from the socket. I pull my pant leg up to find the problem. Three screws have unthreaded themselves and gone rolling around the floor.

I hate my life. Why is this happening to me?

I'm scrambling around trying to pick up the parts of my leg and the contents of my pack when the next bell rings and kids come streaming out of classrooms. Homeroom is only ten minutes. My face burns as a few people stop to help me. Someone gets a wheelchair. Hands help me up into it. I hold my leg on my lap while a girl I don't even know wheels me to the nurse. As if the nurse is a mechanic and can repair my knee.

They call Mom. She rushes from the university with the parts I need to put my leg back together, like I'm Mrs. Potato Head or something. Only Mrs. Potato Head doesn't need tools and two hours of people hovering over her.

And this. This is just a regular day for me.

How did this happen to me?

My entire room smells like coffee. I slide my bra down my shoulders to put on my pajamas. The bra smells of coffee, too, the scent soaked into the lining. My hair wafts dark roast. Ever since I started working at Starbucks in addition to working at the day-care center, everything in my life has smelled like coffee. I *love* it. Even though I drop things all the time—espresso shots, glasses, plates. My grip with these hands is not great. And the mats on the floor behind the counter catch my prosthetic feet all the time. Early on, after I dropped a whole tray of dishes, one of the other teenagers nicknamed me Oopsana. It stuck. I was totally embarrassed, but it *was* funny. I am, after all, a total klutz.

I'm exhausted. Even with the day-care job being part of the co-op program at the high school where kids leave at noon to log hours for a job, working two jobs and staying present at school is a lot. But I want to start helping Mom out with rowing costs—going to a race with the club costs five hundred bucks when you add up the cost of gas, food, lodging, entry fees, and who knows what other expenses that a teenager never even thinks about.

I save on lunch money with my discount at Starbucks. For my free staff drink at the end of a shift, I order a venti no-water chai with espresso. I've long since discovered how to trick my stomach into feeling full, as if I were actually feeding it. I used to pick apart a single piece of bread and spend as long as possible eating it, taking tiny bites and chewing for what felt like hours. A venti chai is a feast. If I'm still hungry, I snag some of the animal crackers at day care that are always out in bowls for the kids. I'm not proud of that, but it does the trick.

Even with the jobs and school, rowing takes precedence. It's my voice when I can't speak things, don't even know how to express them, except by pulling on the oars as hard as I can. I stop cutting. The nightmares subside. I even stop going to therapy.

And I slowly stop taking those damn pills.

The idea of choosing to be fully in control of my mind and body is foreign. Intriguing. I think that maybe this is the heart of why I love rowing. Why I can live inside the pain of a long row. Because *I'm* doing it to *myself*, and I can stop anytime. Or I can choose to push myself through to the other side, all the way to the end. *I'm* in control.

In that moment, I'm normal. I'm *me* in that moment.

Being on the water becomes my therapy. It's not just about being physically healthy. It's about being mentally and emotionally healthy—which is monumentally harder for me than getting physically healthy—and there will always be more distance to travel on that road.

I pull on my pajamas, and my forearms ache from yesterday's session on the water. Because I don't have muscles in my fingers, I'm always overusing my forearms to compensate for grip. They've become strong and toned. I crawl into bed, and when I reach to turn out the light in my coffee-scented room, I admire the tone in my arms even while I avert my eyes from my hands in a move so practiced it's nearly unconscious.

In the sudden dark of my bedroom, my body tenses, like always.

There will always be more distance to travel.

"Have you heard of the Paralympics?" Randy asks me one Saturday.

I'm sitting on the goose-poop dock putting my legs back on. I've just gotten out of the boat. My body is high with endorphins from the row, and my head is blissfully clear and quiet. I look up from my routine of liner-socket-straps.

"Huh?" I say fairly unintelligently.

"Look it up. See if it's something you're interested in. You've got potential. We can talk about it next week."

I go home and immediately look up *Paralympics* on our dinosaur computer. They're the Olympic Games for people with physical disabilities. Elite athletes in their sports. They're held right after the Olympics, same venue, same arenas, Opening Ceremonies, Closing Ceremonies. But what really lights up something in me is the idea of representing your country. Of being part of a team. I'm seventeen years old, midway through my senior year in high school, and I've still never *truly* been part of a team.

I've raced before, but only 5K head races. I'm no elite athlete. I don't see the potential that Randy does. Mostly, I like the thought of rowing more. I like the thought of having a goal to push myself toward. It's been such a long time since I had one. Maybe since ice-skating.

I tell Randy that I'm interested. He says the next step is to convince Mom.

Randy sits at the head of our dining room table. He has the binder he always carries—I wonder what's in there that's so important it needs to come everywhere—laid out in front of him. Mom sits in the chair up against the wall. I'm across from her, watching her face. I know she's on board with whatever I want to do, as long as it's safe. Her question is always just how to make it work.

"In Beijing, in 2008, is the first year that the sport of rowing will be included in the Paralympic Games for trunk and arms." Randy launches into an explanation of the categories: Arms and Shoulders, the only solo rowing category, for athletes who mostly don't have function below the chest; Trunk and Arms, my category, male/female partner boats for athletes who row with a fixed seat without the use of legs; and Legs, Trunk, and Arms, four-person male/female boats for athletes who can row with a sliding seat. Before my second amputation, I could have competed in this category.

I'm still trying to sort out all this in my head when Randy looks straight at me. "Oksana, Bobby and I think you can do this. If you want to."

My head whips from Mom to Randy; I'm surprised at my spot at the steering wheel for this decision. I just nod. I'm awkward with the power to control my own future.

"If you're serious about this, Bobby and I will do anything and everything we can to get you there. We'd make the time to get you out on the water a couple days a week. Bobby would work with you on coaching."

I worry a little at this. Even though I've known Bobby for a while, with him I always feel as though I've done something wrong, that he doesn't like me, doesn't want me around. I don't realize that this is just his personality: he's impassive. I'm still just a self-concerned teenager, after all.

"We'd do the legwork of finding you a partner, since we're connected to the other rowing clubs." Randy pauses, looks me in the eye again. "But you have to give us a promise that you'll work for this. That you *are* serious. No more rowing with Kim, no more social hour."

I flush with embarrassment. "Yeah. Yeah, I will!" I say quickly to cover it, and too excitedly, with none of the adultness I'm hoping to impart. In my head, I'm already on Team USA.

"Oksana, do you understand what he's saying?" Where I'm over-animated, Mom stays even-keeled. "This would mean that rowing isn't just for fun. They'd be giving their time to you, donating it, to train."

I try again. "I want to do this. I'll do anything and everything, too. I'm ready."

Randy nods, satisfied. Mom smiles at me, no doubt thinking of that day a few years ago when she told me I might like rowing. But, as usual, she doesn't rub it in that she was right. She just turns to Randy and unleashes her questions on logistics.

———————

Later, lying in bed and for once not dreading the night because all I can think about are the coming days of rowing and the Games, I realize that, outside of my mother, Randy and Bobby are the first people who've ever said to me, "You can do this." Not *can't, shouldn't be able to, will never be able to.* Not *no.* They're the first people who've ever believed in me and said *yes.*

After I graduate, I'm going to Beijing for the summer Paralympics. I'll be at those Games.

part

three

chapter

ten

"You can't just muscle through this," Bobby says, floating beside me in the coach's scull. In these first few weeks since we've been training seriously, he's been trying to teach me to let go of my death grip on the oars. My thinking is that the harder I grip—especially with my mangled hands—the better I'll be. He blows that to pieces.

"It's not a formula in life that working harder means doing better. Rowing is more of a *feeling* sport. You have to respect the boat and the conditions of the water, and that's always changing. You're fighting too much."

I've been fighting my whole life, I think. *You want me to give that up now?*

He maneuvers space between us to demonstrate. "The oars know the perfect spot to pop in. You just let them. *Then* you can yank on them. And then you keep your hands open—don't force the release—just guide the oars through, and you'll *feel* that pressure, that resistance against the water when they want to come out." He shows me, leaving calm water under his blades every time. "You don't want to be creating rapids. You want the water clean."

Facing backward in the boat to row, I begin to pay attention to the mark I'm leaving behind on the river. The new strokes are bold, defined, beautiful, as the farther ones slowly fade and blend and return into the whole of the quiet surface.

The rower is always leaving a mark, and trying to leave the best one possible. And if one mark is imperfect—or it's a whole series of ugly, messy marks—the next stroke is an opportunity to improve it, build on the mistake. It doesn't matter whether my seat slides or not, whether I have legs or not. The water is honest no matter what the body can do. It tells the truth of a good stroke.

And this despite that you're not looking where you're going, since you're sitting backward in the boat. You look over your shoulder once or twice, just to make sure your path is straight and you're going in the direction you want. But rather than constantly staring at the end goal, you trust the process. You just go.

I want to live like I'm rowing. I want to leave a mark.

I'm just not sure how.

—————

I start rowing in the evenings on weekdays, after Randy's finished with school stuff and Bobby's done working with his house-painting company. They're volunteering their time for me, and I'm well aware of it. I start going to Frazier Rehab to use their gym for free to strengthen my arms, even though I have no idea what I'm doing and I'm not disciplined about it. I spend more time on the rowing machine at the club than at the gym.

I'd always been on the river in the early mornings when the air is crisp and fresh, never when the sun is starting to set, when the afternoons are exhaling and breezy. If someone asked me which I prefer, I wouldn't know how to answer—they're that different in sounds, the way the river smells, how the air feels on skin. But to me there's something indescribable about rowing in the late afternoons with the city in silhouette against a winding-down sky, and with the Big Four Bridge—the tangible outline upon which I've pinned my goal—stark against the sunset.

Before, we'd always rowed in the kilometer-long chute between shore and the island, in the calm water. Reaching the bridge, though, means leaving the tranquility of the chute for the river itself, with its wind and rip and waves and violent wakes from the barges. Bobby doesn't let anyone out there who's not capable of handling their boat. And given this is an adaptive program, that's not many people.

But he said he thinks I can row out to the bridge today.

I'm standing around impatiently as Bobby sets up the boat on the side of the dock, stretched out on his belly and reaching down to fix the seat in place and adjust the straps. I barely register the line of girls from the university novice team getting into their long boat behind me on the other side of the dock, I'm so buzzed with the prospect of a strenuous row and how to prove to Bobby I can do this.

"Okay, I'm ready for you," Bobby says, rising from his horizontal position.

I roll my concealing sweats down to my hips, exposing the shorts I'm wearing underneath, then reach down behind me with my hands to support myself as I sit down on the dock. I ease off my liner, socket, and entire leg as one unit on one side, then the other, in a practiced motion, then leave them there in the sweats: two legs complete with shoes in a pair of pants—my adaptive ensemble. I still hate taking off my prosthetics in front of people, but I think it's hilarious that they look like half of a body just hanging out there. By now, the whole process takes me less than a minute.

I hobble over on my stumps, climb down into the boat, and strap in. Only when I look over my shoulder to push off the dock do I see the girls from the novice team sitting motionless in their boat, all their mouths hanging open.

"See?" Bobby says to them in his characteristic deadpan, walking past the team toward the coach's scull tied to the dock. "If she can do it, you have no excuse." Bobby doesn't smile often, but I love it when he does.

That morning, I row all the way out to the bridge for the first time. I feel like I've made it as a serious athlete.

I have no idea how far I have to go to earn that title.

Back at the dock, I wrestle back into my sweatpants. I get the legs up, grope myself onto my knees, pull them up my hips over my shorts. When I finally get to my feet, the sweats are stuck in the mechanical knees. I have to stick my hand down my pants to fix it. One ankle is eating the sweatpants cuff today, too, so I have to get all the way down there to pull it out, nearly toppling over.

It's a process. But it's worth it.

The first potential partner comes to *us*.

Scott, who lost one leg in a car accident in 1987, has been rowing on the US national team for a handful of years. He's deep into the sport, working hard to promote it and MacGyvering boats and gear to work for adaptive rowers. His wife runs the Bayada Regatta, the biggest adaptive rowing race in the country, on the Schuylkill River in Philadelphia on Boathouse Row. It's my favorite race; I've been going to it since I learned how to row years ago. That's where Scott sees me row with Kimberly, where he hears that I'm looking for a partner for Beijing.

Scott's regular rowing partner is on the ocean competing in a trans-atlantic race. He's worried she might come back from that too injured to race in the Paralympics, or that she might not want to race again at all after such an epic experience. He's shopping for a new partner, too. He calls up Bobby and sets a time to come down to Louisville for us to try rowing together.

Before I even meet him face-to-face that first day, I sit behind the boathouse and watch him talk to Bobby. I want to get a sense of what kind of person he is. That he's quite a lot older than me is the first thing I notice. He spends most of the time talking *at* Bobby, telling him what he needs to do to make the boat I row perform better. Bobby might not be part of the US national team, but he knows a lot. I don't like the way Scott talks to him. Scott's bald, polished head gleams in the sun like it can't get enough of its own shine.

Oh no, I think, sitting back against the wall. *I don't like him. What am I doing?*

I don't think Bobby likes him much either. But then, it's hard to tell sometimes with Bobby. And Scott's doing so much to push the sport forward—he's the one responsible for starting the trunk and arms category in the first place.

And he needs a partner.

Just then, he spots me in my not-so-hidden hiding place. "Oh, hi." He approaches. "I'm Scott."

"Hi." I rise casually like I just coincidentally found myself hanging out in earshot. Up close, I notice the lines around his eyes. *Will I have to say that this old man is my Paralympic rowing partner?* I hate being judged on my appearance, and here I am judging hard. Little do I know that it's not me making the choice here. It's Scott, taking a chance on a young girl with little experience. I can't see through my own selfish misgivings, though.

"Reach *farther,* Oksana," Scott says firmly. We've only trained together a few times, but he doesn't seem to hesitate to tell me what I'm doing wrong. "You need to get stronger. You need to follow me to the nth degree, and that means you have to lengthen out your stroke."

Scott has an old-school way of rowing. He wants me bent over in half like a tortilla press, reaching as far as I can, then pulling to the point that I'm leaning way back in the boat. It's like he's putting the erg, the rowing machine that functions best on muscle and mass, straight onto the water. But my strength, lacking both muscle and mass, is technique and speed.

And there's the obvious fact that Scott has one leg that he's bracing with. He could technically race in the Legs, Trunk, and Arms category, although the nature of his injury would make it hard for him to be competitive, and so he chose this category instead—figuring out the complicated rules for para sports still makes my head swim. But the bottom line is that I can't brace with my legs. My back aches after our sessions on the water.

I lift my head from the toilet seat in the Porta Potti, where I've just emptied the entire prerace contents of my stomach. This is relatively new for me. I desperately wish it weren't happening. Vomiting in a Porta Potti is *gross*, for the record.

I exit the hot little plastic box and head back to the boat waiting on the dock. Scott and I are about to compete in Head of the Hooch here in Tennessee. The nervousness still roils my nauseous stomach. Ever since that conversation with Bobby in our dining room, ever since everyone else began to invest in me because they believe in me—for no good reason—all I can think about is how much they all have to lose in supporting me. I can't let Mom down. I can't let Bobby down, or Randy. Or Scott, now. I can't look like a waste of space and time for them.

I don't remember anything from the actual race. I black out. Which is not unusual for me. But we do pretty well.

"It's a faster boat with you in it," Scott says to me, a rare pure compliment he delivers at the end of the day as we prepare to go our separate ways home. "It just runs better."

He wants to come down and train with me, he continues. Even though he has this other partner that he has history with, he wants to compete with me in the US trials for Beijing. "I want you and me to be a boat."

"Okay. I'm committed."

I am. I want so badly to do my part to be better out there. To be what he's saying I need to be. I'll row however he wants me to row, even if it turns me into a tortilla press. Maybe I won't let anyone down after all.

But weeks go by, and Scott doesn't come down, even though he keeps telling me he wants to train with me. I begin to get nervous. I've been telling everyone—at school, at Starbucks—that I'm going to the Paralympics. I keep training, though. Every chance I get, I'm out on the water. Making my mark.

"Mom, I'm going to a movie with Kimberly."

Mom looks skeptical. I know she thinks Kimberly is a bad influence on me. Mom's face tells me she suspects that no movie is involved—and there's not, it's just a cover so she won't worry about me. But I'm nearly eighteen. She lets me do what I want. It helps that I often don't tell her things that I know will make her worry.

Like that time at the bowling alley last week. Kimberly and I were out late. We'd been about to leave, heading out to the parking lot, when a couple of guys standing outside their BMW smoking cigarettes started flirting with us. They were at least ten years older, and they had an edgy, badass vibe that I liked. It was probably around midnight when one of them said, "Why don't you guys come for a ride with us?"

We looked at each other, gauging the other's reaction, and nodded. The guy opened the driver's-side door of the two-door sports car and flipped the seat back for us to crawl in. Which is when I notice, climbing inside and folding myself into the back, that the car is at least three different colors from repairs and ugly junkyard replacements.

"Maybe we shouldn't be doing this," I whispered to Kimberly. "We don't know anything about these dudes."

"Oh, it will be fine." She flipped her thousand-watt smile to the guy settling himself in the passenger seat in front of her.

We drove around, talked, smoked. They took us back to their house. We hung out, smoked some more.

And now Kimberly and I are, just like Mom suspects, not going to a movie. We're going to hang out with those guys. But—even though Mom is often two steps ahead of me and I can't always hide things from her—this is why I don't tell her about all my decisions. I don't want her to tell me when they're bad.

I haven't had a boyfriend in high school. I guess I've dated guys, but each only for a few months, and always on and off. And they always cheated on me. I didn't tell Mom about those guys either. Part of me feels guilty. She'd never gotten married herself. I would never want to upset her. Maybe that's the heart of why I don't want her to know any of my bad decisions either. I want to protect her from them, to the end.

And my work at Starbucks doesn't cover the expenses of training and races. Mom still writes the checks for me to hand to Randy and Bobby, supporting me on her single income. I can't disappoint her.

In June, I graduate from high school. I walk across the stage, my prosthetics hidden by my gown, to receive my diploma. I sit back down with all the friends I've made. I never liked school, but I take a few seconds, sitting there while the principal wraps up his speech, to marvel at where I am and the twisting road I've taken to get here. In my head, I give that little girl that I was a long time ago a hug for sticking through it. Suddenly I feel Laney's familiar presence with me, next to me, at my back, for a moment experiencing this, too, and it's all I can do to keep in the tears.

The loudspeaker calls the class of 2008, and hundreds of caps go sailing through the air.

I turned eighteen a few days ago. I've been thinking about what I want to do now that I'm a legal adult, and the artsy piercings decorating Summer's ears have inspired me. But I don't want a piercing.

I want a tattoo.

I love the look of tattoos. One night a few months ago, I told Mom I wanted to get a full sleeve someday. She exploded. She told me she would never help with my wedding, or my wedding dress, if I did that. It seemed like a weird ultimatum, but I got the point: she doesn't like the idea of tattoos. Now that I'm eighteen though, I can do what I want.

I've barely gotten out of bed when I call Summer. "I'm going to get a tattoo today. Will you come with me?"

For years, in my school notebooks, I've been doodling my name. Not just the American name Mom gave me. But my full name: Oksana Eugenia Alexandrovna Bondarchuck Masters. In cursive, block letters, printing, with designs. Now, I tell the tattoo artist exactly what I want: those initials, in that order, in a fancy, cool font on the inside of my wrist. I did no research before we got here. We just looked up the closest tattoo parlor, and Summer drove us here. Now that I'm sitting in the chair and the woman bends toward me with the tattoo gun, I wonder if I should have thought this through more.

When she makes the first marks and the pain of the needle rushes through my veins to my heart, Summer, sitting on my other side, says, "Wow, I can't *believe* you're getting a tattoo!"

Now I definitely have second thoughts. Maybe I shouldn't have just woken up and decided I would do this. I'm too spontaneous when it comes to permanent things that can't be erased.

But no turning back now.

As the gun paints the letters in ink and blood on my skin, I remind myself why I wanted this.

The American initials are my identity now. The Ukrainian ones are to remind me to never forget where I came from. They're part of who I am. Even though my dark Ukrainian memories outweigh the happy ones by a magnitude, I'm still proud to be from there. It makes sense, but it doesn't make sense at all. I do know this: I want to have a story on my skin that represents something of my own choosing. I want a mark on my body that is my own story, not one that someone else has written.

I'm still too young to entirely wrap my head around this, but I know this is the start of something.

I didn't do this on my actual birthday because I hate celebrating that day. It's the day I came into this world a reject, valueless, 100 percent on my own, left to face everything alone. I celebrate before and after—I love the concept of birthday month—but not that day. I don't commemorate that day with anything. I won't start with my first tattoo.

When the artist is done, the tattoo looks pretty bad. The initials are upside down so that only I can read them, and it's uneven and sort of rushed. But I don't care. It's mine.

At this year's Bayada Regatta, I race with Kimberly again. I haven't heard from Scott in months, which both mortifies and angers me. But I do my best at the race; Karen's here, the national rowing team performance director, who decides which athletes are worth investing in—essentially, who's a candidate for the Paralympic Games. I've met her before at other races over the last couple years. But right now, so *badly* right now, I want her to have a good opinion of me.

Right off the bat, though, it's clear she doesn't have a lot of interest in this new mixed Trunk and Arms category for Beijing. Her focus is on the Legs, Trunk, and Arms (LTA) four-person boat that's apparently shown some promise in the last couple of years and has the best chance to medal at this year's Games. But I'm trying not to let that bother me. I don't have the use of my legs to row, so I'll never be part of that category anyway.

I walk right up to her after my race. I ask her, pulling zero punches and ready (I hope) for the answer: "Realistically, what are my chances for going to the Paralympics?"

But she didn't pay attention to my race. I've heard this about her— that she uses mostly erg machine performances to determine whether someone's even worth putting *in* a boat. Simply stated, is the person worth investing in?

I've never been strong on the erg, where size and strength trump skill, speed, and technique every time. This time is no exception. After my twenty-minute workout under Karen's watchful eye, she checks my performance stats.

She considers me. "You're too small."

She's not wrong. I'm well aware I don't look like an athlete. Most rowers are jacked. I've been small since I was a malnourished toddler. I know that I'm *still* petite. It's my weak point. Scott alludes to the same thing, although he never actually says the words out loud as Karen just did. He's more about the backhanded compliments, the ones where I say, surprised that he even complimented me at all, "Thank you," and then think, *Wait a minute. What did he* actually *mean?*

"This is an unrealistic goal," Karen continues. "Find opportunities where you'll be able to go somewhere. You're never going to make it as an athlete."

I stare at her. I didn't expect this.

Even Scott says the boat runs faster and better with me rowing in it. But Karen won't deign to give me the opportunity to show her what I can do on the water. She has no idea how hard I'm willing to work for this. She simply decided for me. I feel my fuse burning, the incredibly short one attached to the bomb of the concept *you can't.*

I won't quit. Everything in human society exists because someone dreamed that it was possible. Of course some things are *im*possible. But those are often the things we have no control over, such as that I'll never be able to flex a real knee again. But I have control over this, and I believe, hard, in finishing what I started—no matter what it is.

To Karen, I say nothing. My face likely says it all as I look at her hotly and then turn to walk away. But in my head, I say everything that matters.

I will make the team. And I will come back and say to you, "Remember that day when you told me I couldn't?"

Just before trials, we hear through the rowing grapevine that Scott's racing with his other partner, who's back from the ocean and wants to compete after all. He was afraid that she'd easily find some other guy to row with and beat his boat with whomever Scott had partnered with. So he pairs up with her again. Without telling me.

It's too late for me to find someone else.

I'm not going to Beijing.

Realizing that, I'm introduced to the first thing I've found frustrating about rowing. I can't compete solo; the only solo competitive para-rowing category is for arms only—for people who don't have the use of their body below the chest—and that's not me. So to break into the sport, it's necessary for me to rely on someone else. I can only do 50 percent of the work in the race. I'm only as good as the partner who's willing to row with me. And being young, I don't have much street cred to pull in a good partner.

But I won't be young and inexperienced forever.

"I *will* go the Paralympics," I tell Bobby, when we're back home in Louisville and stroking side by side on the river.

And Bobby, who's never been a hold-your-hand, affirmations kind of coach, replies:

"Prove it."

chapter

eleven

I have no idea what to do with myself once I don't make Team USA. It was all I'd planned for. I feel directionless. My friends are going to college, and that seems like a logical next step. I start community college in Louisville. I do better in my first semester there than I ever did in high school, even though I still hate school. I like learning, but I'm not a school person. It comes so easily to Mom, and I watch her absorbing information and processing it. My brain seems to fight it. So much so that in Ukraine, they thought I had a learning disability. (Partially because I didn't talk until I was three years old, apparently—but who's going to blame an orphan girl for that? Who was I going to talk to?) CT scans since then, though, have shown the effects of shaken baby syndrome and damage from too much cortisol from constant fight-or-flight mode.

My past. It *still* has a grip on every single aspect of my mind and body.

I find an apartment in Louisville, not too far from Mom, and I move into it. All on my own. Well, not exactly on my own; Mom still helps me pay for some of it, since Starbucks isn't the most lucrative job on the planet. For a while, that's my life: work, row, class. It's not too different from high school. Except that I'm looking toward London now, where the 2012 Games will be held. And except for the independence.

I love making my own schedule, deciding when I'll study, see friends, spend time with Mom, be on the water. It suits me.

I meet him at the river.

He's there, randomly it seems, a new face in the usual crowd at the clubhouse. He's seven or eight years older than me, maybe older, in a wheelchair but still with some use of his legs. He's quite charming, but everyone else thinks he's bad news. So of course I gravitate toward him. Joe, he introduces himself. We start dating, and soon he's moved into my apartment. I almost don't notice that I'm paying the rent for both of us.

I do notice that Joe doesn't drink coffee. He hates the stuff. I tease him about it. He teases me right back: how I'm so careful to select beans, my ritual of grinding, brewing, drinking, how I only drink it black. I call myself a connoisseur. He calls me an addict.

Joe used to row more. He had a chance at trying to race competitively, he says, but he's vague about what happened and why he doesn't row much now. I don't press him on it. But he becomes very involved in *my* rowing. He knows my practice schedule. He offers opinions on where I can improve, train better. I mostly only listen to Bobby on this, but I let Joe think that I take his advice.

"You know, Oksana, you have a really flirtatious personality. Even when you don't know it, you're flirting with all the dudes."

I'm surprised. "I'm *friendly*. Is that what you mean? That I'm friendly and I actually talk to people? You think that's flirting?"

"Yeah. You do it all the time when you hang out with Kimberly. And it's really disrespectful."

I don't say anything. Which isn't like me, not at all. But I learned when I was little that sometimes it's easier that way.

I unlock my car door after hiking up to the parking lot from the dock. I reach for my phone in the passenger seat—I always leave it in the car, never take it with me on the water. I'm such a klutz, I'm bound to drop it to a wet grave at the bottom of the river.

The screen shows a row of missed calls and texts, all from Joe. *Where are you? Why aren't you answering? Who are you with? If I don't hear back from you . . .*

I walk into the apartment, a sense of foreboding squeezing my chest in a heavy hand. The air is skunky with weed. I'm amazed at his capacity for smoking such quantities of it.

He comes toward me from his post at the coffee table, face a dark storm.

"Where have you been?"

"Rowing. I've just been training. On the river with Bobby."

"Why is Bobby giving you all this attention? Why is it *just* you? Have you noticed you're the *only* one he coaches?" Joe keeps talking as he closes the distance between us.

I'm getting angry myself. "What are you—" But I don't finish my sentence. He's too close to me. I can feel the lurking violence. I change tack. "You don't have to worry." I soothe him with platitudes. He backs down, and I breathe freely again.

Then he returns to his charismatic, sweet, engaging self. It's easy to write off the episode as an anomaly.

———————

The next week, it's the same when I get back to my car after rowing: missed calls, texts that get angrier for lack of an immediate response. This time, though, when I get home, he's escalated his theories.

"Why do you spend all your time with him? Are you banging him on the side? You're *cheating* on me. All these times you're out 'rowing,' you're really just laughing at me behind my back."

I don't think how ironic this is. He's already cheated on me twice—that I know of. Instead, I remove myself from my body just before the first blow comes.

We meet my second potential race partner in Boston at an indoor world rowing race that Bobby and I have driven to. His name is Gustavo, but he goes by Goose. He seems like a nice guy. But it becomes apparent fairly quickly that his ego is enormous. He competed in the Canada Winter Paralympics in curling and has an outsize pride in those accomplishments. *Is curling even a sport?* I think uncharitably. He wants to try rowing though, and I need a partner.

Goose comes down to Louisville a couple of times to train. Mom puts him up, since there's no funding for this partner search—or for anything else. She gives him her bedroom, her TV, the internet password. Instead of thanks, he tells Mom that he needs *this* kind of potato chips. *This* kind of yogurt.

"I'll take you to the store and you can see what you can get," Mom replies.

He's taken aback, apparently having thought that Mom would be his personal shopper and pay all of his expenses to boot.

I discover that Goose always seems to have an excuse for why he can't do things such as train, work out, polish technique. His head hurts. He's hungry. He's sleepy. He speaks so quickly and flamboyantly in his Spanish accent that I find myself exhausted from listening to his constant complaints, like I've just run a marathon.

Such as today. It's raining. That always makes it harder for me to grip the oars with my crazy hands. I wrap tennis grips around the handles, inside out so the sticky side offers tack for my grip. The friction eats up my palms, just tears them apart. But it works.

We've been rowing for an hour, Bobby in the coach scull next to us. Goose has been complaining for most of that time. "My carpal tunnel. I can't do this," he whines.

Bobby, who rarely slips from his calm monotone, finally loses it and snaps, "Goose, turn around and look at Oksana's hands. She can do it. She's *doing* it. So find a way to do it, too."

Goose shuts up.

It's clear that Goose and I are forcing this. We aren't good partners. But he's my only option. Maybe it's worth settling; the London Games are creeping closer. No doubt Goose is thinking the same thing, looking at this skinny girl with her hands taped to the oars.

———

Mom drives me to the US trials, where Goose will meet us. Bobby drives separately. He rigged up his pickup to fit the boat for transport, so he wouldn't have to rent another vehicle.

In the lead-up to the race, I try to talk to Goose about our strategy. But all he can talk about is the event he's going to next. He's getting into kayaking, with a different partner. He's obsessing about whether it will go well with this woman. When I'm *right here* and our race is *right now*.

Ten minutes before the race, I rush to the ladies' room, expelling the contents of my stomach in a fit of nerves.

When I emerge, scrubbing my mouth, Bobby takes me aside. "You've got to get this under control. You don't ever want your competitors to see that you're weak or something's bothering you. That's when they know they've gotten to you mentally, and this is a mental game. They will pounce. You've got this. You're strong. Go get out there."

There's only one other boat in this race. They pull ahead right off the bat. It's windy on the water, and Goose and I struggle. Halfway through the race, I feel him give up. He's behind me, so I can't see him. But I can feel him stop stroking. He's convinced we're being beaten, and he just stops trying. I don't forgive him for that. I keep rowing. I pull with everything I can.

Just because we're not winning doesn't mean we quit. I don't care if we're in dead last place. I will finish this race. I will pull us across it because you finish what you start. *Who cares about the result when we've come this far.*

"Power of ten!" I shout at him, my code for picking it up to max effort, for giving it all to the oars. "Just ten more strokes!" But he gives nothing. It's like trying to move a rock that's been sitting in a flat field for eons.

When we finally do finish, five *minutes* after the other team, the woman in that boat yells over to us, "I thought you guys were supposed to be good!"

I have no response to this. I focus on getting myself out of the boat. I don't speak to Goose. But he says, "Well. Good thing I have kayaking to fall back on."

Right. He wasn't investing everything into this because it's not all-or-nothing for him. This *is* my all-or-nothing. And I'm at his mercy to fulfill my dream. Or no one's at this point, because Goose will most definitely not be my partner and I have no other prospects.

When I get home, Joe makes it sound like I got what I deserved. I wasn't good enough to win that race anyway, he points out. Maybe he's right. Maybe I haven't been trying hard enough. It probably *is* my fault, somehow, that we lost.

I begin skipping training sessions, classes, seeing friends. I put Joe and his wishes first. I'm on pins and needles trying not to do anything wrong. I schedule a time to train with Bobby, and Joe sees it as sneaking around. I put a coffee mug down too abruptly and Joe calls me careless. I wake up in the morning and Joe complains I'm breathing too loudly.

Kimberly doesn't like him. Bobby doesn't like him. Mom hates him. She sees right through him. I'm still paying for everything in our relationship, which is probably one reason Mom can't stand him because she's supporting me financially, too. By helping me, she's helping him. But she also won't stop supporting me. It's a vicious catch-22. Joe doesn't like her either, though. Because when I'm with Mom, I'm completely myself. Not who Joe wants me to be.

As always, rowing is escape, even though I let my training slip and I'm late more often than not to meet Bobby these days. In the boat, I don't think about anything except what's right in front of me: the motions, the sensation, the speed, the power, the repetition. But while getting to the boathouse, and during the time between my sessions on the water, I can't stop thinking about what I must be doing wrong. *Why can't I make this person happy? How can I be better?*

Sometimes, when Joe is remorseful, he talks about how his father was abusive to his mother. He was exposed to a toxic relationship from the very beginning, and he doesn't know any better. I can't fault someone for not having an example of a loving relationship to follow. I know exactly how it feels to be raised without love.

The third potential partner comes as a surprise. A coach in Washington, DC, calls Bobby asking if we have plans for me for London. He's looking for a partner for his rower. The Games are less than a year away.

Rob Jones is a retired Marine Corps sergeant. I know he's only four or five years older than me, but it seems like he has a whole generation more of life experience. He spent two tours as a combat engineer in Iraq and Afghanistan. Just last year, while serving in Afghanistan, he was struck and wounded by a land mine. Both of his legs had to be amputated above the knee.

Above-the-knee amputees are rare. Like diamonds. I've given up on the idea that there's a good rowing partner out there for me, but at least Rob and I will have something to talk about.

Bobby and I drive up to DC. Rob and his coach, Patrick, are waiting for us on the shoreline. Rob's sitting on a cement wall, looking out at the water, his buzzed blond head in profile, a hooked nose prominent in an unlined face. His expression is stern, almost as if he's smelled something bad. *He has resting bitch face,* I think. Just like I do. He wears shorts, apparently unselfconscious about his prosthetics. I'm wearing my characteristic sweatpants, characteristically sweating my ass off.

Bobby and the other coach call hellos and immediately slip into talking rowing jargon. Rob looks at me as I walk up, trailing Bobby.

"You Oksana?"

"Yeah."

"Rob." There's a silence. "Well, this is awkward." He speaks in a curt monotone. "I guess we're supposed to go out and row? See if they like what they see?"

Even though he seems so serious, I think that there's a dry humor under there. "Yep, another painful blind date," I reply.

But then we have nothing else to say to each other, and it *is* awkward. I ask him about his knees—I've never seen that kind of mechanism. It's all I can think of to ask him. We're quiet as we prep on the dock, gear up in the boat. I settle in the bow. Bobby and I have long decided that I can't be in the stroke seat because I won't stay true to my own race. Every boat has a race plan that's independent of that of the other boats—if I see that we're losing, I'll just start laying down strokes like a beast. But in stroke seat, the job is to set the stroke rate, to be stable, solid, strong. In bow seat, my job is to follow that stroke and be in sync. And to steer. And to call the shots. I've been rowing for years at this point, much longer than Rob, and I'm used to trusting my instincts on when to lay on the surges of energy. I can feel the *Not yet, not yet* switch to *Right now, RIGHT NOW.*

The minute we take our first stroke on the water, it's instant. We click. We match. And we *fly*. It's like we've rowed together our whole lives. Bobby and Patrick, following in the motorboat with a megaphone, say nothing to us. They just let us row. We stay on the water for a while, and the whole picture is clearly there. It needs some detail work, some erasing here, some filling in there. But the sketch is complete.

When we get back in the car to head home to Louisville, I immediately turn to Bobby. "He's the one."

"Yep."

Typical stoic Bobby.

I spend most of the rest of the drive home in silence. But I'm not thinking about rowing anymore. I'm thinking about Joe. I've been wanting to tell someone about the way he treats me in those moments when he's not kind and fun and charming. But definitely not Mom. I've been defending Joe to her, hard, and I don't want her to be disappointed in me. And not any of my friends. I don't know why. It just doesn't feel right. I don't want sympathy, I don't want pity. I don't want them to look at me differently. But I'm also not a little girl anymore, and I don't want to stay silent about this.

"Bobby, I have something to tell you," I finally muster, less than a hundred miles from home. He glances over at me, then leaves his eyes on the road, waiting expectantly. "I . . . I don't know. I don't know how to say it."

"Okay, what'd Joe do?"

I look down at my lap, surprised and embarrassed. I didn't think it was so obvious. I'm quiet for a minute. Then I tell him, just a little bit, about how Joe treats me when he doesn't like whatever I'm up to.

"You need to get rid of this jerk," Bobby says almost before I've stopped talking. "He's going nowhere, and he's dragging you down with him."

My stomach drops. For the first time in the many months that I've been dating Joe, I let myself hear this, actually *hear* it. But I can't make myself believe it. I'm in too deep.

"Oksana, *you have potential.* But I'm not going to waste my time on you if you're going to waste *your* time with some lowlife."

I don't break things off with Joe. But I do step it up in rowing, stop missing training, stop showing up late. I won't let Bobby down. I won't let Rob down, either, now that I've found him.

Rob and I have only had a week or two of rowing together, between traveling back and forth. If we're serious about the Games, which are less than a year away, we need to get more time together. And we need to do it somewhere that the cold temperatures of winter won't interfere with our schedule on the water.

Through his military ties, Rob has a connection to a community rowing program in Orlando, Florida, with two coaches who want to develop a Paralympic training program. Katy and Justin have agreed to host us for free, Rob says. To take a chance on us. It would mean moving there for the winter to train. The coaches already have a family willing to host me as well, living in the upstairs of their house, and Rob's got a living arrangement lined up.

If I'm willing to go.

I've never left home before. Sure, I moved out of Mom's house. But at twenty-two, I'm still in the same town I grew up in from adolescence. The idea of leaving . . . it's intimidating, to say the least.

Joe hates the idea. He thinks I'm dating Rob on the side. Or Rob must be after me. This idea is so off base that it would be hilarious if Joe were the kind of person who could laugh about it. He's not.

"Guys don't talk to girls unless they want something from them," he says. "There's always a motive."

Yeah, like winning a medal? I think. But I don't say it out loud. I rarely do, these days.

He doesn't want to move with me. He refuses to leave Louisville. He doesn't think it's worth it, that I'm being stupid to take the risk of training for something I don't have a chance of winning. To placate him, to make him happy, I tell him he can keep living here in our apartment and we'll visit each other when we can.

I can't see Joe as clearly as can my mom, Bobby, and all my friends. I can't see that he should win an Oscar for his acting skills—that he's a world-class manipulator.

It's been nearly two years now, and he's my first serious relationship. I don't even think about ending it. I don't see a reason to.

I approach my Starbucks manager after my shift, my hair wafting the scent of coffee ahead of me.

"So . . ." I stop. I'm nervous. He looks at me expectantly from his desk in the back office. I take a deep breath, start over. "I'm really serious about rowing. I'm planning to go down to Florida this winter to train there. I wanted to ask . . . can I take a leave for a few months? And come back?" I see his face change. I hurry on. "I've worked here for years, you know I'm a loyal employee."

"If you leave, you're done," he says before I've even closed my mouth. "You won't have a job when you come back."

My stomach sinks. It's hard enough to get a job when you're disabled. It's all people see in an interview. They'll see my gait—never my legs, always covered, but my gait still gives me away—and my hands. Definitely my hands. I look down at them now, curled into fists to keep myself from crying as I turn to walk out of the office.

––––––––––

"Why don't you open up a few credit cards?" Joe says when I come home upset and frustrated. "You can charge stuff, and you only have to make a ten-dollar payment every month and you're fine."

I stare at him. "You don't have to pay right away?" How have I never thought of this?

I start paying for our rent, our groceries, other expenses, with credit cards. I'm so naive, I have no idea that I'm accruing debt, that I suddenly owe quite a lot of money. Joe still hasn't paid a single dime.

––––––––––

I also need to put my studies on hold at the community college. Mom isn't happy about that, and it makes me second-guess my decision.

"Don't do it, Oksana," she says. "Everyone says they're just going to 'take a year off.' Then it turns into five, and then all of a sudden it's forever."

But I know that this is my chance. I don't want to live my life as a what-if. That's terrifying to me. When I'm sixty, I don't want to think, *I wish I'd done that, I wish I'd taken that chance, what if I had?* My education will always be there waiting for me. My body, on the other hand, is at its peak, and there's a time limit on that. Even if I don't make the Games, I'll never have to wonder whether, if I'd just tried harder, I might have had something more to lay down. I know now, after going through two partners and qualifying races that weren't successful, what this will take.

I lay it all down. I step off the cliff, with no idea where I will land.

––––––––––

There's still one major obstacle: Rob and I need a real Trunk and Arms double scull to train with, rather than the rigged-up boats we've been rowing. Bobby applies for a grant from the Challenged Athletes Foundation, which covers half the boat. Bobby covers the other half. Himself. And he drives it down to Florida, caravanning with me as I move away from Louisville for the first time since Mom and I landed there so many years ago from Buffalo.

chapter

twelve

One of our first days out on the water in Florida, my stroke rhythm is interrupted by a loud thunk. I glance over to see what my oar hit. It's a damn *alligator*, hanging there with its scaly nose and eyes, which are now trained right on me, sticking out above the surface. I let out a scream.

"Focus, Oksana!" Rob snaps. "It's fine. It's just an alligator. Just focus."

It's the most words he's said at one time since we landed here.

I worry that Rob doesn't say much. He doesn't talk at all. He's so closed off. At times I think he's *weird*. I'm thinking like a young, naive girl though, often forgetting that he only recently came back from Afghanistan, where he had his accident. I can't comprehend the demons in his head, and he doesn't tell me. At twenty-two and so far away from home for the first time, I can't get out of my own head to sympathize. I don't tell him about my demons, either.

"Mom, we're supposed to be a team," I say to her over the phone one night, "and we don't even do anything together. We're supposed to be in total sync. But he doesn't even talk to me!"

We row six out of seven days a week. Rob's attitude is that training is our job. He's just so *military* about everything. I'm not like that. I'm committed, yes, but I also want to check out the city, go shopping, drink a glass of wine somewhere new (not that I can afford it—I'm still eating cheap Taco Bell and McDonald's meals to stretch my money). But I have no one to do those things with. No one to talk to. No one to tell me I'm making the right choice here.

Alone in my room in Orlando, I question myself endlessly: *What am I doing? Why did I move down here? I don't even know Rob. Why are we chasing this dream that we don't even know if we can achieve?*

———————————

This afternoon, Rob and I have a breakthrough. It has nothing to do with rowing, though.

"There's this new movie out. Want to go see it when we're done here?"

I snap my head around. I'm floored. *Did he just ask me to hang out outside of a boat?* "Um," I reply, stumbling. "Okay."

"I'll come pick you up."

I'm immediately terrified. My first thought is that everyone who sees two people with prosthetic legs walking around will think, *How cute that all those people are friends.* My second thought: *This is going to be awkward.*

An hour later, still nervous, I climb from the hot afternoon into Rob's air-conditioned car. He doesn't say anything as he pulls away from the curb. Of course. I tune in to the music instead. It's heavy rock. I wouldn't have pegged him for that, although I can't say why. I would have guessed he didn't listen to music at all. The song that's playing is vaguely familiar.

"Who is this?" I ask, grasping on to it in my desperation for something to talk about.

"Five Finger Death Punch."

It doesn't ring a bell. But the chorus is totally familiar: *Bad company . . . Until the day I die.*

I notice he's tapping the steering wheel in time, a little animated for once. "This is your jam, huh?"

"Oh, yeah. That chorus? I think of it like racing. Every time you give a hundred percent of yourself to a race, you die a little bit. You never get that part of yourself back because you put it into the unit, the team, for that race."

After I get over my shock at this wildly long speech from him, I realize that I *love* this idea. And I'm thrilled to discover that Rob is not, in fact, a robot. He's a philosopher in military disguise.

"I'm always so impressed with your gait," Rob says to me as we carry our gear down the dock. I snort—it's such an amputee thing to say. We amputees are the only ones who'd ever even use the word *gait*, let alone examine someone else's to the point where it's a discussion topic.

I don't tell Rob that it comes from an embarrassing model scam I got taken in by in high school. I wanted so badly to get into fashion then (the irony of this—from a girl with no feet who loves shoes and has to wear jeans two sizes too big to cover prosthetics—is most definitely not lost on me) that I jumped at a scholarship opportunity to learn to be a model. Turns out the "scholarship" only led to my paying a stupendous amount of money to be on some list to *maybe* get a call *someday* about modeling. But what I did get out of that debacle was learning the runway stride: one foot directly in front of the other, ramrod-straight back with relaxed shoulders. I never had a physical therapist. I had model walking.

Rob, on the other hand, walks with his arms, swinging them forcefully. He rehabbed at Walter Reed, where the military teaches the most efficient way to walk. I will never walk like that. Guys can pull it off. I would look like a maniac.

"It's why I walk down stairs so much faster than you," I tease him. I've settled, surprisingly easily, into the annoying-little-sister role.

The thing about Rob's prosthetics that I *really* notice, though, is this: he never covers them up. And there's no foam or other trappings to make them look like real legs. They're just unapologetic metal and plastic sticking out of his shorts. He's not ashamed of them in the least.

Down at the dock, I slowly stop wearing sweatpants over my shorts. Everyone knows everyone down there anyway, it's a small community. Katy and Justin—or whichever volunteers Rob and I can scrounge up— help us bring the boat down from the boathouse every day. (We can't do it without help, which aggravates both of us.) They work with us on the ergs every day. They already know what I'm dealing with. Popping my legs off without having to wrestle with the sweats makes things a few seconds quicker. Putting my legs back on after without the sweats is life changing. No tottering onto my knees to pull them up, no sticking my hand down my pants to tussle with fabric and hinges. *Why didn't I do this a long time ago?!*

Everywhere else is another matter, though. Like at the gym. Rob asked a CrossFit connection of his to give us a workout series. I've never done legit training like this before. I trained with Bobby, but he taught me to row. I never even knew what a strength plan was, let alone had one to follow.

The first time I wear shorts to the gym in Orlando, I'm convinced that everyone is staring at my prosthetics. *They're judging me for my legs.* I try to ignore it. I get through most of my workout, then I have to wait for a flat bench to do my dumbbell rows. And wait. And wait. There's only one bench, and this guy has had his water bottle and towel on it for the last ten minutes without doing anything with the bench itself except use it as a table. He'll pick up a weight, put it down on the bench, look at himself in the mirror, pump himself up, lift the weight once. Then take forever to repeat the whole process.

He probably thinks a puny girl with no legs couldn't possibly need the bench. Finally, I'm impatient enough to blurt, "Are you actually using this? Or can I?"

"Oh," he says, surprised. "Yeah, yeah, yeah." He hustles to move his stuff. I situate myself on the bench, one knee and one hand on it, one leg standing beside it, and pull the weight up to my ribs. I can feel him watching me.

He's staring at my prosthetics, I know it. I keep lifting, change sides, try to brush off his evaluation that no doubt finds me lacking.

He finally breaks his silence as I rise to rest between sets. "That's impressive. I've never seen a girl row that much weight before."

Oh. I flush but don't say anything, just smile quickly and finish my reps. Not until I'm driving home, music blaring, does the epiphany hit me.

I've been so afraid of people judging me based on my appearance—based on *what's wrong* with my appearance. Yes, inevitably, some people stare. And some people try so hard *not* to stare that their eyeballs nearly pop out the sides of their heads when I walk by. But what if they're actually the minority?

How much have I been feeding my paranoia about outside judgment, then projecting my negative thoughts onto other people? I've wasted so much time agonizing over what other people think and how they view me, when everyone is not, in reality, staring at my legs. Or my hands.

I think back to all that time I spent on the Louisville dock being so careful to never show my legs. All the energy I spent in middle school and high school to make sure my prosthetics looked like real legs under my jeans. How exhausted I made myself trying to look normal—and how I probably made the situation worse by hiding it. I used to get so mad at my peers for teasing me. But I never let them see it to understand it.

Now I realize, like a jolt to the heart, *It didn't matter anyway.* Look at Rob. He doesn't care in the least what people think of him.

I can't just let it all go in an instant though, all those years of conditioning myself to avoid attention. I still wear pants everywhere except at the dock and the gym. And the next time I go to the gym, I get a comment from a woman passing by—a line that reminds me why I spent all that energy hiding what's different about me. "Good for you!" she says with an indulgent, incredibly annoying smile.

I think it's mostly the pity veiled in encouragements that gets me. Especially from strangers.

"Mom, I can't do this. I don't want to be here," I sob into the phone. This is probably the fourth or fifth time I've called her crying since I moved down here. "I don't want to do this anymore. It's not what I thought it would be."

I'm exhausted from this training schedule. And I'm so lonely. The German couple I live with are so kind, but they're not my friends. Rob and I are warming up, but we still don't *hang out* together. I miss Mom so much.

"Oh, honey. It's hard to leave home for the first time. It's a big transition."

"It all just feels so big." Who was I to think that I could handle this?

"I know. It is. But remember that you've worked really hard, you've prepared for it. You're ready for this, Oksana. Home will always be here. But this is your moment. I know you can rise to it if you want to. And I'm right here behind you."

I sniffle my sobs into submission. As much as moms can be corny sometimes, the thought of mine at my back always makes me feel stronger.

My arms are on fire. My vision is tunneled. My back screams. And I still have a hundred meters to go.

The girl on the erg next to me wants it, I can tell. And she's a lot bigger than me, so much stronger. *Look at her, she's going to win.*

Erg times are one way that coaches for the national US Rowing team evaluate athletes. I know this all too well from Karen's sum-up of my abilities—three years ago now. Trials for the national team are coming up in a month, hence my stationary race against this girl. Rob currently holds the men's erg record. I need to be strong for our team, too.

I disappear inside the pain. My vision darkens. There's a deep searing in my lungs. Finally, I pull the last stroke on the machine. I think I might black out. I want to collapse. My arms lock up, cramping in agony.

Behind me, Katy kneels down, fast. "Whatever you do, sit up straight," she whispers. "I know it hurts now but it will hurt more if you collapse. I promise she will see you and she will believe she's beaten you, whether she did or not."

I glance over, and the other girl is heaving, doubled over. I feel like my body is dying inside, but I sit up straight. I wrangle my breath into shallow sips. I try to look like I could do another round if I needed to. I can play this game of hiding weakness. I was born into this game.

On the water, in training, Rob and I both give it our all. We start to sync almost flawlessly. When we row, our heartbeats begin to match. The most successful teams achieve this phenomenon in their boats.

Maybe we actually have a chance at this.

Rob sets a box down on the dock. He reaches for his keys to cut the tape on it, glancing up at me with a look that I think is excited—for Rob, anyway. It's the day before we're to drive up to Princeton, New Jersey, for US trials, the race to determine the national Trunk and Arms team for US Rowing: the team that will represent the United States in all international races for the year—including the Paralympics, if we can qualify. People often confuse the Paralympics with the Special Olympics, which are essentially all-inclusive sports for anyone over the age of eight years old with a cognitive disability. The Paralympics, though, are basically the

Olympics for people with physical disabilities: where the world's most elite athletes in their sports have to qualify to earn a spot to compete against one another. If Rob and I can win in Princeton, we'll be the team that goes to the World Cup in Serbia to try to earn our spot in the London Paralympics. Soon, we'll be racing for my dream.

From the box, he pulls out two shirts, one black, one red. He hands the black one to me. I hold it up. The front reads in red letters: TEAM BAD COMPANY. The back: TODAY WE DIE A LITTLE BIT. I look at Rob, delighted.

We're both feeling pretty confident going into this. We've been training six days a week, hitting good times on our one-kilometer practice races. And Rob has the American erg record. We're strong.

"I love it," I say.

We're gearing up on the dock in Princeton—or gearing down, depending on how you look at the removal of two sets of legs—trying not to look too hard at the competition. I've only recognized two of the teams at trials, and we're racing them both now in the final. One consists of the woman who quipped nastily to me after Goose gave up at the Bayada Regatta, "I thought you guys were supposed to be good!" Her rowing partner is Oz Sanchez, who won gold in cycling in Beijing. They both look built, strong.

The other boat is Scott and his regular partner.

We are screwed. The anxiety begins to build in the bottom of my stomach. I know that it will soon rise into my chest. But I've taught myself not to vomit before every race. So at least there's that. And Mom isn't here for me to worry about letting her down—I still don't let her come to my races. I try to focus on just breathing.

It's been a series of mishaps even to get to this moment. On day one, as we were unloading our equipment, Rob began pulling the boat off

Justin's trailer, and the whole right-side rigger—the piece that spans the hull and connects to the oarlocks—fell right off.

"Oh, shit," Rob said in disbelief.

If we don't have a rigger, we can't race.

Most riggers are prefabricated out of fiberglass, but Bobby welded ours out of piping in a cost-saving measure. Bobby, who met us up here for the race, is generally an equipment MacGyver, and he was horrified—as much as Bobby gets horrified—at this malfunction. He took the rigger to the Princeton University boathouse and welded it back together. We're all wondering whether it will hold.

The anxiety is rising through my torso in a threatening swell. But something else is in there, too, and it's hotter than the nerves.

"Rob," I say, a little under my breath so the sound doesn't carry over the water, "I will be *damned* if one of those other boats wins."

"Well, they're not going to," he says, as if it's evident. "So you don't have to worry about it."

We come in first. By twelve seconds.

There's not much fanfare. It's all pretty matter-of-fact. Or maybe that's just how it seems to me, still in disbelief as we get out of the boat. On the dock after, I'm slower putting my legs on and getting my clothes back in order. Rob, who doesn't care what he looks like or what he wears (which is usually obvious), is waiting.

"Rob, you can go. I'm fine."

"I'm not going to leave you. You're my partner. We'll walk off together."

That's what we do, each carrying our oars. Now I can't stop smiling. Rob even shows some animation when his parents swarm him.

"Good job," Bobby says succinctly. I think there's a little pride in there, though.

Because we've done it. We're the national team.

I turn, and Karen is approaching me.

My breath catches. I've been imagining this moment for four years. In my mind, it's been a *Pretty Woman* moment, the one where Julia Roberts walks back into the swanky department store all dolled up and says to the clerk who wouldn't serve her when she was down, "Big mistake. Huge."

"Congratulations. That was a good race." I can't tell if her tone is condescending. "You looked really strong and powerful out there."

My entire body is shaking, even my legs inside my prosthetics. My blood has gone hot and rushed to the surface of my skin, where it feels like I've been stung by a thousand bees. I know what this burning is. It's me trying to contain the bomb that wants to go off. Because I'm not the same person I was four years ago. I no longer want to bestow on her that power—the knowledge that I'm only here because she didn't believe in me, that her words *you can't* drove me all this time.

I'm driven by so much more than she'll ever know.

I smile lightly. "Thanks." I turn and walk away.

I don't look back.

———

I don't celebrate that night. Or at all. Now that I've proven to Karen that I *am* a serious rower, it occurs to me that I haven't thought seriously of a goal beyond that.

But now, we're really doing this. We have to prove that we *earned* that slot, that it wasn't a fluke. We have to prove that we belong on this stage.

"You know, it's only luck that you made the team," Joe tells me on the phone that night.

The thought wiggles its way in and sticks there.

I have to read the email sitting at the top of my inbox in the morning twice before it registers. It's from Allison, the media head at US Rowing (I have to keep reminding myself that I'm actually *part* of US Rowing now, I still can't fully believe it). She says that ESPN is requesting an interview and photo shoot with me for their Body Issue. They've been looking all over for how to get in touch with me, since I'm not on their usual roster of athletes they follow. Obviously.

I tell Joe about the ESPN request. Rob and I are heading to Serbia soon for the World Cup, but I'm back in Louisville for a quick weekend, in my apartment with Joe. I keep thinking that if I can just see him more, maybe we can repair this. I've put too much time into it to end it now. Joe reads over the email.

"They want *you*?" His tone is a mix of excitement and anger. Since we won at trials, Rob and I have had a few small media hits. It's increasingly clear that Joe doesn't like these new spotlights on me. I think it might be jealousy, a feeling of missing out on his nonexistent rowing career that went nowhere. I try not to rise to it, try to be understanding and downplay any achievements on my part. Which is easy, given I'm a champion of self-doubt anyway.

I stay calm. "Well, what is it?"

"What do you mean, what is it?"

"The Body Issue! I've never heard of it."

"Are you serious? It's where some of the best athletes in the world from all different sports pose naked for ESPN."

"*What?*" I google it immediately. *Oh, hell no.* I'm not going to stand naked in front of a camera. I can't even stand naked in front of a mirror by myself.

I type out my reply to Allison, which basically says that I'm so honored and this is amazing. But I'm not sure I'm ready to do this. Or want to.

She replies almost immediately, *I understand. But I think you should take a little time first to reflect on what this has the power to do.*

She tells me that I'm only the second rower, after Olympic gold medalist Susan Francia, to be offered a spot in the Body Issue. Susan Francia was my idol. I watched all her rowing videos growing up.

And, Allison continues, I'm the first double amputee to be invited. *Think about what you have the opportunity to represent. You have the opportunity to show what's possible.*

All I can think the photographs will show, though, are my scars, the imperfections, the lack of muscles. I'm not jacked. I'm not a real athlete like these other people whom ESPN features.

I'll wait until you tell me No again, and then I'll let them know. Think about it first.

I sit there staring at Allison's response for a while. Then I take my cup of coffee into the bedroom to go get dressed for running some errands. I have a to-do list as long as my arm before I leave again, and I need to focus on it. Not on this terrifying idea of standing around naked for a photographer.

In my room, I'm having one of those days. My hair looks like shit. Nothing looks good on me. I hate my closet. *Why do I have so many pairs of jeans when they all make me look awful?!*

Then I realize, *Everyone has days when they can't stand to look in the mirror. It's not just me.*

And on the heels of that another thought: *I'm making my day worse because I'm trying to hide things. I'm wearing pants to cover the weird bulge of my prosthetics around my thighs, and shirts with longer sleeves to cover my hands. I hate that I feel I have to hide, fit in.*

I give up and throw on the closest pair of jeans. I go about my day. But I can't stop thinking about the mirror. Hours later, at the wheel driving home, it finally sinks in.

This isn't about me and my anxieties. It's about everyone else who looks in the mirror and can't find beauty in their reflections, who, instead of embracing the things that make them different, hate themselves based on what society has told them they *should* look like.

I still hate my reflection. But maybe, by showing society that beauty— a little of it anyway—comes in all different shapes and sizes and forms, I can empower someone *else* to begin to love the way they look.

That night, long after it has gotten dark, I sit back down at my computer. I go through old ESPN Body Issues. I'm so nervous at the idea of being naked in front of a crew of people. But as I click through, that thought fades to the background. This clearly isn't about *exploiting* bodies. Because athletes' bodies aren't in general viewed as beautiful—they're sort of the opposite of models' physiques, after all, with huge shoulders or quads and weird lines or impossible definition. But every ounce of muscle and cut is there because the athlete has worked for three years, five years, more, for *that* particular muscle or the structure of *this* back for a determined purpose. The point seems to be about celebrating these bodies not for what they look like, but what they *do*.

Then there would be *me*, a girl with no legs. An image that goes beyond the traditional mold of an athlete's body, to show that athletes are in wheelchairs. Athletes are blind. Athletes are limbless.

I open up my email.

I'll do it.

When I show up to the set—which is a house on a lake on the border of Connecticut and New York—a *ton* of people are there. I'd told Allison that I don't think I can be fully naked. That I'm nervous about the crew's being all men. She tells me I'll be given a nude thong that they'll airbrush out, and that there'll likely be some women there. That once everything's all set, the crew leaves anyway, so it's just the photographer and me. But right now, dozens of people are milling around and my heart is in my throat. *This was dumb, what the hell was I thinking?* For the shortest of seconds, I wish I'd let Joe come with me.

I'd wanted him to come. I wanted him with me for support through this. Once the shock of that first email wore off (for both of us), he kept telling me what a cool thing this was. But the closer we came to the shoot, the faster his support bled away.

"They're not even paying you for this?"

"No, Joe, I've told you that. It's more of an opportunity for me. It's an honor to be invited."

"You're such a slut. You'd pose naked for nothing?"

I was angry, but I just rolled my eyes. I was accustomed to our knock-down, drag-out fights by now. This was nothing, just the runway before the explosive takeoff.

"Jesus, Oksana, you'd do anything for attention."

I snapped. "What the fuck is *wrong* with you?!"

Liftoff.

Before the shoot, the ESPN writer interviews me. I've done some interviews by now, but not many. I usually let Rob do the talking for both of us. I can't wrap my head around what I'm supposed to say, how I'm supposed to act. The interviewers all want the story of my past—I've already seen the kind of inspiration porn they're after. But only parts of my story are the pretty, inspirational pieces people want—Mom adopting me, overcoming the loss of my legs, finding purpose. The rest is ugly.

The writer's asking me about my body (of course), and I'm so uncomfortable and nervous about my body before the shoot that answering his questions is like pulling a nail from the wall with your fingertips. He starts with what he probably thinks is a simple question, presumably to ease me in.

"What do you like about your body?"

I almost start laughing. But I have to be somewhat positive here—not my strong suit. The moment goes on too long while I rack my brain for something to say, and I start to panic. "My forearms," I blurt. "They're really jacked."

He smiles and waits expectantly, giving me an opening to try again. He's good at this, I can tell. Because he's not pushy, I take my time to think a little.

"I don't think people realize how difficult it is for me to row with my hands." I talk for a while, then naturally flow into telling him about the way I was born and all the obstacles those deformities created.

Then, also naturally, he asks, "What about your life in Ukraine? What hardships did you face there?"

When he says "Ukraine," the old familiar feel of hunger strikes me instantly: the hollowness down to the bones, the desolation spreading to the core of me. Hunger is something people can understand. This feels like a safer subject.

"I was in a poor orphanage in a very poor village. There wasn't much food. We'd only get one meal a day, maybe some soup if we were lucky, usually just a piece of bread. I was only thirty-eight inches tall and weighed thirty-four pounds when I came to America"—I've long memorized these stats the way other people memorize their grandparents' names—"and my three-year-old neighbor was bigger than me. To protect myself, I think, my mind learned to ignore the hunger."

Blink.

Laney creeps down the stairs in front of me in the deep dark, down into the smell of potatoes cooking in sewer water.

Blink.

It's only a flash in my memory before I wrench myself back. The writer's looking at me, waiting for my next thought. *Not that one.* I focus back in. We talk for another half hour, and he helps me open up a little more about how my childhood experience with pain—such as hunger, or the "physical abuse" I refer to only once and only with that single phrase—translates to rowing ("I can endure pain," I say simply). It's the most I've ever talked about my past with someone who's not a therapist.

"And why did you decide to pose for the Body Issue?" he asks, the last inquiry before we expose the body in question.

I hesitate, trying to form words for all the things I've been thinking about since that email came through. "There's no one perfect model, or, you know, *ideal* of beauty. Just because you have this color hair or that color eyes doesn't mean you're beautiful. I think that as humans, we're drawn to what's inside—that when we think a person is beautiful, we're connecting to something on a different level. It's something inside, it's . . . it's *confidence*," I finally articulate. "It's confidence in yourself that makes you powerful."

I get my hair and makeup done in the master bedroom. Not much though—they want to keep it natural. I joke that they should feel free to photoshop in some abs, maybe airbrush in a tan to fix the ugly tan line I have from my rowing uniform. The woman doing my makeup laughs, but says it's unlikely. This is all about what's real.

They give me a white robe and show me to the bathroom to change—or strip. I have zero confidence in myself right now, even for all my talk in the interview.

I can still back out, I think as I slip my clothes off. *Yeah, right. It's too late now.*

I'm ushered outside to the edge of the lake, where a single scull is inexplicably suspended from the limb of an enormous tree. The crew positions lights and me until the photographer is satisfied (of course it's a man; I researched all his work before I agreed to this, wanting to know what I was getting into), while I try to tamp down the anxiety building in my throat.

Finally he says, "Okay, ready?"

The knot of anxiety free-falls into my stomach.

"Actually, wait, wait," he says, holding up a hand.

I stop holding my breath, gasp, and halt my shaking hand that's reaching for the robe belt.

He runs over to one of the lighting crew and talks to her for a second. She takes off her shoes, and the photographer brings them to me, these black Nike skateboard shoes. *Are you kidding me? I have no clothes on, but we're gonna fixate on shoes?* I'm not sure why I can't just go barefoot with the shell feet of my prosthetics, but I'm not the artist here. I slide them on.

"Okay, you ready?"

I want to say, *No, never mind, I can't do this.* I'm terrified. I want to walk back into the house and put my clothes on and drive away. But I close my eyes and remember this isn't about me. I drop the robe.

No one leaves. Ten people are holding lights and extra cameras, watching me be fully naked.

I seem to be having a lot of trouble breathing today.

"You're going to stand just so." The photographer directs me so that my front is away from the camera. Thank God. I *like* my back. It's the strongest part of me, more than my forearms. I should have said that in the interview. Maybe I can still tell the writer.

"Go ahead and lift that boat above you, just enough that the muscles activate. And look back at me over your shoulder." I follow directions as best I can, trying to focus only on the commands, not my bare butt mooning everyone in sight. "*Yes*, that's perfect."

He takes several shots, has me move into different positions—without the boat, holding an oar, no props. He's so supportive, and all the lighting people are, too, that it's like a gentle wind starting to blow on the hard cloud of nervousness until it slowly, slowly wafts away. In its place blooms something else. Not confidence, I don't think. Motivation, maybe. I discover I want to try everything the crew suggests. Next thing I know, I'm naked holding on to a rope swing in the tree and *having a good time.*

I'm exhilarated by the time I finally put my robe back on. It feels like I've just rowed a race.

When I get back to the hotel hours later, I feel light. Like a weight I didn't know I'd been carrying has been lifted. I'd been vulnerable in a way that I could never be on my own, alone with the bathroom mirror. Because it had been for a bigger purpose. To try to break a mainstream perception of what *perfect* is supposed to be.

———

Not until the photographer emails me the proofs of the final photos does it dawn on me: *Oh, shit. Rob's going to see this. Bobby's going to see this. Mom is going to see this.* How naive could I possibly be that I didn't think of that?!

I spend the next few weeks worrying, but I don't have that much time to focus on it. The Games are around the corner.

———

The World Cup in Serbia in May 2012 is the first race I tell Mom I want her to come to. Now that Rob and I are on the national team, there's finally some funding to pay our way. So, for once, I don't have to lean on Mom for financial help, and she can use that money to come herself.

"Wait. It's in *Siberia?*" she says over the phone.

"No, Mom. Serbia."

"Oh," she says, as if that makes more sense.

"Rob's dad and stepmom are going, too, so you'll have people to hang out with."

"I don't care who I hang out with, honey, I'd come alone. I'm just excited to see you race."

I close my eyes. *Don't let her down.*

My Team USA uniform comes in the mail. I rip it open and pull it out, holding it up to memorize the front, the back. I find myself not wanting to put it down. Ever.

I would never have guessed that the first uniform I put on would be for Team USA. It's overwhelming. Most people probably go from Little League uniforms to middle school jerseys to high school team uniforms, a graduation of seriousness to orient them as part of a team. I never had that, not even for volleyball.

I sleep in my uniform for the first two nights. It's not exactly comfortable—it's a lot of spandex—so I take to hanging it in my doorway instead. It's the first thing I see in the morning and last thing before I close my eyes at night. To remind myself why I'm doing this, through all the questioning of this outlandish dream. I don't think it's until right now, seeing the uniform hang there, that I grasp what it means to be racing for my country.

When I meet Rob at the airport, I'm still flush with excitement. "Did you see the uniforms? Did you like yours? Did you try it on?" I know I'm babbling like a teenager, but I can't help myself.

"Yep, it fits. Threw it in the suitcase. It's fine."

Well. I won't tell him I *slept* in mine, then—because that's clearly not what you do with a uniform. I follow him into Departures, cheeks burning. But as I walk, I lovingly pat the suitcase that contains my uniform.

At the waterfront in Serbia, Rob and I are kneeling above the boat that US Rowing rented for us. It's the same model as the boat we row at home. We brought our own oars though. Which didn't show up at the baggage claim with the rest of our luggage. So we're fitting rental oars into the oar-locks, and I'm praying I have enough tape and time to make them work for my hands. Twelve teams are all gunning for the two spots left for the London Games.

Among them are the Brazilian team, with the woman who won bronze in the last Games, and the Australian team, whose rowers are both medalists. Between them, those four rowers are swimming in world championship and Paralympic medals. Only first and second will qualify their boats, and it's already clear who that will be. At most, Rob and I can get third. Maybe. We haven't even been rowing together for a year. We're the smallest team out here. No one even knows who we are or a damn thing about us, other than we're the team with the new rower and the girl who's too small.

We only won trials because the weather was good, Rob was so strong, the stars aligned. All the stars have to align again for us to qualify here. We did it once. But the continuing test will be whether we can do it again, and again. This is our first international race, and we have to win it if we want to keep going down this road.

This is impossible.

We come in first in our heat.

I tell Rob that we only won because they put us in the slow heat, which is true. Now our lane in the finals will be on the outside, where the underdog boats grapple with the wind while the best boats get the inside lanes protected from weather.

The finals. Where we go up against the Brazilian and Australian boats.

We're in lane 6, on the outside. I'm nervous, I can feel it all through my body up to my skin. Mom is around somewhere, set to watch the race with Rob's parents. I try to shut out the idea of her being here, the idea of her watching me fail after all the things she's done for me. I have to do well enough eventually to be able to pay her back financially for supporting this dream. To pay her back for . . . well, everything. The sinking feeling in my stomach tells me it's not going to be this time, though. I shouldn't have invited her.

There's a crosswind, so Brazil, the number one seed, is right next to us where we block the wind for them. I feel like a horse that needs blinders, I'm so aware of their presence and how it affects me. All the boats sit at the start line for a full three minutes, each one a little lifetime. I try to banter with Rob to distract myself.

"You know that since I'm in the back of the boat, I'm first across the finish line—which means I'm pulling your ass across it." He snorts. It's like bantering with a rock. *I* think it's hilarious, anyway.

"One minute to go!" an official calls to the racers.

Rob turns his head slightly so I can hear him: "Today we die a little bit."

I feel myself steel. I feel what's becoming a familiar certainty, foundational and powerful, that rises up through the nerves: *I* have the ultimate control in this moment. *I* had control of my training, *I* had control of what I did up until the race starts. *I* have control in this race over every single thing that I do.

Then the beep goes off, and Rob and I are pulling. We have our own race plan, with a start-stroke sequence, and we stick to it—Bobby, Justin, Katy, they've all coached me never to race another boat's race. We stick to the plan. At the 250-meter mark, I cue Rob with a faster stroke rate. "Pick it up to thirty-six!"

When I do dare to look up, Brazil is right beside us. I don't even see any other boats. *Where the hell is Australia?* We can't be beating them, there's no way. They're probably just playing mind games. They'll pick it up out of nowhere.

But we're so far ahead, no other boat is in our peripheral vision. We're right next to Brazil, just a hair behind them. *Holy shit, we're doing it. We just have to keep this, keep this spot.*

Then something in my head switches. I don't want to just maintain. I want to *beat* them. I want to win.

"Rob!" I shout.

He nods, once.

I don't look over my shoulder. I focus in. "Right here, this is all for London! *Power of ten!*"

I don't look up until we cross the finish line.

On the podium, I can't stop smiling. We not only qualified for the Games. We *won*. The World *Cup*. It's my first gold medal. I'm holding my flowers and waving and vibrating—giddy—and Rob is standing beside me completely unemotional. He looks like he just smelled rotten socks.

I'm scanning the crowd for Mom, but I can't find her. I'm sure she's up there somewhere though, and I smile wider just for the knowing.

Mom is frantically looking around for me. From their spot on the shore, she and Rob's parents couldn't tell who won. They waited without breathing, Mom clinging to Rob's stepmom, until the announcer boomed over the loudspeaker, *"USA takes first!"* Then they ran for the stands, jostling for a place to be able to see the medal ceremony.

And there Rob and I were: on the tallest step on the podium.

After, on her way to find me to give me the biggest hug of her life, Mom got swallowed in the crowds. She can't find me. She asks one official-looking person where to find me.

"She's over there." He points.

I'm not there. Mom asks another.

"No, she's over there." The official points in a different direction. She still doesn't see me.

A third official says, "Oh, some woman came and got her, a team doctor, I think. Something about drug testing."

Forty-five minutes later, Mom's convinced someone's kidnapped her daughter in a foreign country. Finally, we glimpse each other as I make my way back from the medical tent, which is in a totally bizarre location that Mom would never have found.

"Oh my God, I can't believe you did it!" She wraps me in a huge hug, desperately relieved to see me.

"I know, I know!"

"Where have you been, though?"

"She made me drink two bottles of water so I would pee! She made me drink so much I have to go again and I can't find the damn bathrooms. Let's get to the hotel!"

Not the celebration I envisioned sharing with Mom after my first World Cup win. But there's time for celebrating later. Right now, I have to pee.

"What's the hottest color you can visualize?" Brad asks me as I sit on the erg in the boathouse before my workout.

Not just Brad. Brad *Alan Lewis*. Only one of the most famous rowers in the world. He won a gold medal with his partner in the 1984 Olympic Games, the first American team to win a gold in any rowing event in twenty years. Rob fell in love with Brad's book *Assault on Lake Casitas*, about his journey to that medal. Brad's email apparently shows up everywhere in the book, so Rob thought, *Why not?*—and emailed him, asking if Brad would coach us for the Paralympics. Brad, shockingly, said yes. If we came up to his turf to train in Charlottesville at the University of Virginia for the summer, he'd coach us.

"Red," I say definitively. It's the color that powers anger—which powers my rowing.

"No."

I snap my head up, caught off guard.

"It's white. The hottest color, the color at the center of a flame—it's white. That's the color your focus needs to be. White-hot."

I can get there, I think. *Oh, I can get there.*

Since our Serbia win, Rob and I have been getting more media attention. *Sports Illustrated* publishes an article on us titled "The Marine and the Orphan." Other outlets pick up on the theme, as if they can't think of anything else.

It's so incredibly frustrating. An orphan girl is who I was when I was seven years old. I'm not an orphan anymore. They make it sound like Rob, who gets the cool moniker, is taking pity on me and making this poor, sad girl's dream come true. What about "Legless Man and Badass Girl"? Or "Mr. What Not to Wear and the Stylish One"?

When do I get to be more than my past?

"It has to be Bobby," I say again to Rob. "I'm not going if Bobby's not going."

Rob rolls his eyes. "You understand that Brad is a gold medal rower, right?" Rob thinks I'm being immature.

US Rowing allows us to choose one coach to accompany us to the Games. Rob wants Brad. Rob has bonded closely with him in just these two months. Rob is convinced we need Brad there. I want Bobby. We've been arguing about this for a week. We stopped speaking to each other for two days straight over it. It's been horribly awkward, and we're only just now broaching it again.

"Look, I understand the value we'll probably both miss out on if Brad's not there," I say. "But *you* don't understand: Bobby is the only reason I'm here."

I still don't know if Rob gets that this is more than just a gold medal or a goal or a Games to me. It's the whole process that drives me: from the first day that I sat in a boat and discovered I could silently scream with the oars to this person I've become—who I think is maybe powerful, if I could just let myself believe that for more than one single second at a time—and who I might be able to become with rowing as my guide.

"I literally won't go to the Games unless Bobby comes because I won't go through this journey without him. Period."

Rob eventually gives in. He knows by now that my stubbornness is final. He chooses Roger Payne—the boatman in charge of the boathouse at UVA, who also helped coach us, and who arranged for us to keep our boat down at the dock so we didn't have to rely on anyone else to get it in the water to row—to come as our boat mechanic, which assuages the both of us. I call Bobby.

Mom's not sure she can afford to come to London. She doesn't have to fully financially support me now that I have some finances from fund-raising and US Rowing. But she just paid to go to Serbia. She's not sure where the money's going to come from to go to London, which is one of the most expensive cities in the world, on top of the international flight.

She borrows from her retirement account so she can be there to cheer for me. It's far from the first time. But she never tells me that. She protects me as much as possible, still, after all these years.

Just before the Games, I discover that Joe's cheated on me. Again. For the fourth time (that I know about).

I finally, *finally*, think, *The hell with it. This isn't sustainable.* In my mind I cut myself out of the relationship. I begin to use going to London and the Games as a way out. When I'm home in Louisville for a weekend, the last time I'm home before I leave for the UK, I sit Joe down on our couch. *My couch,* I think, for the first time.

"This isn't a sustainable relationship. It isn't healthy for either of us." I take a deep breath. I look him in the eye. "After this, when I get back from London, things have to change."

His whole face transforms. I knew it would, but I'm still not ready for it. "Fuck you. And London?!" His voice is rising with each word. "You're gonna lose. You're not even gonna be a blip on the radar. You know you don't even deserve to be there." His anger is searing. White-hot.

I'm terrified to leave this apartment for the Games. It's in my name. I'm scared he'll trash it, ruin my credit, ruin the name I've only just started to make for myself. I backtrack somewhat to soothe him and bring the tension down. I'll save everything else I have to say for later.

thirteen

It's early at the Louisville airport, the sun just rising. Rob and Bobby and I are wrestling bags and gear in through the sliding double doors of Departures. Rob came to Louisville so we could fly to London together. The boathouse threw us a little celebration last night, Randy almost in sentimental tears by the end of the short party. But now that we're at the airport, it feels a little anticlimactic. Some teams—for example, those that compete in the sexy sports such as track or basketball—get huge send-offs. We get Mom. Who'd probably turn herself into twenty people if she could, just to make me happy.

As Bobby and Rob head toward the desk to check in, I look back through the doors. Mom is still standing there outside her car. She'll be coming to London in a few days, but I know I won't have the chance to see much of her there. I wave. She waves back, encouraging, happy, nervous for me. I turn and walk into the airport.

Here goes nothing.

Waiting for boarding, I'm in one of the little shops with snacks and books and magazines, and there it is: the ESPN Body Issue on the stand. My heart nearly stops. I'm not sure I want to see it. At least I'm not on the cover, thank God.

I pick it up. I flip through the athletes—José Bautista, Maya Gabeira, the whole US women's volleyball team—and then there's me. It's the picture of me swinging from the rope and smiling like an idiot, the boat down low in the frame and barely noticeable. It's not even obvious what sport I do. I'm mortified. I look around the shop. It's not like thousands of double amputees are walking around this airport. *Everyone's going to know this is me,* I think irrationally, as if every single person has simultaneously seen what I've seen and is on the lookout for a girl with no legs.

I flip through the text of the interview. I don't even remember saying most of that. I put the magazine back on the stand and creep out of the shop, my face burning, hoping we board before Bobby or Rob sees it somewhere, too.

———

Shortly after we land in London, it's clear that some of our equipment didn't make it. *Of course* it didn't. Something always has to go wrong for Rob and me.

My custom-fixed seat, which a prosthetics company made for me to lock in so I don't lose energy and power in sliding, doesn't arrive. Neither does Rob's prosthetic pylon he made for himself that straps into the foot structures for him to anchor himself into the boat. I always thought that was just dead weight anyway—we have the luxury of a lighter boat because of the absence of legs, why are we putting them back in?—but now he has no anchor. We have less than a week to practice on the course before the race. We're set up to fail.

———

The scene isn't quite like I pictured it.

We're staying with the other rowers in a satellite village three hours from the main Olympic village. We're out here in the boonies so we can compete on Eton Dorney, the man-made lake where all the rowing competitions will happen. The boat races are early on in the Paralympics,

175

and after that we can move to the main village with the rest of Team USA—which I'm already looking forward to. There's not much fanfare here. Although I'm not sure what I *did* expect, given it's the Paralympics and not many people pay attention to para athletes. But I definitely didn't imagine sitting around twiddling my thumbs.

Eton Dorney is nothing like the calm reservoir Rob and I trained on while based in Charlottesville. It's *windy*. Whitecaps roil the surface. It would be great to be able to practice our technique in this gale, just like all the other boats out there on the water getting a jump on us with every single minute.

Instead, Rob and I are decorating our oarlocks. We wind red, white, and blue ribbon around them and then down the oar handles until they resemble American flags. But then we're done, and we're faced with empty time and a boatload of anxiety.

"Why don't we do that workout that Brad had us practice?" Rob says into our silence.

One morning in Virginia, the skies had opened up into a downpour just before we were about to get on the water. *Amazing,* I thought, *I can go back to bed.* But no. Brad went to the janitor closet and came back toting a broomstick without the broom. He stepped between two ergs set up side by side, taped the stick to either erg handle, and told us to row. In being connected to each other, we could feel who was rushing or slowing their stroke, the catch, the finish, everything that the other person was doing.

Now that's what we do, because we have nothing else.

In the afternoon, we sit on a bench and watch the other boats. The British mixed-four boat strokes by, a blond woman in the bow.

"Wow," says Rob. "She's hot."

I look over at him.

"Make sure you're staying focused here," I say, half-teasing, half-serious. He's still watching the boat speed away.

The next day, I'm checking my email in the little business center of the building we're staying in. There's a message from the ESPN photographer. He chose that photo for print, he says, *because* of my smile. Because I look so happy and confident. Confident. It's the first thing that jumps out before the absence of my legs. *That* was the powerful image that he wanted people to see, he says.

I realize, reading his note, that since I saw the issue, I've been falling into a trap I tried to avoid: comparing my photos to those of the other athletes and caught in the endless loop of *I'm not strong enough, I'm not beautiful enough, I'm not on the same level.*

Over the next days, the feedback starts coming in: emails, comments, social media, coverage of the coverage. Some comments are bad, horrible, and I try not to absorb them, especially while we're here trying to get our act together before our race. But most are positive. Bobby just says it's great, doesn't mention it again (thank God). Rob is similarly stoic, but I know he's happy for me. And Mom. Mom is just proud when she texts and emails me after she sees it, even though her daughter is naked for whoever wants to look. She knows what it took for me to do it.

I hope I touched even one person. If someone realizes you can't judge yourself by other people's standards, that thought could ripple to three more people and grow further until it wakes up everyone it touches. Change doesn't happen overnight. It starts with one tiny pebble.

Our gear finally shows up with two days left for Rob and me to practice. Now that we're out on the water, contending with the wind and the nerves and the excitement, we can feel the tension in the boat. After we finish our session for the day and we're cooling down on our row back to the dock, Rob, who's far more used to stressful situations, says, "Want to play H-O-R-S-E?"

He does a fancy trick with the oars, taking a stroke, flipping them backward for a back stroke. "See if you can do that."

I try, and I flub it, letting out a laugh despite myself.

"You've got an *H*! Your turn."

I think. I take the oars, stroke, spin the handles so the blades rotate in a three-sixty just before they hit the water for the next stroke. Rob drops one oar on his attempt, and we're both laughing. We play that way all the way back to the dock, and I feel the tension flow from my shoulders.

As we put our legs back on, I watch Rob's neck twist as his gaze follows that British woman on the LTA 4 team.

"Rob, just go *talk* to her! You talk about her, you look at her, you could cut the air between you two with a knife. I need your mind to be present on the water, not looking over your shoulder for her. So just get it over with and go say hi!"

He brushes me off. I can't help but smile.

It's funny how I used to think that Rob wasn't normal. I just didn't know *his* normal.

––––––––––––

We don't go to the Opening Ceremonies. It would be a six-hour round-trip bus ride to get to the main village where they're happening, and our race is early tomorrow morning, one of the first races of the Games. Twelve boats are competing for gold, starting tomorrow with two heats of six boats each. The top boats in each automatically head to the final race two days later. In the intervening day the others get one more chance, at the repechage, or runoff heat, to try for one of the four remaining spots in the final.

All of the rowers, just shy of a hundred athletes, have our own mini-celebration in our little satellite village. We dress in our country's Opening

Ceremonies outfits—ours are sort of like business suits, which I don't love, but I'm still so excited to be wearing any iteration of a uniform that I don't care—and gather in front of a big TV to watch.

As I watch all the countries entering the Olympic Stadium three hours away in London, upward of four thousand people experiencing exactly what I'm experiencing—pride, joy, nerves, even though mine are a little muted here, removed from the festivities—I'm hit with a sudden understanding.

I've been so deep in the trees that I've lost sight of the forest. I'm here for something bigger than me or my own goals. I'm here for my rowing partner. I'll give everything for Rob. And I'm here for all of Team USA. I'm representing something as significant as a *country*.

And not only that. I'm Ukrainian, an origin I still wear with pride despite all the scars. I'm representing Ukraine, too. And I'm representing adopted orphans—all the children who've been given a chance at a new life and opportunity—on a world stage.

Somewhere along the way, I've allowed this dream I've had from the first time I sat in a boat—just a misty idea then without clear edges—to take a back seat to appeasing Joe. I realize that I'll never be able to follow my dream if I can't put away the anger that I often feel when we're together.

After the Opening Ceremonies, when I have a moment of quiet in my room, I write down all the things I'll say to Joe to officially end this when I get back to Kentucky. I get the lines out of my head and onto paper, then I tuck the paper in my luggage and turn my focus to this moment.

The Games.

And the start line.

179

We're lowering ourselves into our boat for the first heat. I look over at Rob. He's got some nerves going, I can tell. But I understand him enough now to know that this doesn't mean for him what it means for me. He's here for a chance to represent his nation again, look strong, win.

But for me. For me, this is *everything*.

He flashes me a quick smile, then he sings a few lines, way off-key, from "Bad Company," to ease the tension. I can't help but laugh.

Bobby's presence on the dock helps, too. I can never tell if Bobby's nervous, so he always seems calm to me.

He kneels down beside us. "You know what to do. Just go out there and row."

I nod. I tighten the straps across my thighs. *This is it.*

Rob and I pull our oars out in sync and use the blades to push off the dock. Bobby reaches and pushes mine to guide us away because it's getting crowded out here—all the boats are leaving the dock at the same time. *This is happening.*

Bobby rises and picks up all four of our legs, unwieldy and heavy in their lengths and mechanisms, to shuttle them to the finish dock. For the first time, it hits me how undervalued para coaches are—they're doing *so much more* than are the coaches of able-bodied athletes. One more reason I can't fail. I'm so nervous I can feel my throat closing around it.

As we row out to the start line, I try to focus on anything but rowing. "Look how beautiful this water is, Rob. And how cool is that bridge?" I can't stop chattering.

After we get situated, Rob swivels his head to me and says, "Okay," cutting off the stream of nonsense coming out of my mouth. "I'm gonna say *locked*. Then you're gonna say *cocked*. And then together we say *ready to rock*. Got it?"

"I'm not gonna say *cocked*," I scoff, falling into my little-sister role. "What the hell are you talking about?"

He sighs. "Okay, I'll say the first two. You say the last part. And it's the last thing we'll do before the start."

I know what he's doing. And it works, to a degree. I focus back in. My throat opens a little. And then it's time.

"Locked." Pause. "Cocked."

"Ready to rock," I say firmly, decisively.

We go all out.

And we lose our heat to China, which is blisteringly fast, by a solid margin of five seconds. We're relegated to the repechage tomorrow, where we have to come in first or second to secure a spot in the final the next day. It's the first time Rob and I have lost together.

We're in the big leagues now.

That evening, while scurrying around my room in an old historic dorm located in the satellite village, I plug my electric hair straightener into the bathroom outlet. I don't know why I even use a straightener—my hair is straight as a board anyway. I go out to dinner with Mom, and right when I return to the building, the fire alarm goes off. I file back out with everyone else, grumbling about how mad I am that I can't just take my exhausted body to sleep.

When we're finally allowed back in, I'm mortified to discover it was *my fault*. I'd left my flat iron on to smoke up the place and set off the alarm.

Finally ensconced in bed, I text Joe, *You'll never believe what happened*. I tell him the story.

Of course you almost burned the place down, the response comes. *You're such a screwup*.

I barely sleep that night.

"I just want to make it to the final," I say to Rob's back as we row out to the start line for the repechage. "I don't even care if we get a medal. My goal is to make it to the final, and I'll be happy with that. I can walk away with that."

"No," Rob says without turning or missing a stroke. "You're not just going to make it to the final. We'll make it onto the podium. I think we can beat these people here."

In your dreams, I think.

We come in first in the repechage.

When Mom finds me after, the first thing she says is "You know what this means—that whatever happens tomorrow, you're one of the *top six* rowing teams in the whole world!"

I allow myself to be proud for a while. Over that night and into the next morning, I reset my goal.

I'm hungry for the podium.

I begin to believe that we can do it.

What the hell was I thinking?

The final is about to start. Rob and I have already raced two days back-to-back. The favorites, France and China, are fresh after their day off. Great Britain is next to us, on their home turf, where rowing is huge. So many fans are here cheering for them, it's like being at a football game in the United States. It rattles me a bit—no one even follows rowing at home.

These are all incredibly fast, strong athletes. There's no way we'll be on the podium with any of these people.

On the dock, Rob took to singing stupid songs to make me laugh, to ease the adrenaline pumping hard through both our hearts. But that ease is long gone. I'm trying to focus on our race plan instead of how built the China team is or the throngs cheering for the British boat. Our strategy today will be the opposite of what it was for the last two races, where we blasted off the line and tried to hold on—"flying and dying," it's called. Now our plan is to start slower and build toward the end.

The beep goes off, and we go with it.

We start out alongside a couple boats, then they pull away. We're dead last. China is far ahead, France on their tail. We spend at least half the race in sixth place. But we stick to our plan. We slowly pick it up.

We move into fourth place, right behind Great Britain.

My shoulders are searing. My forearms are numb. I'm praying my hands don't fall off the oars.

At the 150-meter mark, the finish buoys turn from yellow to red. It's our cue to sprint.

"Power of ten!" I scream to Rob. I keep screaming to him. "Ten strokes for Roger!"

I'm tired as hell and pulling everything I've got from some deep well.

"Ten for Katy and Justin!"

The sound of the crowd roaring is distant, like it's coming through a deep sleep.

"Ten for Bobby!"

I'm watching Rob to follow his technique as mine breaks down. The roaring gets louder and louder until I can't ignore it because everything is vibrating with it. But they're not cheering for us. We're neck and neck with the British boat.

They're cheering for Britain.

My body is burning and I'm trying so hard not to flag, to speed it up instead. I feel like I can't get enough air. Then, from inside the pain cave I'm currently occupying, I feel the lightest of touches on my shoulders, like an insistent wind, pushing me toward the finish line.

"Ten for Team USA!"

We fly across the finish line. We stop stroking, burned-out, still burning, ablaze. The big screen says *1: China. 2: France.*

Third is blank.

It stays blank. For the first time ever in all the time we've been rowing together, I can hear Rob panting, like a big German shepherd when it's 105 degrees, in and out from his gut. Under the clamor of the crowd is a silence on the water, where you can hear a pin drop as the teams stare at the screen. We look over at the British boat, nod our heads to them. They return it solemnly. An eternity ensues.

The screen flashes: *3: USA. 4: GB.*

"Oh my God, oh my God!" I scream.

Rob pumps his fist in the air. Without a word, he reaches his hand back to me in a low five. I smack it.

———

In the stands, Mom had started out the morning sitting with Rob's parents. Well before the start, she'd moved away, all three of them joking that they were making one another more nervous than they already were. So she screamed at the top of her lungs among strangers as she watched us creep up from behind, and now she waits, alone in a crowd of people, to hear what the loudspeaker says about that blank spot on the board.

The loudspeaker roars, *"USA!"*

Mom is silent among the cheers.

A woman turns to her. "Are you okay?"

Mom blinks, dazed. "Did they say US?"

"Yes."

"My daughter just medaled," Mom says wonderingly. "Oh my God. She won bronze."

"Wow, really? How are you not crying?!"

Mom is so beyond tears—such a small expression of all her emotions—that she doesn't even know what to say.

Rob is calmly rowing over to the medalists' dock, where the podium is, while I, unsurprisingly, continue to freak out.

"Are you sure this is happening? Maybe there was some mistake. Did we actually do it? *Is this actually happening?*"

At the dock, Bobby is there with our legs.

"Good job," he says simply.

We wrestle ourselves into our prosthetics. Even in this moment, I spare some time to agonize over how, under my tight uniform, my liners and sockets make me look like I have a butt in the front and how the screws are sticking out on one side of my prosthetic. Then we're walking on the red medalists' dock and it feels like walking on a red carpet. The Paralympic anthem is playing, and the loudspeaker calls our names first for the bronze, and we walk up and situate ourselves. The medals come out on a tray, and a woman hangs the bronze medal over my neck, and it's so long, so much longer than I thought, and heavier, and I've forgotten all about my second butt. The Chinese anthem is playing and it's not ours and it doesn't matter in the least, because I can't contain the feeling rising out of my chest.

It's the same feeling from the first time I rowed on the Ohio River so many years ago, when I still had one leg and a head full of nightmares. I'm years away from that girl, even though she's still there inside me. On the podium, I can't stop smiling, can't stop waving.

Rob is stoic, as usual.

Mom is there with Rob's parents holding a US flag, people from US Rowing are there, and we're surrounded by media. People expected things from the other boats. No one expected anything from us. But we've just won the first-ever medal for the United States in Trunk and Arms rowing.

Us. The smallest, least experienced team out there.

I close my eyes and raise my face to the sky. We did it. This is what it feels like. I wish this moment would last forever.

———————

After the ceremony, I finally find Mom in the little friends-and-family section, which she'd made her way to after realizing we came in third. She pulls me into a bear hug, laughing. When we part, she lifts the medal from where it hangs down my torso and admires it. Watching her, I understand for the first time that something more than this is possible, and this road could be a long one—if I want it to be.

"Mom."

She looks up at me.

"The first gold medal I win in the Paralympics . . . it won't be mine. It's yours. The minute I get it, I want to give it to you."

This will be my way of thanking her. For everything. Supporting this dream. Saving my life. Even the things I can't articulate. Especially those things. For all of it. As I say it, I can see us, the surroundings blurry but the two of us clear, standing face-to-face in a bright and colorful arena, beaming as I drape the ribbon around her neck.

Mom smiles. "Oh, honey, that's so sweet. But I don't need a gold medal. *You're* my gold medal."

I roll my eyes. Leave it to a mom to cheese up a poignant moment. But I feel a small seed of anxiety take root, and I sober. What if we only succeeded because Rob was the muscle? He's so strong. I'm not sure how much *I* earned this medal, whose weight hangs proudly around my neck.

Who am I to promise a gold medal, to anyone?

———————

Now that the boat races are finished, we get to move to the main Olympic village, and I understand what we've been missing way out there in that quiet satellite. This place is buzzing with athletes and people moving about with purpose, accents and languages of all kinds mingling with the low hum of activity. The Olympic rings are still up everywhere, and they're joined by the Paralympic symbol: the three arcs in red, blue, and green that represent the colors most widely included in national flags around the world. We stay in the Team USA high-rise apartment building in the heart of the village. All the athletes are walking around wearing the same clothes as us, since we all get the same kits, and I've never felt more like I belonged in my entire life.

I immediately head to the coffee hut outside our new digs. This isn't automatic espresso, where you push a button and your drink streams out. There's an actual person in there, actually pulling the espresso shots. There are croissants and other grab-and-go snacks. And it's all *free*. I have a hard time wrapping my head around this. I still carry an irrational fear of starving, and I snatch pastries and apples and bananas to hoard in the backpack I carry around the village. Even if I'm not eating it, I feel more secure with a pile of food. I make a note to come back to this hut every single day for an afternoon coffee. I've died and gone to heaven.

My phone beeps with a text. It's from Joe, who, thanks to time-zone differences, has just seen the coverage of my race.

That should have been me.

I put the phone back in my backpack and leave it there.

That first night in the main village, the rowing athletes from Team USA—Rob and I have become close with the LTA 4 boat—go out to celebrate. We're a drink or two in when the British LTA 4 team shows up. I watch Rob's gaze zero in on the blonde. After a few minutes, I get up to head to the ladies' room, the route to which just happens to pass the British team. I stop next to the blonde while the other three keep talking. I'm tired of Rob not making a move. I'm making it for him.

"Hi, I'm Oksana."

She smiles and shakes my hand. "Pam."

"I just wanted to let you know that my rowing partner thinks you're gorgeous." I point him out. "He's the military-looking guy over there."

She smiles wider, and I keep walking to the ladies'.

An hour later, our teams have mingled at the same table. Rob's finally talking to Pam. *That's two wins for today,* I think happily.

I'm out on a brief exploration of the streets of London when I see it. It's in a door on an ancient cobbled avenue.

A skeleton keyhole.

Blink.

The floor is so cold, but Laney and I piled a few of the old clothes on it to keep from freezing. She has her face pressed against the keyhole. She giggles at something on the sliver of television screen visible through the opening. Or *barely* giggles—we know to be quiet. But even that soft sound makes me feel better than I've felt all day. She moves aside to let me look. Then we settle back down, leaning against each other for warmth, to watch the white and gray flares flash under the door and light up the dark around us.

Blink.

I've stopped in the middle of the avenue. Someone nearly runs into me, offers an apology in a polite British accent that I don't really hear. I look around. Skeleton keyholes are everywhere.

Blink.

Laney and I are locked in the upstairs room. The only light comes through the keyhole. She can always read in my face what I need, and even though we can barely see each other, she knows I'm scared. She pulls me in and wraps her arms around me.

Blink.

Mom's told me that even though I had no family, no idea what love was for seven years, I was affectionate with her. I think it's because Laney taught me that.

That touch on my shoulders the other day in the race. I've felt her before, I think, on the water.

An image forms right there on the old street of London: a key tattooed onto my rib cage, close to my heart, protected under my right arm. It's in a secret spot, not for display. It's only for me, to remember that she's locked with me. She stays with me, carrying the good and the bad.

To remind me that I'm living for her.

Back home, even after everything, I still can't bring myself to end things with Joe. The lurking thoughts win out.

What would happen to me if I broke up with him?

I might never find love again.

Because who would ever love a girl who looks like this?

chapter

fourteen

The woman with the blond braid sits down next to me at the lunch table, her manner conveying obvious purpose. We've only just met; we're both panelists at an adaptive event at this CrossFit gym. Rob and I were invited here to San Antonio by the owner to discuss how to adapt exercises to wounded military men and women. The whole thing is hosted by Concept2, which makes stationary ski and rowing machines like the ones we train on. It's a surprising move on their part. Brands don't tend to see value in adaptive sports, let alone treat Rob and me as "real" rowers. Rather than offers for sponsorship, the sentiment that often comes our way is "how cute that they're still trying to do this sport thing."

I'm not used to "making appearances" either, which is apparently something medal-winning athletes do. It's October, just a few months after London, but I don't think of myself as a Paralympic athlete—I'm just another rower. So I'm totally awkward throughout the talk we give, preferring to get to the demonstration part.

My back aches on the erg. It's been bothering me more and more. I know that if I stay on the machine and try to work harder, the pain will get worse. I can push through it, and I do now, a pro at hiding the discomfort. It worries me, but thankfully I have no time to think about it. Now that we've wrapped up, I'm relieved to be done with being the center of attention, with no remaining duties other than to chat casually with people at lunch.

"Congratulations on your bronze medal," says Eileen, the compact woman who's plunked herself next to me. I don't know much about her, other than that she's the able-bodied coach for one of the other athlete panelists, a Paralympic cross-country skier. "Have you thought about what other sports you'd like to try?"

I fumble a little. Other sports? All I've been able to think about since London is how much further we could take rowing. Rob's already been saying he thinks he only has one more year in him and then he's done. He says he has other things he wants to accomplish. My mission over the last month has become to keep him in the sport. Less than subtly, I drop hints about Pam, who's aiming for the next Games in Rio de Janeiro—surely Rob wants to be there, too?

To Eileen, though, all that comes out of my mouth, sort of unintelligibly, is "Um. I really like winter."

I do. I love the idea of snowboarding and downhill skiing. I love the look of it, with the goggles and helmet, which are so, well, *cool*, especially compared to the awkward-tan-lines look of rowing.

Eileen looks pleased. "I coach for the Paralympic Nordic ski program, we're always looking for new athletes."

While she explains that they have an introductory cross-country camp coming up in Breckenridge, Colorado, and extols the virtues of skiing, I think secretly that training to ski looks so . . . *boring*. I watched her cross-country athlete on his stationary machine. It looked mind-numbing. He's sitting here at this table, the quietest, least animated person in the room. What if all skiers are like that?

"We'll introduce biathlon at that camp, too," Eileen says.

I snap back to attention. "The sport with the shooting?"

"Yeah. There's a really cool mental aspect to it that other sports don't necessarily have. We call it 'the rabbit and the rock.' You go from being the rabbit, skiing as fast as you can, pushing your body to the limit. And then you come into the shooting range, and everything changes in an instant, and it becomes precision. Biathlon is about actively having strategies to take a step back from where you were in the skiing portion, so deep in the pain cave, and relax into a very narrow present."

I hang on her every word, completely rapt now.

"Come to Colorado in December. I'll teach you how to ski."

I suddenly see myself on a snowboard flying down a mountain, a total badass (once I've learned how to snowboard). I see myself toting a .22 to a target, hitting each shot cleanly, then dashing away through the snow with the gun smoking. Then, just as suddenly, I'm eight years old, skating on the clean ice after the Zamboni has polished it, with cold air flowing across my skin and into my lungs.

I look at Eileen and I smile. "Okay."

Rowing is and will always be my first love, my priority, my therapy—but what could it hurt to try this? She's probably not serious anyway. She'll forget all about this interaction in a week. I reach down and rub my sore lower back, focusing on my lunch plate.

———

After lunch, Eileen steps outside and calls John Farah, the performance director of the Nordic program. "She doesn't know it yet," she says, "but I have our next medalist."

———

The rain runs in sheets down my windshield. My wipers can barely keep up with it. In the dark—the clock on the dashboard flashes 1:45 a.m.—the falling water blurs everything. The light turns red ahead of me, and I brake hard, skidding to a reckless stop partway into the intersection.

I stormed out of the apartment an hour ago, unwilling to let the torrential rain prevent me from getting in my car and just *going*. Joe slammed the door behind me, threw something that shattered into pieces against the wall. I'd discovered that he's cheating on me *again*, with a coworker this time. My throat burns from screaming.

His text on my phone on the passenger seat lights up the dim interior of my car: *It's over, it's done.*

The stoplight turns green as his second one comes in: *Good luck finding someone who's actually going to love you.*

I floor the gas, and the car leaps forward in sync with the surge of tears.

Soon, I can't even see the stoplights. I don't know where I am. Water is running down my face in what feels like the same volume as all the rain outside. I pull over into an empty parking lot, and I just let myself go. It's like someone pulled the lid off a boiling pot of water, the pent-up steam racing out in an explosive cloud. I cry, hard, until I'm hyperventilating, until my eyes hurt, until there must not be any fluid left in my whole body. An Aretha Franklin song plays on the radio, keeping time with the rain drumming on the roof. The R&B beat pulls everything out of me, like a magician pulling scarves from a hat.

The sobs rinse my brain clean. It's a wild, deep release. When they finally stop, I sit there. I'm exhausted. But into the clearing created in my mind comes a thought:

I don't care about what comes after.
I'm going to be okay.

It's 3:00 a.m. when I walk back into the apartment. He's on the couch, head in his hands. He looks up when the door opens. I can't read his expression. Maybe he thinks this will be like all the other times. We'll make up, pretend everything's fine, and keep descending into this insanity.

This is not like all the other times.

"Get your shit," I say calmly, "and get out."

I erase him from my life. I trash everything that reminds me of him. I throw away pictures. I delete photos and comments from social media. It's like a ritual burning.

It's hard to cope with love or sadness. Anger is always easier.

I'm driving to the waterfront. I *need* to get into the boat today. That rain-soaked night in the car opened up something in me so that, for the first time, I can see. Everything, all of it. I know now that my relationship with Joe wasn't healthy. It wasn't safe. Only familiar. Just like moving from the orphanage and the darkness and fear and all the horrible things that happened there, to a warm bed and color and love. Except with Joe there was no real love.

It's so easy to overlook all the bad things because we're comfortable in the familiarity of the moment.

The same Aretha Franklin song, "A Rose Is Still a Rose," is playing. The lyrics settle around me while I beat myself up for making terrible decisions, for letting someone else control me like that. Joe hated that, with rowing and the Games, I was slowly becoming a happy person, *without* his being able to control it. When he saw the happiness creep in, he had to break it down, break it, break it again.

My mind goes to my scars, like it often does. I can pretend the scars on my mind, my heart, aren't there sometimes. But I can't ever forget the ones on my body. There are some I don't even remember getting, a couple on my arms, some on my legs. And there are the ones I can map every detail of: hand surgeries, amputations. And that damn slash low on my belly, the one I hate so much.

'Cause a rose is still a rose, baby, girl, you're still a flower, comes Aretha's voice through the speakers.

My body is covered in stories that were written *for* me. They happened *to* me. I don't own them. I survived them.

I want my own story. One I choose. One *I* want.

I realize that I have the power.

The image comes to me with perfect clarity: a rose, a dying one, morphing into a beautiful, thriving red one. It arcs over my hip bone, curves down across my pelvis. Right on top of that slash.

———————

I go alone for this tattoo. I don't tell anyone about it. This time, I do my research. I make sure the artist is good. For all the situations where I didn't have power, for all the people I gave power to—this story on my skin, this rose of my own making, is my way to take back that power.

"This is likely to take three sessions," the tattoo artist warns as he preps his tools.

I lie down on the table. I pull my pants down as low as they go on my hips. "I want to do it in one."

He stops what he's doing and looks at me for a moment. Gauging, maybe. He nods gravely, then begins.

The pain of the tattoo gun is calming. I know this feeling. It's cool, then icy, then stinging. When it gets to my hip bone, the pain changes to vibrating, tingling, ticklish. I don't want it to stop.

"You're fucking tough as nails. No one just sits here smiling while I go across bone."

I hesitate. "It feels good." I try to say more, but I'm not sure what. He seems to understand anyway, and I'm grateful for that.

The image takes form on my skin. The colors are deep, jewel-like, the living rose like vibrant blood over the scar.

That scar. It's all so tied together. The second-floor room. When

Laney died. How, once she was gone, the world got so much darker and I understood how much she'd protected me.

Blink.

It's the first time they've ever put me up here alone. There are two beds, one against this wall and one against that wall. No sheets are on the bed. The inky blackness is choking. I can't escape it.

The door opens, a triangle of light expands. A pair of ugly shoes steps, steps, steps. The door closes. The light is gone. There's a rustling. Then a hot weight is on me and hands and pain and terror. I struggle, a gut reaction to protect myself.

There's a curse in Russian above me. A metallic flick in the scary hush. Then so much white searing fire below my belly button that I forget where I am, who I am, everything except that unnameable pain. I black out. I leave my body, the wetness of my blood on my skin somewhere and the encompassing agony, floating above the hot weight with its pair of shoes that stays on top of me and the dirty bed.

Blink

I know, with a certainty that hits me every single day of my adult life, that I'm lucky I got out of that orphanage alive. It was run as an underground brothel, and I was put in that room every night from five to seven years old. I could easily have slipped into a subterranean system where my existence didn't matter. And no one would ever have known.

It took me a long time to understand that the upstairs room was something I didn't have any control over, that my presence there wasn't about misbehaving. To this day, I don't know why women have to feel so disgusted and ashamed of this—why *I* feel like that, even still.

I think this is why I've always been attracted to the uglier things. Dandelions, perceived as weeds by everyone else. Bare, gnarly trees. Even dying roses. To be attracted to imperfect things is to understand what they've been through.

A rose always is and still will be a rose are the words I ask for, inspired by Aretha's lines. The artist is inking that into my skin in a wave along the fading stem. It doesn't matter if it's living, dying, broken. It is, and always will be, a rose.

This, for me, is a reminder. It's a declaration of something I couldn't believe for the longest time. Ugly things happened to me. They. Are. Not. *Me.* No matter how ugly I feel, how much I hate my body, how much I hate my memories, I'm still worthy of love. Of a good life.

And this. This is what I wish everyone who's experienced physical or emotional trauma, some of us unfortunately more than others, could grasp:

You are not the product of where you came from. You are not what happened to you. Regardless of the taint of how you were treated, there's beauty in you.

When we rewrite, we heal. When we rewrite, we get stronger. When we rewrite, we're unstoppable. There is never an end point, or a cap. Because we are only and always moving forward.

fifteen

This is *not* what I expected.

I'm stuffed into a sit ski, perched on the snow with a few other sit skiers and a couple coaches, including Eileen—who had, it turned out, been completely serious. She emailed and called in the weeks after San Antonio, explaining that the program would support me financially in coming out there, all the equipment was there for me to use. The slopes and ski runs of Breckenridge Ski Resort are all around us, and I was buzzing with excitement as we drove up here from the airport. *Oh my God, I'm actually doing this.*

But we never went to the lifts. I haven't even laid eyes on a snowboard. Instead, we've been on a trail. A flat one. Now we're sitting at the *bottom* of a hill. It's minuscule, sure, but this is literally the opposite of downhill.

Turns out I had no idea what cross-country skiing is.

Two days before, I'd been shouting down the hall at Mom, "Where are we even going to *find* a helmet in town?!" I was panicking, having left packing for this camp to the last minute, and discovering that—of course—there's not a single alpine shop in Kentucky to buy ski gear. Mom and I wandered all over the city trying to find winter clothes at all, which I haven't needed since we lived in Buffalo. We spent a lot of money just on those, and I felt so guilty about it. And that was even after I'd told Mom I wouldn't be going because we couldn't afford the airfare. When I'd told

Eileen that and tried to back out, the program bought my plane ticket for me.

Thank God I didn't show up wearing a helmet, I think now, mortified at the idea. Although it's not as if I look any less embarrassing. I had no idea how to dress for this. I look like I'm ten years old and headed out to make snow angels in our yard in New York. I'm wearing a pink fleece headband from the seventies, and these enormous red, white, and blue sunglasses I'd gotten from the London Games. The look of this sit ski is most definitely *not* badass the way I'd envisioned downhill skiing. It's an open bucket that makes my hips look twice their size, and my legs are *freezing* in this thing. I'm only wearing my liners, and I have to cinch my quads down so tight in the bucket that I'm probably cutting off my femoral artery. *I'm going to get frostbite and have to amputate the rest of my legs.*

I eye the short little hill before us. "How am I supposed to get up there?"

"You ski up it, of course," Eileen says, in what I'm learning is her characteristic no-nonsense but relentlessly optimistic way.

I've been a little distracted from the disappointment of flat skiing by the truth that this sport is challenging with my hands that refuse to grip anything with strength, including ski poles. Especially these neon-yellow poles that have been whacked off from the top as if for a little kid. I've been skiing so slowly, trying desperately to hold on to these poles that make me feel actually disabled, that it must be the movement equivalent of crickets chirping. And now to push uphill like this . . . ? *Challenging* is definitely a good word.

Once I've gotten to the top, out of breath and sort of annoyed, I'm exposed to another truth—of physics this time. We have to go *down*. I have no idea how to stop in this thing. I'd thought that falling on snow would be forgiving, but apparently it's a low-snow year here. The trail is covered in a thin layer of man-made snow, but the sides offer only exposed rocks and grass.

Something rises in my chest. It's fear. But not the old kind of fear that I've experienced so much of. It's an exciting, exhilarating fear. Because this is unknown. I watch the other sit skiers push off and make it down without incident, so I know it's obviously possible. It's just that I don't know how to execute it.

"I don't know if I can do this," I say to Eileen, beside me, "but it seems really cool, if I can figure it out."

"It's just a small hill, with a long run-out. It's a perfect start."

I push off, gather speed, fly . . . and I'm completely out of control. I don't figure it out. I explode onto the ground, poles flying, hitting my ribs on a pile of rocks. Once I recover my breath, though, I'm laughing.

Eileen skis up, laughing, too. "That's the one place you weren't supposed to end up!"

She tries to explain how to get myself back upright, but my short T. rex arms are making it hard. She ultimately helps me get up. Then she has to do it again. And again. Because I want to perfect this without exploding, but when I get scared, I just bail and eat shit.

I have no idea what Eileen sees in me.

———

In the common kitchen of the hostel-like accommodations at this training camp, I make a beeline for the kettle to make hot water for my tea. Two guys are sitting at one of the tables—*Aaron and Travis,* I remind myself of their names—hands wrapped around coffee mugs. I'm about to pass by without saying anything—they're deep in conversation, and I don't know them anyway, other than that the two of them always seem to be together—when my eyes land on the object sitting between them. A French-press coffee maker. I change course immediately.

"Where did you get that?"

They look up, surprised. I cringe. What about *Hello* or *Excuse me?*

But Aaron's brown eyes light on me—I feel a jolt of electricity—and he smiles anyway, despite my clumsy tone. "We brought it, actually." That wide smile through his dark bushy beard is genuine. Infectious. "Do you want some? Grab a mug and come sit down."

I don't need to be asked twice. I return and sit, and as he pours me a cup from the press, I say, "I absolutely *love* coffee. I can't believe I didn't think to bring my own French press."

"I'm sorry we don't have any cream to offer you, though," Aaron says. "We drink it black."

"True coffee connoisseurs!" I exclaim.

The three of us chat, but it's Aaron I keep my eyes on. He's about my age, maybe a few years older. Although he's sitting in a wheelchair, it's obvious that he's tall. And built. His arms disappearing into the sleeves of his T-shirt are muscular and ropy. It's also obvious that he's confident. But not overbearingly so. Just enough to make other people—such as me—feel likewise confident in his presence. He and Travis banter back and forth, quick-witted and quick to laugh, and sure to include me. It's the most fun cup of coffee I've ever had.

But then it's back to the schedule. This camp is short and packed tight. I don't have time to talk with Aaron much more.

I'm done with men anyway.

Turns out the biathlon rifle is not the kind that releases gun smoke. It's an air rifle. And there's no sexy black mat to lie on to sight the target. Nope. We're stretched out on an old shag carpet that looks like it might have been a mop dog in a previous life. There's also no cuff to put our wrists in to stabilize the stock of the rifle. I have to just hold it. But the wooden stock is so wide, I can't hold it properly.

"You want to do it like this," says Rob Rosser, the biathlon coach, leaning down to adjust the stock.

"Um, I can't, really, I can't hold it this way." The rifle slips. I can't reach the trigger. *Damn hands.* He relents, lets me experiment until I find what works for me.

"We call it *clean* if you hit all your shots. It's *dirty* if you don't," Rob explains to us prostrate shooting newbies.

I aim at the white aluminum square with its fifty-cent-size black circle, and at the dime-size bull's-eye in the center of that. We're closer than the traditional 10-meter range to start, which is probably a good thing.

I shoot fifteen times. I miss every shot. I don't hit a thing. I don't even come close. I should have known. My favorite drink is a dirty chai. I like men that have a dirty—read *rugged*—look about them (I flash to Aaron's beard). I guess I'm stuck with the theme.

I hit the target on my sixteenth shot.

"I got it!" I shout. Now I have to do it again. I have to prove that it wasn't a mistake, I didn't just get lucky. I know what to do now.

I don't know what to do. I miss the next ten. But now, paradoxically, I love this. Because it's so hard, and I'm determined to figure it out.

———————

"There's a World Cup competition coming up in Wisconsin next month," Eileen says to me over our last dinner at the camp before I head back to the hot Southeast. "We'd like to invite you."

"*Me?*" Has she already forgotten how many times she picked me up on the ski trail?

Eileen laughs. "It's a rare thing to have a World Cup in the US, and it's our next opportunity to all be together, the next opportunity for you to move forward. I'll be honest, you're probably going to get your butt kicked out there. But that means it's a chance to really try out the competition aspect of the sport without any pressure for results or success." She pauses here for a moment, considering me. "But I have a feeling that getting thrashed is actually good for your motivation. And you have potential. If you want to stick with this."

"*I* have potential?" I know I need to stop parroting her, but in my disbelief at what's coming out of her mouth, I can't come up with anything better.

"You have the ingredients of a successful athlete. As someone who's tasked with finding people who can be successful at a very high level, I meet a lot of people who start off by telling me why they're amazing—they were the first person to do this, the only person to do that. Those people aren't going to search to continually be better. You, though. You're passionate. And you have an inherent respect and understanding for how hard it is to be good at something."

I stare at her.

"And, you actually enjoy the process of being in the pain cave, which is illustrative."

How did she come to these eerily accurate conclusions about me in only a few days? She reads my expression and laughs again. "When I knew you were going to be at the CrossFit event in San Antonio, I did my research on you. I wasn't going to pass up the opportunity to convince a medal-winning endurance athlete to try my sport."

Lying in bed that night, blissfully exhausted from the last four days and trying not to think about my ridiculously early flight back to Louisville, I let myself think instead about what Eileen said. I don't know that I see this capacity for success in myself that she does. But I do think that if I want to prove I belong on an international competition stage—that I can earn it on my own as much as I can with a partner—maybe this is my chance.

First, though, I need to focus on the World Rowing Championships coming up. Rob and I have to defend our title. I'm already looking forward to rowing in Rio in 2016, to what, I hope, will be that gold medal I can give to Mom.

Rob knows I've been having back problems. But I don't tell him how much it hurt through our first heat, or how much it hurts during our practice sessions on Tangeum Lake, where the races are held. It's the World Rowing Championships in Chungju, South Korea, and the final is in an hour.

We have so much potential. We're third best in the world right now. We've been training for nine months. Rob even went back and trained with Brad for a few months while I trained with Bobby, so we could work on individual strengths. It gives me hope I can keep Rob in the sport.

Rob's in the bow this time. We're trying something different this year. But it doesn't seem to be working. We're dropping back.

In the last hundred meters, I know that I'm not racing our race. I'm trying to outrace the boat next to us, instead of matching Rob's stroke. And then that thought is obliterated.

Pop.

Something snaps in my back. I can hear it as much as feel it. Excruciating pain overtakes my entire core. I don't stop rowing. I can't stop. But I know immediately, deep in my gut, that something is very, very wrong.

We come in fourth. *Fourth.* The only thing that makes it okay is that Ukraine wins the third medal. But my back hurts so much that the disappointment doesn't quite distract from the agony.

Pam is on the podium. Her LTA 4 boat won gold. Rob and I are in the bleachers watching her medal ceremony. I'm so bitter about our loss that I can barely pay attention. All I can think about is my back. Anger at myself and resentment toward my traitorous body rolls through me in pulses.

It's all my fault that we're in the stands instead of on the podium for our own ceremony. I shouldn't have taken time away from training to ski. I've let Rob down. He's only out here because third wasn't good enough for him. He wanted first place. He'll be done now, I'm sure. Because I failed.

I'm not ready to give this up. I can't be done with rowing yet.

A tap on my thigh pulls me out of my turmoil. A little girl in a shirt that denotes her as maybe the tiniest volunteer at this World Cup event is looking into my eyes. She smiles and holds a stuffed animal out to me. It's a white bear wearing a blue scarf.

"Sochi," she says in her Korean accent, pointing to it. Then she smiles again and walks away. She doesn't give one to Rob.

I stare after her. Sochi is where the 2014 Winter Games will be held.

I did go to the Nordic World Cup a few months ago. I did get my butt kicked, just as Eileen predicted. There was one mean downhill corner that I exploded on every time I practiced the course, so Eileen placed coaches there to keep me from hitting a tree at Mach speed. I did sessions on that hill over and over, until she had to pull me away. Still, I crashed on it during the race. But Eileen was right there, too—losing so badly only made me more determined.

As the ache in my back slowly ebbs from a scream to a dull roar, I look down at the bear in my hands: the mascot for the upcoming Winter Games.

I don't believe in coincidences.

———————

"You have unstable spondylolisthesis," the sports orthopedic specialist says. While I'm still trying to pronounce that word in my head, he strides over to my X-rays pinned on the backlit wall. "Essentially, one of your vertebrae in the lower spine slips out of place onto the vertebra below it, pressuring the nerve. In addition, the small bones on either side of your spine are broken, which means they can't support it. Every time you execute a rowing motion, your spine slips back and forth. If you want to continue rowing, we need to put rods in your back."

I hear Mom inhale next to me. I take a moment to absorb what he's saying. I expected this. I reassured Mom (or myself, maybe) as we drove to this appointment, "They're just going to tell me what I have to do to fix it. Maybe I'll have to have a little surgery, but it's going to be okay." Another surgery doesn't mean much to me, I've been through so many of them. And if it means I can keep rowing . . .

"But," the doctor says sternly, "as a double above-the-knee amputee, putting rods in your back means you'll need to be in a wheelchair. Walking with prosthetics, where you lock the knees out, will create the same issue where the rod meets the bones, putting the same load and pressure on your lower back. And the thing is—there's no guarantee the rods will solve the problem if you keep rowing at this level."

What?

He can't be right. This can't be the choice.

I'm still under Mom's medical plan from the university, and we go to a few other surgeons and specialists, Mom is always helping me ask the clarifying questions and advocating for me and taking notes. But they all say the same thing: rods and wheelchair. Or stop rowing.

No. This is just the beginning of this crazy dream I've been dreaming. I finally have the right partner in Rob, and if we go to Rio with four years of training, we can get that gold medal. We can row that perfect race.

But I know it's more than that.

If I can't row, what will calm the storms in my head? Where will I find that elusive feeling of contentment, of happiness?

Mom and I stand looking at the tiny apartment. We're in the little mountain town of Winter Park, Colorado, where the Nordic team trains. I decided to move out here before the start of the official season to train, looking at it as an investment in my skiing so that I can get my feet under me and not make a fool of myself in front of the rest of the Paralympics hopefuls. Although I don't fully acknowledge it to myself, I'm looking at skiing as the solution to getting my body healthy enough to go back to rowing. If I can strengthen my core, I can solve my back problems. It's also an investment in the longevity of my rowing career. But this depressing apartment is currently making me doubt my choices.

The Murphy bed is folded into the wall, a little table folded down in its place. The good news, I think, is that when the bed is down, I can reach over and turn the coffee maker on without getting up, it's that close to the kitchen counter. But that's the only good news. It's dark, with only one window letting in dim November light. The laundry room is shared, down an even darker hallway with creepy flickering lights. And this place is *expensive*, even though there's nothing in Winter Park except a ski hill and a movie theater with a bowling alley attached to it.

Mom wanted to book a place for me for the whole season. But, as usual, she's helping me out financially, and I can't ask that of her. I know a couple of different training camps and competitions will take me away from Winter Park, and we shouldn't pay for a place when I'm not here; it's cheaper just to book a series of Airbnbs for when I *am* here. It means I have to move in and out, but that's worth the savings.

And I'm not even on the national team—I'm trying to make the US Paralympics Nordic Skiing Development Team—so I have no stipend to train. I'm running on hope, my own disappearing savings, and Mom's bank account to keep me afloat right now. I already feel bad enough about *still* having to rely on Mom.

"Are you sure you're going to be okay, honey? I can find somewhere to stay in town for one more night."

"Oh my gosh, no, you should get on the road while it's still light," I say to Mom, even though I want nothing more than for her to stay. I know it will feel so lonely here once she leaves. But she already drove with me all the way out here from Louisville in my cheap Jeep Cherokee. We can't spend the money to change her flight to stay another night.

I drive Mom to the airport. I'm reluctant to say goodbye. I know one other person out here, Beth, a woman I roomed with at one of the few competitions I skied last winter. She and I hit it off immediately. She's the one who planted the idea in my head that I come out here early to get a jump on training. I'd envisioned hanging out with her some evenings and skiing with her during the days. But she lives forty-five minutes outside town. I won't be seeing nearly as much of her as I thought.

I hug Mom at Departures. Then I slowly drive back alone to the silent room and all the new unknowns staring me down.

I have no idea what I'm doing out here.

I'm directionally challenged on the best of days. On the trails in Winter Park, I can get lost in ten seconds flat. And I have, a couple of times. The trees all look the same to me.

Another athlete is often out skiing, and I know he's training to make the team—I met him briefly at the introductory camp last winter. I'd love to approach him to ski together, but he's the opposite of approachable. I take to chasing him on the trails anyway, just so I don't get lost. Which is what I'm doing now, although the falling snow makes it harder to keep my eyes on him up ahead. I pick up my pace a little to avoid being left behind. (Which implies you're *with* someone, which I'm not.)

At least there's finally snow on the ground. I spent the first few weeks training indoors and getting the lay of the land here, and, inevitably, wondering what the hell I was thinking to pursue this. Self-doubt in skiing is easy to come by when there's no snow to ski on.

As the guy ahead of me fades into the falling snow around a corner, the winter air swoops across my face. My nose is cold, my cheeks are cold. Everything else is warm, even as the cold air moves across my body. It *is* just like ice-skating. I love the glide on the skis, when I can get it right, that feels like the glide on the Zamboni-fresh ice. Back when I had two legs. And then one.

And now I have none.

I slam the poles against the snowy ground. I slam all my loneliness, my misgivings, my sadness at my malfunctioning back that's taking me away from my first love. My frustration at my inadequate hands that keep sliding off the handles—I hurl it through the poles as if they were the oars and the snow a river.

I try not to think about last night, which was the same as all the other nights here. I poured a second glass from a bottle of cheap wine and blasted music so that the background noise would mask the emptiness. I made the same dinner I make every night: rice in a pot and salmon baked on foil. I put the salmon in with the rice to eat, fold up the foil and throw it in the trash, and the only dish I have to clean is the pot—so I can make my same oatmeal out of it the next morning.

As I sipped the wine, I came to an unwelcome realization. I don't know myself anymore. I'd been in a relationship for so long, living for someone else, that I don't know who I am. I don't know what I like to do. I know little of what makes me happy. And here I was closeted in a tiny room that only made me more depressed.

Back in the present, I hit the snow hard on each stroke. It's not the same release that happens under the oars. But it's *a* release. Each time, I come away a little lighter than the last.

I look up from beating up the snow to realize I can't see the other skier anywhere anymore. I'm all alone out here in the silence. My stomach drops, and the desolation crawls its way back toward my chest again.

Then a snowball hits me right between my shoulders. Gently, like it's made of the lightest snow that poofs into nothing on impact. I whip my head around. There's no one there. There's no one anywhere. But I felt that playful hit. I know I did.

The key tattoo pulses slightly under my arm. My lips curl into a smile. I turn and push on.

I'm leaving the grocery store, a bag in each hand. I spent most of the time I should have been shopping talking to Mom on the phone from a corner of the produce section. I don't know why I'm doing this, why I'm here. I'm not good at skiing. It's cold and lonely—Beth lives so far out of town—and it's all I can do to keep myself from crying over the zucchini. The funk is like a storm cloud over my head as the sliding doors open, a cloud that even the new snow on the ground shining in the early-December sun can't dissipate.

A car pulls past me toward a parking spot, and I make accidental, awkward eye contact through the window with the driver. A second later, I realize it's Travis. Aaron's in the passenger seat. I wave furiously like a total dork.

I walk up as they're exiting the car into their wheelchairs. Aaron's big grin cracks his bushy beard.

"What are you guys doing here?" My voice rises a whole octave, I'm so excited to see them.

"We just moved here for the winter," Aaron says. "Got here today, actually."

"To ski?"

"Oh yeah. We're both pretty dead set on making the US team for Sochi." I remember his quiet confidence. Travis wheels up beside Aaron and nods. "What are *you* doing here?"

"I moved here for the winter. Beth and I are training for the Games, too."

I feel, all at once, like I'm not on my own anymore, like a team is coalescing. We chat a bit more, then part, driven back to our original separate paths by the cold wind.

But not before Aaron makes sure he has my number.

———————

The first time Jane gets in my car, the cold air sweeping in with her when she opens the door, she tells me all about herself. She's an accomplished summer athlete trying her hand at winter sports now, and the US Paralympics Nordic skiing program is paying her whole way here, including housing. The program asked me to drive her to trainings, even though she lives in the opposite direction from me to the training center. In the way she carries herself, she shows me what it would be like if I had sponsors and funding and people backing me.

She was also an orphan from Eastern Europe, she tells me, adopted at a bit earlier age than I was. She tells me that she had a serious birth defect. It's a miracle she lived at all. It's a miracle her parents adopted her, and that they gifted her with a normal childhood. They introduced her to sports when she was young. Now she's hoping to compete in Sochi, close to her home soil. Unlike me, she's already met her birth parents, she tells me. She went back to her orphanage when she was twelve years old and met them there.

In some ways, I'm envious of how easily she tells her story. Like she's told it a hundred times. And it's so palatable, so easy for people to be inspired by.

I wish my story were like that. I wish I didn't remember all the details of every horrible night, forced to relive them through the rest of my life because my body doesn't know how to process peace and safety, can't process that those things aren't happening to me anymore.

So I sit in silence in the driver's seat of my cheap car instead of sharing *my* story. I'm relieved when she doesn't ask.

Over the next couple of months, I see Aaron more and more. At training, on the courses, at his house, which he shares with Travis and a few others, for dinners, board games, coffee. Always with a group. Aaron always reaches out first. I always respond.

I start to learn his story. In venues such as this, people with injuries are pretty open about how they got them.

Shortly after Aaron was born in Minnesota, his father joined the Air Force. Aaron spent his youth in South Dakota, then Idaho, then Virginia, and graduated from high school in Germany.

In the middle of all that bouncing around, at thirteen years old, he went hunting on the Virginia coast with his father. It was early in the morning, still dark, and the pair saw only one other hunter through the thick woods. With his father fifty yards off and walking parallel to him, Aaron stepped into a clearing where he could walk freely without navigating the tightly massed trees. He must have snapped a twig underfoot or maybe rustled a branch. A loud report broke the silence. He didn't remember hitting the ground.

He came to lying in the dirt, confused. The rifle he'd been carrying lay four or five feet away. He tried to get up to retrieve it. But his legs wouldn't move. He couldn't feel them. He had no idea why.

He was still struggling to move, increasingly freaked-out, when his dad got to him. Aaron wasn't bleeding much, but his father found the spot in Aaron's back where the bullet had entered at about the same time the man who'd fired it found them on the ground. Aaron remembers his father shouting at the hunter over and over, "What the hell, man? What the hell?"

The man at least had a cell phone, a rarity back in 1999, and called for help. Four and a half hours later—with the tide out too far for a boat to get to them and the regional hospital's helicopter broken down—

a Maryland Coast Guard chopper doing exercises in Chesapeake Bay arrived to extract him with a long-line cable. He doesn't remember much of that, either, or arriving at the hospital, other than a quick glimpse of his mother sobbing in a waiting room.

Aaron convinced himself he would walk again. Lying in bed a month after his injury, he noticed movement under the sheets toward the foot of the bed. *Leg spasms,* he thought. Then he realized—the movement so foreign to him after a month of paralysis—*Wait.* I'm *doing that. I can move my toe. It's coming* back. In physical therapy, he began focusing on training himself to move again and regain strength.

One afternoon, Aaron's physical therapist introduced him to a man in a wheelchair, a former Navy SEAL with a similar spinal cord injury. The PT knew that before Aaron's accident he'd loved to play sports: baseball, with whoever in the neighborhood would play, basketball and football on school and club teams. The PT steered the SEAL toward Aaron.

"You know, when you're ready, there's some really cool stuff in this area for athletics," the vet told Aaron. The vet ran a youth team for track wheelchair racing. He showed Aaron photos of the wheelchair basketball team. "When you're ready," the SEAL said again.

Aaron was polite. But in his head, he thought, *No, man. I'm gonna walk again.*

He made it a goal that he would walk at his high school graduation. He went to physical therapy three times a week. He woke up an hour early most mornings before class to stretch, stand, walk, and exercise his legs, although he still used the chair most of the day—which he was getting more and more used to. He also took up the SEAL vet's offer of athletics and joined the basketball team. Because Aaron's competitive and hates getting his butt kicked, he practiced as hard as he could. He'd drive an hour and a half to where the team met once a week, practice for just as long, then drive the hour and a half home. He began dabbling in racing as well. The physical outlets kept him from slipping into depression.

He began to get a decent return of movement and strength on his left leg, although it remained weak. His right leg was even weaker. He could only be up and about for a maximum of twenty minutes, and even that still required a crutch and a brace on one leg. He knew that, even with the gargantuan effort he'd put in, he'd reached a plateau. It would never be enough mobility to be independent of the wheelchair.

Aaron walked across the stage at his high school graduation. Then he gave up on walking entirely.

Aaron received offers to join college wheelchair basketball teams from University of Wisconsin, University of Texas at Arlington, and University of Illinois. He chose Illinois. Now, though, he prefers marathon racing—he raced in the 2012 London Games—and he's becoming dedicated to cross-country skiing.

"I like how in individual sports it's all on me," he tells me one night as we're setting up a game of Risk on the dining room table at his house. "I have so much more control. It's completely up to me."

I look at him. It's like he's echoed what's in my own head. But I don't say it because we're already sitting down with Travis and Beth to start this board game, which I've never played but which I've heard is epically long.

I take Ukraine right away. "You can take any country fair and square," I tell them. "But you can't take Ukraine. It's mine. You can't have it."

"Um," says Aaron tactfully, carefully. We don't know each other that well yet, but he does know that I'm stubborn. "You know that in order to win this game, you have to conquer the world, right? So we can't let you have Ukraine forever."

"Just don't take it. It's not that hard."

We play for another hour. Risk truly takes *forever*. I imagine us playing this game all night, too wiped to ski at all tomorrow.

Then Travis takes Ukraine.

Meeting my mother for the first time. She arrived when I was asleep and woke me with a gift. It was my first toy, so I had no idea what it was or what to do with it. I found out years later that my mom's mom had made it for her to give to her daughter someday, and she knew right away that it was meant for me. *Courtesy of author*

The boarding school where I spent my fifth birthday. The orphans lived in this wing. The interior was always dark and looked even worse than the outside. When my mom arrived, she saw the staff scraping ice off the floor. *Courtesy of author*

I had seven surgeries during my time in this orphanage. They tried to lengthen my leg multiple times and also performed the first surgeries on my hands. The other children and I didn't usually look this good. The staff only placed bows in our hair when trying to persuade prospective adopters to take us. *Courtesy of author*

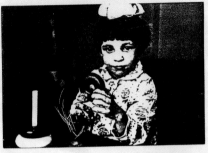

Oksana Bondarchuck was born on June 19, 1989. The girl was born by the first normal pregnancy. The parents were young healthy people. The child was born with multiple deformities of hands and feet. Oksana is staying in the orphanage now. The parents relinquished her.

The girl will be 4 y.o. soon. She has undergone 5 surgeries. Oksana is well developed for her age, eats, dresses by herself, draws - manipulates well with her hands. She likes communicating with adults, she is very active, has a sense of humor, has her own opinion.

Oksana is eager to have "beautiful" healthy hands and feet. She dreams that kind, loving parents will be a reward for all her sufferings and pain.

Oksana has been waiting for her mummy for half a year. She knows that her picture was sent to her mummy overseas.

"Where is my mummy? When will she come?" - the girl asks.

Two families had tried and failed to adopt me by the time this picture was taken. But one family brought this photo back to America, which led to my future mother seeing it and vowing to adopt me. I can't imagine how this terrible photo kept her determination high through what was a yearslong ordeal. *Courtesy of author*

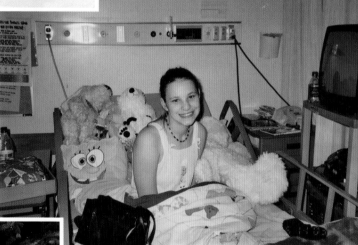

During the operation to amputate my second leg, the doctors removed more than had been planned. While other fourteen-year-olds went about their lives, I had to spend six months in the hospital. To keep up my spirits, I must have watched the movie *Shrek* five hundred times. *Courtesy of author*

Right before prom night with Mom. I was never a girly girl, but I chose this dress because the tulle covered my prosthetics and my limp (a tomboy at heart, I even wore shorts underneath). Plus, I could hide my hands in the skirt. We didn't have a lot of money, but my mom insisted we buy this— the first expensive piece of clothing I'd ever owned. *Courtesy of author*

On the floating dock at the Louisville rowing club on the Ohio River. Only when I was on the dock was I comfortable without my legs. Rowing was an incredible outlet for me. I could be myself there. *Courtesy of author*

Randy Mills gave his free time and passion to managing the Louisville Adaptive Rowing Program. He nagged me until I finally agreed to join, a decision that changed my life. *Courtesy of author*

Bobby, Randy's partner in crime, coached me on the water and forced me to prove that I belonged at the Paralympic level. Together, they were the first people in my life, outside of my mother, who completely believed in my physical abilities. *Courtesy of author*

Rob Jones and me—otherwise known as Team Bad Company. I fed off Rob's confidence as we competed at the 2012 Paralympic Games in London, winning bronze in Trunk and Arms mixed double sculls. *World Rowing Federation*

I appeared in *ESPN* magazine's Body Issue in 2012. I didn't even like wearing shorts then— too revealing—but the photographer made me feel so confident that this is how the shoot ended! I was in the same issue as Ronda Rousey and had a proper fangirl moment when I met her at the launch party. *Martin Schoeller/AUGUST*

Soon after the Sochi Games in 2014, I got to test a high-tech rowing rig for able-bodied athletes. I couldn't help but think that para-athletes would really appreciate having the same kind of sophisticated equipment. But availability, expense, and access are still huge obstacles for para-athletes. *Courtesy of author*

Seconds before I finished in fourth place—off the podium—at Rio. I screamed a furious obscenity as I crossed the finish line, which contrasted horribly with my team's silence as I got out of the bike. I never wanted to feel that way again. *Friedemann Vogel/Getty Images Sport via Getty Images*

Here's my mom showing off my medal at my first ever Winter Paralympics in Sochi. Russia had just invaded Crimea—between the closing of the Olympics and the opening of the Paralympics—and I raced with mixed feelings. When I was announced at the start line, I wasn't "Oksana Masters from Ukraine," but "Oksana Masters, born in the former U.S.S.R." Those Paralympics still stir very complex and unsettling memories, which Russia's recent actions have only made more difficult. *Courtesy of author*

This photo was taken during the biathlon at the Pyeongchang Paralympics. It captures the true difficulty of the sport. You must arrange quite a lot of equipment to achieve maximum stability and focus in order to hit the mark. *Getty Images*

While competing in the biathlon, I'd fallen off the back of the hill because of soft snow and dislocated my already injured elbow. I was in agony. My coach Eileen had to put her foot on my skis to prevent me from staying in the competition. She carried me for almost a kilometer so that I could have my arm seen to. *Chang W. Lee*/The New York Times/*Redux*

The winning moment at Pyeongchang. From my lowest moment to my highest in just a couple days. I was cool, calm, and collected throughout—and it was one of my greatest races. You can see the pure joy on my face. *Jung Yeon-Je/AFP via Getty Images*

My second gold medal for women's 5K cross-country skiing at Pyeongchang. I'm in total shock, especially since I'd just reinjured my elbow. *Getty Images*

Posing for a photo with my boyfriend, Aaron, and his family. *Tiffany Pike*

With the 2020 Tokyo Games postponed for a year because of the pandemic, I had more time on my hands to think about my journey so far, and I became more comfortable telling my story. This photo, from Players' Tribune, reveals my rose tattoo, which carries great symbolism, and some of my scars, which speak of darker things. *Taylor Baucom/ The Players' Tribune*

When I visited Ukraine, I met with soldiers in a military hospital. Only months before, these men were fully functional defenders of Ukraine's Donbas region. I was there to show them what's possible and what they can overcome. By sharing my story, we pushed past the initial bleakness of the meeting to create hope. *Courtesy of author*

This was a beautiful moment. In 2020, after receiving the Laureus World Sports Award for Sportsperson of the Year with a Disability (from Tony Hawk!), I was able to share the recognition with the woman who made it all possible— my mom. *Andreas Rentz/Getty Images Sport via Getty Images*

Never in my wildest dreams did I think I'd participate in a high-fashion photoshoot for Rihanna's Fenty Beauty. But it was glam with a message: that all people, all skin tones, all bodies should be visible, especially since that hasn't always been true. *Richard Burbridge/Fenty Corp*

Standing tall on a building-size billboard in Los Angeles for Kim Kardashian's SKIMS Team USA campaign. If I can help the world see people like me— those who don't make the journey through life in the typical package—then I feel I'm doing something right. *Jason Swing at Swing Media*

"*What!*" I shout. "You can't *do* that!" I was already losing anyway. I am *not* losing my own home country on top of it. "I don't want to play this anymore!" I knock a few of my pieces from the board, which sends a few of Aaron's flying as well. I get up and storm from the room. As I'm stomping out, I hear Aaron laughing.

"Well," he says, "we're clearly never playing *this* game again."

"You have a very . . . unique style," Eileen says as she skis to a stop next to me on the trail.

"No one else does this? It must not be right, then." Embarrassment flushes my cheeks. "We should fix my technique." I'm not sure how to fix it though, given I don't have a biceps on one side—the anatomy of my arms makes certain things impossible.

"No, no. It's about figuring out what works for you and maximizing that. Your style is unique because it looks like you're incorporating rowing technique into it. You have a swing that's a lot like a row stroke. And I think that's a good thing for you."

I think about that for a bit.

The next morning, we're practicing sprints. I blast out at the start, a whirlwind of energy and effort and breath, somewhere in between power and flailing.

"Oksana, you're like a little Tasmanian devil!" Beth teases me as I huff to a stop next to her. I'd like to take this as a compliment, but I don't think elite skiers are usually compared to maniacal marsupials. I know I ski aggressively with no finesse, like a bull in a china shop. At least Tasmanian devils are cuter than bulls.

As we cool down, Eileen skis next to me. "When you're out on the water, rowing, how does it make you feel?"

I'm quiet for a while, caught off guard. I can't figure out how to verbalize that to her. It would require explaining my past, the hurricanes in my head, the drugs, the therapy, the surgeries—the whole damn tangled mess of everything—just to explain the release.

"At peace," I finally reply. "It's so comfortable for me now. Rowing is like coming home."

She nods. "Then I think it's a powerful thing to bring that peacefulness on the water into your skiing. If you're at a big event and you're *trying* so hard to do something, you're probably not going to be successful. Because it isn't about trying, it's about letting yourself do what you already know how to do."

"But I don't know how to just . . . *let* myself do something." I pause for a moment. "If I'm in a race, and you notice that I'm going crazy, just trying too hard, can you say something? Like a safe word, kind of?"

"Absolutely." She thinks for a minute. "How about *find your swing*. That's your cue to relax, let it happen."

I like that.

———

Hey, are you busy? Aaron's text beeps onto my phone. *I had some coffee shipped here—would you give me a lift to go pick it up?*

I smile. He could borrow Travis's car like he usually does. But I like that he's asking me—even if I refuse to admit that to myself. And I like that he has such high standards for coffee that he's having it shipped. So of course I go pick him up.

After he maneuvers himself back in my car with the package, he gets to work on opening the cardboard box right away. As he pulls the bag of coffee out, I catch a glimpse of the label.

"Stumptown? I've never heard of that roaster." I put the car in gear.

"Yeah. I wanted to make coffee for you and Travis." Travis is an amputee, too. Aaron looks sideways at me, grinning, waiting for me to catch up.

"Oh. *Real* mature."

He laughs, pleased with himself.

I break yet another pole in training. I can't hold on to them properly and I end up slamming them on the ground and flinging them into trees when I crash. I'm costing the program money out of their equipment budget every time I destroy another one.

"I know your teammates have decided that your spirit animal is a Tasmanian devil," John, the head of the para Nordic program, says to me one afternoon.

I smile weakly.

"Can I give you a different animal to think about? I want you to be a butterfly. Because those technical corners, the ones that give you so much trouble, are asking for elegant, smooth skiing."

A butterfly. Me. The least graceful person on earth. But I agree, and I *will* try to visualize that. I want to become better.

Later, I'll learn of a conversation that takes place around this time between my coaches:

"I just don't know if she's worth the time investment leading into Sochi," John says to Eileen. "She goes from zero to a hundred. She doesn't know how to harness that power."

"She just needs to learn," Eileen replies. "And she will."

My breath comes heavily from the damn hill I just climbed, which always has me questioning whether I actually like skiing. The trail already looks different at the top here than it did on my last lap. The sun's come out, and last night's new snow is softening, taking on weight. I *do* like this about skiing: It's always changing. It keeps me awake, mentally and physically. I'm skiing alone today, and I know the way well enough not to get lost, finally. Under the noise of my breathing, the trees creak. Snow falls from a series of branches, its thud muffled.

I'm still not used to the Rockies. They're huge. I've always had respect for big elements of nature. Water, mountains. But *these* mountains. Skiing through them makes me feel insignificant. Like a single snowflake. One of the cool glitter-bomb type, for sure. But a speck nonetheless.

Or maybe I'm more like a spark. So many things in this world are so far out of our control, and specks can't do anything about that. But a spark. It creates a fire, with smoke that lingers long after the flames have gone out. And maybe a new spark from that fire catches something else, lights it up, and suddenly the flames are bright and high again.

I stop to take a sip. I always put hot water in my bottle. A tiny cloud of fog rushes out from the lid when I unscrew it. In the hush, I can hear myself drink. I can hear my heartbeat, the thump of it telling me exactly how alive I am.

I win bronze in the 5K Nordic race at the World Cup in Canmore, about an hour's drive west from Calgary in Canada's Alberta province. The win comes as a surprise to everyone, me included. The podium is stacked with athletes from wintry northern countries. And then there's me, standing there in shorts (I have no legs I need to keep warm), wishing someone had told me how to dress for this sport when I got into it so I look as legit as the Russian and Norwegian skiers.

That moment wasn't as embarrassing as that of a few days before, though, at the airport heading to Calgary for the race. I hadn't realized I needed to buy my own ticket and submit a receipt for reimbursement. As we were standing at the airline counter, the team arrayed behind us waiting for this snafu to be cleared up, John leaned over to me.

"Can you go ahead and pay for it? I'll reimburse you later."

I felt my cheeks burn. I only had $57 in my checking account. My credit cards were maxed out. I'm in so much debt it hurts to think about it. I've meticulously budgeted what I need to last out the season, and this ticket was most definitely not a line item.

"I can't," I whispered to him, almost choking on the words. "I don't have this money, I can't pay for it."

He nodded matter-of-factly and pulled out the team credit card. I wished I could just melt into the floor. And I wished this sport were like others—tennis, for example—where the winners are awarded mountains of cash instead of just points toward future competitions. Even though this win gets me that much closer to Sochi, I still wish I'd picked sports that made money.

At least this bronze medal means that John might start believing I'm worth what it's costing the team in time and dollars.

"I didn't make the Beijing team," Aaron tells me one morning over coffee at his kitchen table. "I missed it by one spot. I remember going back into the training room and crying in a corner. Looking back though, I don't think I was ready. Then I was dead set on making the London team. And that was literally the goal, was just to make the team."

I'm stunned. His story mirrors mine almost exactly.

"And I did make the team for London, but I wasn't really able to do anything competitive there. I think it set me up better for later things, though." He's quiet for a minute, sipping from his mug. He looks down at it. "Oh, man, there was this coffee hut right outside my hotel in London. I went there for free espresso every single day. That might have been my London Games highlight, actually."

"The one outside the Team USA hotel? In the village? *I* went to that one every day! Once we got there, anyway. The satellite village had *no* good coffee."

"Really?" He meets my eyes. "What if we saw each other there and just don't remember because we didn't know each other then?"

He looks as if he likes this idea. I do, too. I look away to hide it.

"I think Aaron likes you," Beth says to me the next morning as we're gearing up to head out for a session.

My stomach drops.

I'm not ready to admit there might be some chemistry between us, let alone confirm it to Beth. I don't want to be anywhere near a relationship.

After I podium in Canmore, I get a couple interview requests.

"I don't know if I should do them," I tell Eileen. "What am I going to say? I don't know what to say."

"Well, think of it this way. What would you tell your eight-year-old self?"

As usual, she catches me off guard. But this time, without warning, I just start crying. In front of her. Because I'm suddenly back to being little.

I should have protected Laney.

I should have fought harder.

I should have been more of a good girl, so I wouldn't be put in the upstairs room.

I wish I could tell my tiny, conflicted eight-year-old self, fighting a losing battle against all the things already haunting her from her short past, that all of those things were out of her control.

I look at so many athletes where it's easy to think they knew success right away—sponsors, wins, the straight road to the top—never knowing anything else. Then I look at my backstory of failures and hard, hard things, and a little-girl-Oksana who could never even have fathomed the word *athlete*, let alone dreamed up the idea of becoming one.

Eileen doesn't panic at my tears. She throws me a lifeline, a little more to work with. "Think back to when you had just one leg. The world sees you one way, and you see yourself another way. What would you want to hear?"

I pull in a ragged breath. "I would say, not just to myself, but all the little kids who are underdogs—unrepresented in sports or underprivileged or just beaten down—there's no perfect timeline that you're supposed to follow. There's no perfect path for achieving your goal. Which means that we can *all* go after our dreams, if we want to."

Eileen smiles. "Now, that's a hell of an interview."

A week before we leave for Sochi—after I've won another bronze in Germany in the 12K, and with it my spot for the Games—I realize I've drastically miscalculated my budget. I don't have enough to cover the final three days in this apartment I'm staying in now. I've gone through my own savings. I don't have the heart to ask Mom for more money. I can't fail like that in her eyes. I refuse to tell my coaches or my friends that I'm so poor that I'm sleeping out of my car. I can't take the pity.

I move my things into my Jeep. I park it in the lot of the building. I prepare myself to settle in for the night.

With the engine running to keep it at least above freezing, I crawl into the back seat and gather blankets up to my chin. *Good thing I don't have legs,* I think, reflecting on the only reason this cramped space isn't less comfortable than it already is. I open my computer and start the DVD player. While the opening scene plays out, I pull out the bundles of spinach I bought for less than a dollar. My experience with starving when I was little comes in handy, again. I roll up a fistful of spinach leaves in my freezing fingers. If I eat slowly enough, I can fool my stomach into thinking I'm filling it. *Just like the sugar cubes,* I think. I crunch into the leaves slowly while the wind keens through the unsealed windows of my cheap car.

In the morning, I'll run the defrost for what feels like forever to thaw out the windows, then drive the twenty minutes to go pick up Jane. We'll train. Then I'll hang around the warm coffee shop until it closes and come park here again with my spinach in the cold Colorado winter.

chapter

sixteen

Out the window of the bus that carries part of Team USA to Sochi, an ocean laps at a long shoreline. We landed in Russia an hour ago, and my body clock is all messed up. But I snap awake at the sight of that water. It's the Black Sea. On the other side is Ukraine.

It's the closest I've been to where I'm from since I left.

There's tension here. We felt it immediately in the airport. Right after the Olympics, in the window before the Paralympics, Russia annexed Crimea in blatant disregard of the Olympic Truce, a peace accord between competing nations for the duration of the Games that dates back to ancient Greek tradition. Pro-Russian separatists are clashing with Ukrainian forces in the eastern regions of Ukraine right now. On the streets outside the Olympic village, we've heard, men with guns roam around the city. As I watch the Black Sea slide by, an ominous feeling grows in my chest. But I can't figure out what it is.

The first thing I see as I walk through the village with the team is a life-size version of the stuffed bear the little girl gave me in South Korea. My heart jolts at the sight of it.

I can't untangle my feelings. But I know that one of the threads is motivation. Pride. I will race for both of my countries.

I don't go to *these* Opening Ceremonies either. My first race is the next morning. Instead, I'm practicing dry-firing at targets. It's the biathlon sprint tomorrow, which means three ski laps interspersed with two target shootings. For every shot missed, a racer has to ski one additional penalty lap.

I'm taking extra time at each shot to execute it well. I know biathlon is still not my strong point. No one expects me to do well in this race. No one expects anything from the women on Team USA in biathlon. I don't expect me to do well, either. But that doesn't mean I'm not going to work hard.

I wake hours before we have to be at the venue, the way I always do before a race. It's 5:00 a.m. Beth is still asleep—she'll sleep right up until she has to leave and then roll out of bed ready to go, I don't know how she does that—so I'm careful to be quiet. I grind my coffee by hand. I brew it and savor each sip. By the time I set up at the start line, I'll be vibrating with caffeine. But right now, I'm grounded and thinking about what it means to be ready. With no pressure to win this first race, I can just let myself race. For me.

I think I am ready.

———

I'm skiing well on my first lap and I slide into the range in full focus. I take my time, and I clean the target. It's the first time in my life I've cleaned the target (well, okay, the first time in my combined few months of skiing, but it feels like my entire life is up for grabs right now). Most good shooters are at the range for twenty-five to thirty seconds and are then back out on the ski course. I'm at the range for more than fifty seconds. But that's why I ski so fast on my next lap: I've got a few extra seconds of recovery on everyone else. I more than make up the time on the snow. The same thing happens on the next round: fast lap, clean target. The perfect shots amaze me, but I don't have time to think about it.

As I'm coming into my last lap, another racer is just ahead of me. My biathlon coach, James, shouts to me, "Catch that girl!" Even though she could be at a completely different point in her race—only on lap two after skiing penalty laps, who knows—James knows that having someone to catch will ignite my competitiveness.

I lock onto her like a missile. I tune everything else out. When I race, I block out noise to the point where I jump if a leaf crosses my path because I didn't hear the wind that blew it there. I'm so focused I don't realize that the girl isn't heading to the finish line, but into the penalty loop—with me following. Faintly, as if from far away, someone is screaming my name. The sound gets louder until James's screams pierce my silence: "*Oksana!* Turn around, *wrong way*! Finish, finish!"

I skid to a stop, turn, and frantically retrace my strokes. There's a slight incline back up to the race lane. I push across the finish line. Finally I raise my head.

I came in fourth. By less than five seconds.

Holy shit.

My very first Paralympics race on my own. If I hadn't accidentally skied past the finish line . . . I could have medaled. This is amazing.

No one expected this.

I hug the podium finishers and watch the flower ceremony. Then I look around for Mom in the crowd. Her flight got in last night and I haven't seen her yet. I can't wait to talk to her, to relive every moment with her and say together, "Can you *believe* that just happened?"

But I can't find her anywhere.

She'd said Jane's mom, a veteran of more Paralympic Games than Mom and more knowledgeable about the way things work around ticketing and family spectating, had reached out and offered to help Mom find her way around. She should be here.

I get back to our room to call her. She's already heard about this incredible race I just had. She can't stop gushing. She's so mad she missed it.

"What happened, Mom? Where were you?" I ask over FaceTime.

"Jane's mom told me to meet her at seven thirty this morning in the hotel lobby so we could get our credentials from the Russian government and make it to the race at ten." Even with the crappy connection, I can tell she's still upset she missed the race. "I asked her if she was sure she was going to go to the race, since I didn't think Jane qualified for biathlon. But she insisted. So I wait and wait this morning, and she doesn't show up in the lobby. I tried calling her room but the phones weren't working. Finally, I went and knocked on her door around nine. And she said, 'Oh, I'm sorry. It slipped my mind because Jane's not racing.'"

Mom hurried out on her own and ended up on the wrong bus. She bustled all over Sochi, with different officials and volunteers each telling her a different place to go.

"I was out at the airport when the results came up, and I didn't see your name. And then I realized my face hurt. I thought, 'What's wrong with my face?' I realized it was because I'd been trying so hard not to cry since eight this morning."

"Let's make sure you're there for the next race."

"Oh, I will be," she says fiercely.

———

Later that afternoon, leaving my room on a hunt for coffee, I run into Jane in a hallway. I can't stand conflict to the point that I'm famous for apologizing for things that aren't even my fault. But what my mom went through this morning—navigating the streets of what's become a potentially dangerous city in a conflict zone, by herself and because of *me*, to come watch *me* race—hit me like a punch to the gut. "Look," I say, "I understand that you weren't in this race. But what your mom did to mine is not okay."

"Oh. I'm sorry you didn't get to hug your mom after your race."

I feel a spark ignite. But I turn and walk away. And I stoke that fire to use for fuel.

"Coffee time?" Aaron says.

We're both killing time in the cross-country village. I never noticed this in London, because Rob and I only had one event to compete in, but you have a lot of time to kill in the race areas when you're in more than one event. Aaron and I have discovered that the cross-country village has a cute coffee spot with fantastic espresso, and the café has become our ritual whenever we run into each other.

"Yes." I find myself gravitating more and more toward him, wanting to steal moments with him. I hurry to fall into step with his glide.

As we head across the plaza, we cross paths with Travis. He's psyched to go get coffee, too. I sigh. Yesterday, coffee time included Beth and Mom. Seems like Aaron and I can't ever get a minute alone together. But maybe that's fine. I don't need this to turn into something. I don't need him. *I don't need* any *men in my life right now,* I remind myself, rather unconvincingly, as he holds open the door for me with that damn beautiful smile on his face.

Today's the 12K Nordic race. Jane and I are both racing. One of her big sponsors is here in force, displaying their banners with her face on them. As we line up in our starting blocks, the stadium is chanting her famous name.

Not for the first time, I'm struck by what it can mean as an athlete to have the legitimacy of sponsorship behind you. Thanks to her sponsor, Jane's parents are staying in nice accommodations and have their own security detail—unlike my mom. Jane's had far more resources to follow her dreams. Her housing for training was covered. She's probably never had to sleep in her car—or owed her parents so much money it hurts to think about.

At least I *have* Mom. And at least I know she's here this time.

There's no Rob here to distract me now with off-key songs—to help me focus when it's time. I force myself to zero in on the start line. Here nothing has been determined yet, unlike so many other things in my life that were determined for me. In this race, I'm in control and I *am* control, I tell myself. When the red dot turns to green and the beep goes off and the clock starts, I begin a new journey in this race. I remind myself that even though I may not physically have control of how the race plays out, I have control of how I react and adapt and pivot.

I inhale. Exhale. And the beep goes off.

This is a long race. I stay in my head. Whenever I compete, I don't look up at the jumbotron for where racers are or for times, and I don't do it now. I'm not racing anyone else's race. Only my own. I keep my eyes on my skis. I'm trying to ignore all the noise, the distractions, like I usually do. But then I hear it on the loudspeaker in a Russian accent:

"Oksana Masters, born in the former USSR."

No. I was born in Ukraine.

That reference to the USSR makes me so *angry*. Russia just invaded my home country. I realize, suddenly, what that ominous feeling was that I felt on the bus. It's entirely possible that they'll take over Ukraine entirely. What if I'll never be able to go back to find my birth family, to learn anything about my roots? What if . . . what if they're killed in this conflict?

I hear Jane's name on the loudspeaker, announcers praising. I hear the crowd cheering for her. In my head, even though I try to push it away, I hear a voice saying that I'm not good enough for this.

I hear on the loudspeaker again, "Masters, of the former USSR."

Ukraine. Say it. Ukraine.

I feel like the Incredible Hulk before he transforms, as he ricochets around his human skin that's too small and too weak, in that moment when he silently screams *ENOUGH!* and breaks free from it altogether.

I break free. The noise finally dies all around me. In the hush of my mind, I see nothing except my ski tips traveling forward, ever forward, in the white heat of *right now*. My arms, my shoulders, everything is burning, but I disappear into the pain cave. Into the race.

Usually I can hear, through my focus, John calling my splits to me as I pass to let me know where I am, how I'm doing. But it hits me that I haven't heard any splits in some time. *Am I that far back? I must be doing pretty badly.* I try to pick it up even more. My body is on fire.

I don't know how long it's been when John's voice lasers through my focus: "You're in second!"

I allow myself to look up from the snow for the first time. No one else is around me, no other racers. He's talking to *me*.

"Be a butterfly!" he shouts at my back. He means this downhill curve coming up. He means don't fall, to take it gracefully. He means don't screw this up.

I don't want to be a damn butterfly, I think, and I scream around the corner.

I don't know where the finish line is, I'm so deep in my race. I take five more strokes after I've crossed it before someone yells that I can stop. I let myself finally stop. I raise my head.

The jumbotron says, *2: USA, Masters.*

I won silver. It's the first US cross-country Paralympics medal in twenty years. I throw up my arms, toss back my head, shouting. I can't believe it. I couldn't have been more angry going into this race. But I constructively channeled that fury into a positive outcome and emerge unburdened. This can't be just a sport. It's some magical alchemy.

I look back at the finish line. It looks like me determining what I was able to do on this day in this moment in this race. Suddenly, it's not a finish line. It's not an end point. It's a *starting* point. From which to set the next challenge.

The skier from Ukraine came in first. I'm so thrilled. I push over to her and give her a hug. The rest of the Ukrainian team hugs and congratulates me, too.

I'm celebrating with them, with my teammates, my coaches, with Mom—and I find myself looking around for Aaron, even though I know he's not at this race—when Jane's mother approaches.

In what seems a general announcement, but is really directed at the media surrounding the Ukrainian gold medalist, she says, "Come over here, quickly, Jane's meeting her birth family for the first time."

What? I'm confused. I thought she'd told me she'd already met them. I must have been misled—or misunderstood. But the cameras scurry over to where Jane's tearfully talking to an older couple. You can see it on the journalists' faces that they're rabid for the inspiration porn this story will make: a paralyzed orphan girl turned decorated athlete meeting her birth parents for the first time in the country she was born in. My heart jumps. I don't even know if my birth parents are *alive.*

But I can't even get past my psychic blocks to tell my own story to *myself*, let alone anyone else. The idea of packaging it up neatly for an international audience makes my throat seize. It's one reason why I'm glad to see the cameras swing away from me to Jane. I have no idea how to give interviews. Rob's not here to do the talking for me.

Someone tugs at me, bringing me back to this moment. It's time for the flower ceremony. Someone else hands me a bouquet, and I line up on the snow with the Ukrainian girl and the girl from Russia who came in third. The Ukrainian flag rises, then the US next to it. The Ukrainian anthem soars through the open air. I don't remember the words. But I know the sound, the music, because it runs through my body. I give everything I have not to cry.

The gold medalist reaches over from her own sit ski, pulls me in, and holds me there. The US team, and all the spectators—from all walks of life, facing down all different kinds of issues, hardships, joys, passions—

turn toward the flags, hands on their chests in unison, down to the last person in the stadium.

This must be the most powerful thing on earth.

"How is it so easy for some people to share their story like that?" I ask Beth. We're back in our room with a little downtime before the medal ceremony tonight. "She's able to leverage it, and it will probably get her *more* sponsors, and she'll just keep achieving everything she wants to." Tears are starting behind my eyes. I know this has nothing to do with Jane. It's triggered something deep in my own subconscious.

For the first time, I open up to Beth, just a few details of my past. She knows there's a darkness in me, but she's never known why. I don't tell her much. I only release a few of the monsters, the smaller ones, the least terrifying ones.

"Why don't you start there?" she says. "Why don't you tell that story?"

Because I hate it. People will start seeing me for what happened to me, instead of seeing *me*. I don't want the words "Oh my God, you're so strong." I don't want people's perception of me to change because they feel pity.

But I don't say this to Beth. Instead, I say, "No one would want to hear it. There's no value in it."

My legs are shaking in my prosthetics. Not because this is the first time I've proven to myself that I *can* do this. Just me. Rob didn't pull me across this finish line. They're shaking because we have to wear specific outfits on the podium for Team USA, including shoes with a crazy sole that has no flexion. They activate my knees to bend, and suddenly I feel like I can't balance. I'm so uncomfortable. This is supposed to be the grandest moment of my life, and I'm staring at the ground thinking, *Don't fall, don't fall.*

"Silver medalist . . . Oksana Masters!" the voice booms over the loudspeaker. The head of ceremony approaches, hangs the medal around my neck. It's so heavy that it pulls me off-balance and I take an involuntary step. She raises her hands as if to catch me.

"Spasibo," I say.

"Oh, you speak Russian?" she says in English, obviously thrilled. I smile weakly and shake my head. I've begun a practice of learning *please* and *thank you* in the language of every country I travel to compete to honor all the people who make the events happen—but I can't say much more than that.

After we walk off the stage, I hear John yell, "Champ!" I pretend not to hear it. This is probably a onetime thing. I doubt I'll be able to repeat it.

We head into the media room, and I fumble through the interview, just like always. Finally, on the other side of that, it's just our families and our coaches waiting. Mom gives me a huge hug. When she moves aside, Aaron's there, a huge goofy smile on his face.

"Let me see this medal." He lifts it from my chest to examine it. He's so close. "Good job. My God, you're a freaking beast." He turns to Mom. "Can I get a picture?"

He puts his arm around me at an awkward height, somewhere between my waist and ribs, and I lean into him awkwardly, with everyone watching. It's all awkward. There's so much energy between us that we can barely stumble our way through it.

Aaron and Travis are racing the cross-country sprint today. I head to the stands with Beth and a few other teammates to cheer them on. At the moment, though, Beth and I are far away from the concept of skiing.

This morning, our teammate Monica extolled the virtues of hand cycling to us over breakfast. She's accomplished on the lie-down bike, and I grilled her with questions.

"It's a great crossover sport with training for skiing," she said. "You should try it. You're so strong already from rowing and skiing." She paused for a minute, considering. "You know, I don't think there's a woman on the US team in the H5 category, the kneelers, which is what you'd be."

Now, shivering in the stands, Beth and I are dreaming about summer sports. She's already ridden a kneeler bike, but she's game to try it again with me.

"I just don't know about my hands," I say. They are currently stuffed in my pockets trying to stay warm. "I don't know how I'd shift gears or brake. . . ."

I trail off because, as the athletes mill around the start line finding their places, a familiar prerace feeling begins to build in my stomach. It's anxiety. And I'm not even racing. I'm a little confused until Aaron sets himself up in his position. I can see him take a deep breath. I feel the same breath in my lungs, and the anxiety rises into my chest.

We trained together all winter. I know exactly how hard he's worked for this moment. I know how much he wants this. I'm surprised at how much *I* want it for him. But now I have no control. This isn't my race. I can only watch it unfold.

The beep goes off, and the anxiety leaps out of my throat as I yell his name.

Because of the classifications in Paralympics based on injury and mobility—this is a hard, confusing thing to explain to able-bodied people, like comparing apples to bananas to oranges and then throwing in a tomato, which isn't even widely agreed upon as a fruit—athletes are systematically advantaged or disadvantaged in their final times in an attempt to level the playing field. Some athletes, sometimes many athletes, fudge their classification so they're going up against less mobile people—a kind of doping that doesn't require drugs. Aaron, being the good man he is, would never dream of doing that. He's the only athlete in his class who can't walk at all. I know this means he has to work three thousand times harder than everyone else out there.

At only one kilometer, the sprint is over quickly. Thank God, or I might have forgotten to breathe for even longer. Aaron comes in fourteenth, Travis nineteenth. We stand to make our way down to the snow to congratulate our teammates on their finish. I bring up the rear, made unsure and weirdly shy by all the emotion now ebbing from my body.

———————

My next couple of Sochi races, biathlons, are terrible. I don't hit any of my targets and I keep falling on the penalty laps. This is why I have a love/hate relationship with biathlon. When it's good, it's good. When it's bad, it's *ugly*, and it makes me question everything. It's the same pattern of my life that often resembles a heart-rate chart. Spikes of ups alternate with low plummets to the bottom.

Finally, in my last race—that's also the last race of the Games—I find my swing again. I'm fighting for third place. John starts shouting my splits every time I pass him so that I know where I am, know what I have to do. And I slide into third place.

Since it's the last race of the Games, the medal ceremony is held right there at the finish line. It's quick. I'm still in my sit ski. The medal hangs down in my crotch. It's over pretty quickly, then Aaron is suddenly beside me, in his chair, pulling me into this hug so tight that my hips lift and my sit ski tilts into him. When he lets me go, I lift the medal to show him.

"That is *so* cool." He flashes a wide grin. "Congratulations!"

I've never seen someone so genuinely happy for another person. Joe was never like this. He never even acknowledged when I had a good race. Suddenly I'm second-guessing everything I feel, everything I know. Aaron is *too* nice, too thoughtful, too caring. No man is like this.

As soon as I can, I take the medal from around my neck. It feels weird to be wearing it. I don't know why, I can't explain it yet, but it sort of feels like walking around without pants on.

After the ceremony, we all head to dinner on the mountain—Aaron, me, Mom, Beth, Travis. I'm acutely conscious of Aaron the whole time. When we file out to head back down the mountain to our hotels, which takes a couple of gondolas and a bus ride, I walk slowly. Aaron's at the back of the group, talking to a few acquaintances he's run into. I walk slower, looking totally awkward. The others get into a gondola. Aaron's still talking.

Finally, he wheels up beside me just as I'm about to step into the car. I sit down abruptly as the car bumps onto the fast cable. I'm so close to him I can feel his body heat.

"Let's take a picture," I say. I want to remember the high from the Games, my first achievements solo. This moment. I hold up my phone and turn it toward us, and we lean into each other. He puts his arm around me. I click the button, lower the phone. He keeps his arm there. I turn toward him, and we wrap our arms around each other in the first real hug we've ever had.

This hug is different from any other embrace I've ever had with a man. It's authentic and real and . . . *humanizing*.

Then the gondola shudders, slows, and the doors open. The ride is over.

———————

Our departure from Sochi the next morning is stupidly early. Or maybe it's really late. It's hard to tell which at that hour. All of the Nordic team is stumbling, bleary-eyed at three in the morning, through the airport. I'm bizarrely energized though. Aaron is wheeling along next to me.

"What seat are you in?" he asks.

I check my ticket. I'm at the front of the plane. He's somewhere in the middle. Once we get to the gate, I go up to the desk and ask to change my seat. We sit next to each other at the gate, waiting. We just want to be close. A sense of unspoken urgency is between us. After this flight to Munich, we take separate flights to our separate homes in separate cities: me to Louisville, Aaron to Champaign, Illinois. We won't see each other again until next winter. Assuming we both keep skiing. Assuming one of us doesn't meet someone else.

Unless we make a conscious choice to do something about it.

After we board, though, I can't keep the exhaustion at bay anymore. I immediately fall asleep, cutting short our last time alone together.

"Oksana, wake up." Aaron's voice wafts into my deep sleep what feels like hours later. I drag myself awake, my head lifting from where it's drifted, comfortably, onto his strong shoulder. I don't wake gracefully, finding myself annoyed to be woken at all.

"I'm sorry, but the sun's rising. I thought you'd like to see it."

He's right. It's beautiful. I lean over him to try to take a picture.

I look at the image on my phone. "Damn, I can't get it to come out. It's never as good as what you actually see."

"Yeah. Pictures of things like sunsets or the moon never quite match real life."

I marvel that he takes the time to notice such things as moons and sunrises and thinks to share them with other people. Then the captain's voice comes over the intercom, telling the flight attendants to prepare for landing.

"There's this place that sells incredible butter pretzels and coffee," Aaron says as we shuffle out of the plane in the Munich airport. We have a little time here before our separate connections. We can make up for my falling asleep. If we can just slip away from the rest of the team, who are milling around talking to one another, also dragging out goodbyes.

We make it to the little restaurant alone, just the two of us. As we sit down with our coffee (which *is* incredible, another point for Aaron's being right), a couple of teammates trickle in. Then a couple more. Suddenly six more people are at our table. Aaron and I can't have the conversation we'd prefer to be having. And a few teammates are on my connection, so Aaron can't accompany just me to the gate. We leave the restaurant in a convoy. I give Aaron the same hug that everyone else gives him. I imagine he holds on to me longer than the others.

As I walk onto the jet bridge, I glance back through the clear doors. He's still sitting there. He raises his hand in a wave. I don't want to turn. If I look away, this will be over. Maybe it was just a summer-camp type of fling and I misread everything. It's too good to be true. *He's* too good to be true. I raise my hand. Then I turn, because I have to.

I spend the whole flight thinking about him.

seventeen

"Y ou have to let this go," all the doctors say. "You won't be able to row anymore. Nothing has changed. Perhaps recreationally. But not at the level you want."

My heart won't accept that it's over. It sees a little crack in the door, sees it as a chance, and tries to pry the crack open, no matter what it takes. But my mind knows.

It will take a long time for the two to connect on this. A long time for me to give up this dream for good.

"Oh, man, it's so late. I guess we should go," Aaron says.

The time on his phone screen lights up as 11:00 p.m. He has to drive an hour back to Champaign. I have to drive two and a half to Louisville. I razzed Aaron the first time we met up at this Starbucks for his definition of "halfway."

"But there's literally *nothing* in the actual middle," he pointed out. "And you don't want to actually drive into Indianapolis—navigating the big city would add so much time." I'd gone home and searched the map, determined to cut some time off my drive. He was right (yet again): the true halfway between us is just Midwest nothingness. Plus, he's worth the extra time in the car. We've driven to see each other three times now, each time meaning to stay for only an hour to drive home while it's light, and every time staying far past our self-imposed curfews.

I reluctantly rise from my seat, and we head out the door together as the barista gratefully begins to close down behind us. I lean down to kiss him, lingering in the warmth of that incredible embrace. I don't want to pull away.

"I have a race in Michigan in a couple weeks," he says into my ear. It's early May, less than two months after Sochi, and he's already deep into marathon season. "Would you come up? It's in Holland. We could camp on the lake."

I pull back. We've never had more than a few hours alone together. We've never spent the night together.

We are who we are because of our life experiences. We think the way we think, move the way we move, because of them. For me, my experiences mean that I've become an absolute expert at dissociating my mind and body from certain situations. Before Aaron, sexual encounters with men never mattered. Not even with Joe.

Aaron is so different from those others.

I worry about that.

––––––––––––––

We lie next to each other in the back of my Jeep. It's been raining for hours. It took us forever to light a fire to cook our food (which, because neither of us put much time into shopping for this camping trip, consisted of bacon and sausage) before we retreated to the dry fold-down seats in my Jeep to watch a movie on my computer. The movie's been over for a while now, though.

Aaron traces his fingers along my scars, asking for their stories. This one is from this surgery, I tell him. This one is from that surgery. He gets to the long, welted gash on my low belly, now covered in the arc of a rose stem.

"What's this one from?"

I look down. "It's just something that happened in Ukraine."

Even if I wanted to tell him, I don't know how to say it. I couldn't even verbalize it in therapy. It's one reason I cut myself off of therapy and medication—cold turkey—even though I'd been told I'd need to be in therapy the rest of my life because my damage was so extensive, so deep. So now, I just brush his hand away and snuggle in closer to his warmth.

Even though my mind forgets, my body doesn't.

Since Sochi, I've started to get messages on Facebook in Cyrillic text. The 12K race, where I won silver and the Ukrainian athlete won gold, was televised in Ukraine. Along with the most basic part of my story: I was a Ukrainian orphan.

Google Translate gives me the gist: everyone thinks they've found their long-lost daughter, sister, cousin. Or they think they can convince me that they have, to share in the wealth I must have as a US athlete (if only). I stop looking at them and let the messages build up unread.

This thing is a tank.

"Well, it's meant for someone with two walkable legs," the hand-cycle rep says as I examine his bike. "Also, I'm twice your size."

"I'm used to being too small for a sport, trust me."

Mom and I are at a military event in Louisville meant to showcase options for veterans with disabilities for assimilating back into everyday life. I don't know how Mom found out about it at all, let alone that there'd be a hand-cycling display.

"I don't have another model at the moment, but we can take this one out to the parking lot for a spin," the rep says. "At least you can get a feel for hand cycling."

Mom's gone in search of a bathroom. I text her where I'll be, then I follow him through the crowd.

After I get my legs off and he helps me settle into the shell, I nearly disappear into the bike. I feel like a kid who needs a booster seat. Or training wheels, which the two wheels on the back of the cycle almost feel like, except they seem like monster truck wheels from where I'm sitting now.

"Okay, this is the shifter. This is the brake. And let's see how your hands might want to sit on these pedals." The rep towers over me as he makes a few adjustments. "Okay, ready? Give it a try."

I push the pedals. The movement is completely different from rowing, which requires pulling hard and then smooths out; or skiing, which is also pulling in a never-ending swing. This feels like those times when you just want to *shove* something and it's so incredibly satisfying. Maybe not the healthiest analogy, but it's coming from me, so . . .

I haven't ridden a bike since I was nine years old, when Mom helped me rubber-band my prosthetic foot to the pedal and I used my real leg to do all the work on a bike that still needed training wheels for me. I knew I'd never ride one again when my second knee was taken from me.

This isn't the same as that time, though. After a few revolutions, I'm rolling faster, the wind rushing past my face and in my hair, and I forget all about what bike riding is *supposed* to be. I feel so . . . *free*. I never got this feel of speed when I was rowing, since the seat faces backward. I only do in skiing when I'm going downhill, which is terrifying since I still suck at stopping.

Wait, what if I can't stop?!

I look for the brake and hope to hell my hand can squeeze it. The bike smoothly rolls to a standstill. A breakthrough. *I know how to stop.* I take another lap around the parking lot, faster this time, wanting to see how fast I can go, until I hear:

"Oksana! Where is your helmet?"

Mom is standing, hands on hips. Next to her, the huge hand-cycle rep looks sheepish.

———————

The same rep lets me use his bike for my first road race. It feels like a Buick on steroids. I'm not even strapped down, so I'm swimming in the shell. I've also never done a race this long. Rowing races are three to five minutes, then I transitioned to longer ski races, at forty minutes. Now I'm trying to do a two-hour race with no training. My body isn't up to it. I think I'm going *so* fast, but I only average fourteen miles per hour. Nowhere near the standard for Paralympians, who are averaging twenty miles per hour.

I like the endurance it requires, though—that feeling of working every second of a ride and knowing you can always be working harder.

I'm hooked.

———————

"If I want to be in Rio, it's not going to be as a rower. But maybe cycling," I tell Aaron over the phone. "I feel like it challenges me in a way I've never been challenged before."

"Well, you definitely like a challenge," he teases.

Aaron and I have kept up our long-distance thing, neither of us willing to rush. Which is good. Because I still don't know what to do with his touch, which is so kind and gentle.

My body never rebelled like this before with a man in my adult life. But now it's fighting, even though I want to be with him, and I'm terrified of that. Because this man *matters*. Maybe that's why: it's easier to put up walls with anger. But now, approaching with love, I'm relaxed and safe. And that finally allows me to be vulnerable, maybe.

I don't know how to explain it. In the upstairs room, it was like a sledgehammer beating my insides, the deepest parts of me. Every time, I was just paralyzed. There was nothing I could do. Then it would finally end, and I would be left hating myself. To be back in that moment of hate, but in the middle of a loving experience—to just start crying and sweating and not be able to verbalize why to Aaron—I can't explain that either. Except for feeling so guilty for ruining the experience for *him*. The most intimate thing in the world was robbed from me such a long time ago, and I'll never be able to be normal. Now I'm robbing it from him. That breaks me. Every emotion seems to be wrapped up in a single moment, and it's too overwhelming to even try to process. Many times, after, I go out to my car or lock myself in the bathroom and just cry.

I worry about what he thinks of me, that I must be absolutely crazy, because I don't tell him about those things from my past. I still haven't told *anyone* those things. I'm so scared I'm going to lose him because I can't get ahold of myself.

But Aaron is patient. He's slow and caring. He's the kindest person I've ever met.

"Do you want to do this? We don't have to," he asks constantly. "Are you okay? Are you sure?"

"*Yes*, I want to," I always reply, as I shake and sweat and my body takes control without my permission.

Aaron started a notebook that we mail back and forth to each other, a different way to talk to each other besides over the phone for hours before falling asleep. I've pasted a movie ticket in it. Written memories from growing up with Mom, some of the gushy stuff that's easier to write than say over the phone. I've considered writing to him in there about why I go to cry alone sometimes.

I don't.

"You know," Aaron says now through the receiver, "Champaign is a great place to train for cycling. The Midwest is *super*flat."

"I'll keep that in mind." I laugh to keep it light, still afraid to commit like that to someone else.

Even though I've long since gained control of my mind (thank you, rowing), my body still has reactions from things that were done to me. I'm still terrified of needles every time one comes near me—which is pretty often given my surgical history. Scenes of things that I won't—*refuse to*—remember, or certain smells and sounds, or the way something feels—any of those can make my body react. I'll black out and go straight back to the reality of the memory, forgetting where I am.

It's October, and the US Nordic Paralympics team is in Sweden, where we come to train early season. We stay at a little farmhouse-turned-hotel just up the road from our training site. It has a traditional sauna, with a small lake just down the bank in which to cold-plunge when we get too hot.

The first time we sauna, I take my legs off—sweating in my sockets is a no-go. Eileen piggybacks me in. When we're both so hot we can barely stand it, she carries me down to the lake.

Eileen wades in with me riding on her back. As soon as my legs touch the water, my body jars.

Blink.

I'm being held under icy water in the dirty bath in the toilet room. I've done something bad, I have no idea what it is. I can't breathe. The blackness. It's frigid. I panic. I thrash, fighting for my life, but the caretaker won't let me up. My lungs are about to explode. I'm going to drown in this freezing hell.

"Oksana!" I know that voice. It's far away. It doesn't belong in the orphanage.

Blink.

I come back to myself. I'm screaming like someone is trying to murder me. I'm choking Eileen, bending her painfully backward with my arms around her neck, trying to pull away from the water to dry land.

She's shouting my name. I let go of her immediately and the two of us tumble to the ground, sweaty and shocked.

"It's okay, it's okay," Eileen says over and over while she gets to her knees next to me as I'm gasping in a heap. I've never told Eileen any of my story, beyond the standard *My mom saved my life when she adopted me, I lost both legs, sport is my lifeline.* I've never shared details. Now she must think I'm insane. *I* think I might be insane. But Eileen has worked with a lot of Paralympic athletes toting around pasts heavy with trauma. She's a hard one to rattle.

"We don't have to do this," she says gently once I've caught my breath. "We don't have to do this unless you want to."

I get ahold of myself. "I'm so sorry. Oh my God, I'm so sorry. I do want to do this." I have to face this in myself. I can't let it control me like this. *I'm not that girl anymore. I'm not there anymore. I. Am. Strong.* "I'm sorry."

"Okay. Then we're doing it together. Tell me when you're ready."

I breathe, brace myself. I *need* to do this. I nod. She helps me onto her back.

We jump in together.

After, I tell Eileen about how I was punished (*"abused,"* she emphasizes). How they would hold me under in the bath. Or make me stand in the cold shower. How it was slippery, and it hurt so much to stand on my short leg, and they knew it. How when I fell, they'd kick me until I got up.

She's the first person I've ever told.

Eileen understands. She starts coming with me if she knows I'm heading into the sauna, so that we can jump into the lake together after. Otherwise, she knows I won't go down there.

"This is about overcoming fear," Eileen tells me. "That, to me, becomes so much more important than just a cold plunge. Each time, you're literally facing your fears. A lot of ski technique is about creating new neuromuscular pathways for your body to perform differently. This is another way of doing that. You're creating new associations.

"You can do this. But you don't have to do it alone."

She knows I don't *need* her to hold my hand. But she's also well aware that I don't trust many people. In many ways I'm still like a child who pushes boundaries with a parent: *Are you still going to be there for me even after I do* this? *Even after you see* this *part of who I am?*

Eileen and I are so much the same person in the way we think, the way we approach things. I feel so comfortable and safe with her that she sometimes—often—sees the ugly sides of me. She calls me out on my bullshit, gives me tough love. She talks to me in a way that she doesn't to many of my more pure and good teammates, who'd shatter if she told them they were acting like a bitch and needed to get their shit together.

Eileen always says she's no psychologist. But she seems to get the way the mind works pretty damn well.

I feel so out of place here. I was nominated for a Team USA award I don't even feel that I deserve. I don't know anyone, so I'm standing around awkwardly when this big bald man approaches—probably out of pity—and starts making conversation. He's Steve Holcomb, he says. He makes casual conversation for a while until it emerges that he drove the bobsled that won gold in the 2010 Winter Olympics. I like that he's humble, and I confide that I don't know much about the world of sports, let alone know anyone here.

"Well, the way things work at these is that there's an after-party that's much more casual. That's usually where you can actually meet and talk to people without feeling like it's all official."

That sounds more up my alley. "Where is it?"

He's about to reply when a slick-looking man appears and takes hold of his shoulder.

"I'm sorry, we gotta go," the man says to me, steering Steve, who looks apologetically at me, toward the door. "He's got somewhere to be."

"Oh," I say. *Could that have been more awkward?*

As they reach the door, I see Steve say something to the man and walk on through. The slick guy hustles back over to me.

"I'm sorry, it's just that he has a previous obligation. Here's my card." He hands it to me, waiting impatiently for me to take it before striding off again.

I look down at it and read, *Brant Feldman, agent, American Group Management.*

chapter

eighteen

I've been invited back to Ukraine.

After Sochi, people in Ukraine seem to think that I'm famous (I'm so *not* famous it's almost comical). The US embassy in Kyiv thinks I'll have poignant messages for the people of Ukraine.

Below are some preliminary plans and ideas that we have so far related to your visit to Ukraine. We are really excited and look forward to working with you closely on your programming for this upcoming trip.

The email from the woman at America House, the cultural wing of the US embassy, says they want me to visit an orphanage, as an example of the successful lives adopted Ukrainian orphans might lead, and a military hospital to inspire soldiers wounded in the Russia-Ukraine conflict. They want me to speak on panels, at ceremonies, on radio and television.

It will be the first time I've visited Ukraine since I was adopted.

Reading through the email, I flash back to high school when I was hit with an urgent need to know something of my heritage. I went through a phase of constantly asking Mom about Ukrainian culture and history. But she didn't know much either, other than the various roadblocks to foreign adoption and the abject poverty she observed.

I think I'm ready to return. It's time. If I can help some people there just by sharing my story, well, the journey will be absolutely worth it. I tell the embassy people that I'll come. My only condition for doing the tour is this:

I don't want to meet my birth family.

All my life, I've been constructing an image of who my birth mom is, of what it would be like to meet her and talk to her, of what I'd say. I've daydreamed about how I'd be with her, how she'd be with me. But when this long-fantasized-about prospect seems attainable, I realize I'm not so sure I want it anymore.

Which makes me realize that I still have significant issues. I'm still *angry*. It's the same anger that during my teenage years surged up in shocking waves. I still believe my birth mother relinquished me because she must have hated me: the way I looked, how I'd formed. Because why—*why*—would you put a child of yours into such a horrific system?

I never imagine a father alongside my birth mom, or what his role might have been in the *relinquishing*. Whenever I imagine my birth family, it's only my mother.

Which is interesting, because now I *have* a mother, and not a father, and that's all I've ever wanted. She's all I've ever needed.

"If you're going, I'm going," Mom says as soon as I tell her about the invitation. "You might need me."

We land in Ukraine on October 27, 2015. Our arrival is a blur. A procession of people are waiting for us at the airport, handing me flowers, hugging me, speaking to me in Ukrainian and heavily accented English. Cameras are rolling everywhere. Underneath all my smiles, I'm shaking. I don't know why. We check into a beautiful hotel. This whole city seems to be beautiful. I don't remember this at all. We're jet-lagged, and Mom and I fall into bed.

The next morning, our first morning in Ukraine, Mom and I are scheduled to visit an orphanage in the city. We're being driven to a baby house, an orphanage for the youngest children. I was in a baby house for much longer than my age dictated because I was so small. America House had wanted us to visit that baby house. They'd been willing to drive us all the way to Khmelnytskyi, over five hours away. But there are apparently up to twenty baby houses in Khmelnytskyi, and Mom didn't know which one I'd been at and no one could help us find it. I don't know how to feel about this, relieved or disappointed.

Outside the hotel, we meet the ombudsman for children's rights, a suited man who is, essentially, in charge of all orphans in Ukraine. He'll accompany us to the orphanage. After we're settled in the van with our handlers and translators from the embassy to travel the hour or so through the city, he turns to me. He asks quite casually:

"Would you ever want to meet your birth family?"

My stomach drops. Has no one told him? I think about all the cameras at the airport, all the reporters who are supposed to be at the orphanage this morning, and I flash to Jane in Sochi. Does he want this to be a PR moment, a success story for Ukrainian orphanages?

"One day, when I'm ready," I say carefully. "But I'm not ready now. For now, all I would want is to see a picture of them. Maybe. And to know my family history healthwise." I've come to share my mother's terror at every surgery when the doctor asks, *Are you allergic to this medication?* My standard reply, helplessly sarcastic: *I don't know. We'll find out. Just be ready if I am.* "But I'm not ready to meet them physically. And I don't really want to talk about this right now," I tell the man, the politest way I can think of to get him to stop asking.

I don't say—not to this man, not to anyone yet—that one of my biggest fears is that I'll die before meeting my birth family. Before seeing a picture, even. Before knowing. But I can't do anything about that fear because I'm not ready to meet them yet. Like most of my emotional paradoxes, it's complicated.

It's also possible that my birth parents have *already* died. The Russian-Ukrainian conflict has been raging for over a year now. There's no guarantee they weren't victims of the violence. I've told myself that I probably need to come to terms with this and stop fantasizing about meeting them one day.

My mother doesn't like the ombudsman. She doesn't trust him, she whispers to me in the back seat while he speaks in Ukrainian to our driver. "He has something up his sleeve."

"I don't think he meant anything by asking," I say, trying to convince myself, too. "He's trying to fix broken homes and families so that there are no orphans at all. It's probably programmed into him to want to unite families."

I've learned from the officials who prepped me for this trip that Ukraine is trying to create more of a foster care system, where a child is placed in a home to experience what a *home* is, what a *family* is. Instead of the system I was raised in, with cement walls and pipes frozen over in the dark.

We drive through forests of trees, pass by lakes shimmering in the cityscape. I don't remember trees where I grew up, or lakes. My Ukraine was all tan wheat fields, broken occasionally by sunflowers. Kyiv is not that at all. I feel strangely disconnected. Where *am* I?

Blink.

Laney takes my hand. She never cares how weird it is, my webbed fingers, extra bones. She grabs it in her beautiful hand, and we run into a stand of sunflowers like enormous trees. We hide there, laughing, whispering, picking the seeds out of the centers and taming our ever-fierce hunger with them, in the golden light that I never want to leave.

Blink.

Then the landscape morphs, into the gloom of ramshackle neighborhoods. They're beaten down, sagging with obvious poverty. It's almost menacing, like a dead war zone. These are places where you lock your car, where you tell no one that you're American. We glide past a faded red ball alone on an empty expanse of weedy concrete. I suddenly remember the playground from the boarding school orphanage. The slide was rusty, its sheen completely gone, but zooming down it was *fun* and the feeling of playing outside was the polar opposite of being inside the walls of that awful place.

Even my orphanage had more than the kids living here have.

Sadness floods me. This is going to be brutal. If the neighborhoods look like this, the baby house must be . . . I'm not ready to visit an orphanage like this. I'm not ready for this.

From somewhere far away, outside my body, I notice that I'm having trouble breathing. I inhale. Then I feel so out of breath. I realize I haven't taken another inhale. I'm forgetting to breathe.

In my zoned-out state, the Ukrainian that our embassy guides are speaking in the front seat dances into my head. Into the sadness and panic swirls a nostalgic happiness at the sound of it. Cyrillic words adorn the signs of the buildings we pass. It hits me that *I can read them.* The words click, and my understanding returns in a sudden tide.

"Mom, I *know* that word. I don't know what it means, but I know it." She smiles, puts her arm around me. I know she's worried about me. For good reason. My armpits are soaked. "I'm so happy I'm wearing black right now," I whisper. "I'm sweating to my core."

We finally pull up to a little building, incongruously clean and well-kept amid the rest of this part of the city. We climb out of the van.

"Are you ready for this?" Mom asks me.

I pause a moment, looking at the front of the baby house. Women are already streaming out the doors—the caretakers, I assume. I can see a few small figures behind them in the doorway. I want these people—the caretakers, the embassy people, the government officials, the Ukrainian people—to know that those little kids, that *every* child is worth the same love and care that my mom gave me. Every child deserves a good home, regardless of whether that home is an orphanage or a family's house. I remind myself, *This is what you're here for. You've always wanted to shine a light on this, bring attention to systems like this. This is what you're here for.*

"Yeah." I take a deep breath, my internal systems back on track. "I want to show what's possible." I'm not sure if I mean show the children what's possible for a future beyond the hell they're living in; or show everyone else what's possible from a Ukrainian orphan, why people need to care for these kids. It doesn't matter which. Maybe I mean both.

All the women are compact, happy, healthy, with short hair—just like my memory of the woman who took me home with her when I needed tending. I can get through this. I'll be okay.

Then my foot hits the first of the stairs to the front door.

This is where I came from.

Oh my God.

Right there on the step, as I'm walking into an orphanage as an adult with grown-up eyes and a fully formed opinion of what's right and wrong, the full gravity of what my mom saved me from settles onto me. My stomach falls into knots. I can't stop flipping my hair to get it off my neck, which has gone so hot. But I'm trying not to reveal my distress. Photographers are everywhere, and a video camera is in front of me documenting my every move. I get the sense that I can't go anywhere in Ukraine without the message being broadcast on national news that *Oksana Masters is here.* I don't know how to deal with this celebrity. I definitely don't know how to deal with it right now, in the middle of this physiological reaction I'm having.

Inside the door they ask us to remove our shoes and put on little bootees, so we don't track in mud.

"What is going on with me?" I ask under my breath to Mom, who is thankfully right next to me fumbling with her own shoes. "I can't stop sweating. I don't know what's wrong." I'm not that little girl anymore. I'm not an orphan anymore. I can't understand this.

It's clear that this orphanage is for kids with more intellectual disability than where I grew up. The children are all around, hiding shyly in doorways or holding the hands of the short women. They tell me through translation and show me that each of these children is assigned a specific caretaker who gives them one hour per day of physical contact, nurturing them with playtime and affection.

I can tell how proud these people are to show me this place. The locals, with help from the embassy and the Office of Children's Rights, have worked on this place. They've changed it and improved it, hoping to hold it up as a new standard for orphanages in Ukraine. The first thing I notice is the *color*. The walls, the chairs, the floors, it's all so colorful. It looks more like a preschool than an orphanage. It reminds me of the ball pits at amusement parks, which still make me want to pop my legs off and dive into them like a little kid.

I notice how tiny the building is. The halls are so narrow, the ceilings are so low. *Was my orphanage like this?* I remember hugeness, caverns, hallways going on forever. But this place is made to fit little kids. I also notice that it's warm in here. Although it's October, not full-on winter yet. But maybe it stays warm for their small bodies during the frigid winter.

We stream past the medical room. It's tiny, just like everything else, and mostly empty of any resources. Except on the little metal table, where there sits a pair of pliers. They aren't as rusty as those in my memory, but they're chipped and dented.

My body screeches.

We pass the bathroom chamber. The toilets have colored plastic seats. But they're lined up side by side against the wall. The smell. It's just like what I remember.

No. This is not friendly whatsoever.

Like an faucet of icy water turning on, I realize all at once that *all of my memories were real.* Even with the scars I physically bear on my body, even with all my working through of things over the last years, I've tried to convince myself that those things didn't happen to me. It was fake. Those were just bad dreams. Nightmares.

But it was all real. It all happened. To me.

I'm looking right at it. It. All. Happened.

The tour over, we all sit down in a little common room. I try to remember to breathe, try to get out of my head with the kids and the caretakers arrayed before me and around me, and the video cameras running.

I'm here for them right now. I'm here to show them that those memories don't define me. I drag myself into the moment. I'm embarrassed, suddenly, that I can't speak Ukrainian anymore. It feels like a slight somehow. Smiling, I count to ten in Ukrainian for the kids, since I remember that at least, then I switch to English. I tell them about my journey from orphan to doing what I love, about my dreams of having a *home*, a *family*, a *mother*, all coming true. I tell them about some of the U-turns in my road and the obstacles I've had to leap—just a few, though. I don't want to scare them. I say to them that no one can tell them what they can and can't accomplish.

After, I'm surrounded by children. Beautiful, laughing, hopeful kids. I give out presents, the books and toys we brought. I play with whoever wants to for a few minutes before we have to leave.

A little girl approaches me and looks up into my face. She only comes to my midthigh. She looks older than she should for her short height, and I think that maybe she's like I was, trapped in a tiny body that's too small for her age. She reaches for my hand. I'm amazed; most kids are freaked-out by my hands, don't want to touch them, often shrieking in innocent voices, *"What is that!"* But this little girl takes my hand.

I look down at her, and I'm looking back at myself. Although she has normal legs and lovely hair that they let her keep instead of chopping it off for lice, I'm looking at the little girl that I was. She hugs me. I finally break free of my frozen state. I kneel and wrap my arms around her. My heart cracks.

I get to leave here, I think. *But you'll have to stay in this place.*

She's growing up in a much better environment than I ever had—one that I probably couldn't even have imagined back then. But all the paint and bright colors in the world can't change that this girl is an orphan in Ukraine. I know how these systems work. Putting up a public front and sprucing up the surface can't change what happens inside the walls. How are they punished? Is there an upstairs room full of darkness and fear and horrible men with hot weight? Who holds them when they're scared and alone?

Laney. What a gift she would be in this world if she were still here. How many of these children won't get the chance to live their lives?

I hold the girl tight until she's ready to let go. I'm herded toward the front door, and her little body disappears in the crowded hallway.

The flashbulbs fire left and right. A reporter is in my face. "How did that make you feel? What do you think about this place? What's your message to the people of Ukraine?"

They're bragging about having paint on a wall. One hour of affection. *One hour.* What about the rest of the hours in the day, the night? These kids don't have families, they have no one to protect them, and I know they're thought of as throwaways. These journalists don't *see* these kids. They don't see the situation. Even though they're all aware of what's happening, they just go on with their jobs. And on to the next story. What's my *message?*

You can all go to hell.

This isn't about just a message. It's so much bigger than that. But I don't have the words right now, and I'm well aware that this is nothing but a show-and-tell for the country's media.

I don't know what I say to the reporter. Something short and sweet, with the expected smile on my face. I stumble to the door, rip off the weird little bootees, and head straight for the car.

I'm silent on the ride back through the city. I stare out the window at nothing. My body is numb and heavy. The only other time I've felt like this was in the upstairs room, terrified to death. Back then I was paralyzed into only hearing and feeling things faintly, as if it were an out-of-body experience.

Mom is right next to me. I've never shared with her what happened to me in Ukraine. But she's so smart. She knows why I'm quiet, and she knows how to be there for me. She holds my hand. It's like she was born to be a mother. She was born to nurture. Thank God for her.

Goddamn it, why did I do this? It made no difference at all for any of those children. And I'm in a free fall of memories I now know, unequivocally, were real. *All. Real.*

I don't notice the ombudsman dropping hints about finding my family, asking questions. Mom does, though. When we get out of the van at a stop for lunch, she pulls the other embassy people aside and murmurs to them. Protecting me, always.

I get through the rest of our scheduled day in a haze. I have an interview with the Christian Broadcasting Network. The ombudsman is supposed to be here, but he's late. As Mom and I are in makeup, he shows up with a folder under his arm. He approaches Mom, apparently having decided (inaccurately) that she'll be the friendlier liaison here in his quest to find my birth family. He's pulling photos and files out of the folder and handing them to Mom, sort of triumphantly, as if she's never seen them before.

"Of course I've seen these," Mom says. "These are from her adoption file."

"Yes, I went down to the agency."

"You took these from her file? Isn't that all required to stay there?"

He's unfazed in the face of Mom's anger. He hands her one more picture. She's never seen this one.

I look over. I have no memory of that photo being taken.

The grainy black-and-white image shows a little girl standing against a dark background, maybe a curtain, that hangs above rotting floorboards and does nothing to disguise the threadbare carpet. I'm wearing a heart-printed dress that's clearly too big, tied at the waist to save me from being swallowed. In white knee-high socks, my right leg looks normal, although the arcing left leg (*my Little Leg!*) with its floating knee is impossible to hide. Under the cuffs of the too-long sleeves rolled to the wrists, there's a glimpse that my hands don't look quite right. But mostly it's the harsh expression on my face. I do *not* look happy to be having that photo taken. *Must be the horribly ugly dress,* I think.

"Ugh," I say.

"Good thing this wasn't the first photo I saw of you," Mom jokes. The ombudsman must think he's done something right since Mom has dropped her acid front to laugh with me for a moment. We head out for the interview.

When we're finally, mercifully, back at the hotel, Mom says to me, "You know, Oksana, at the orphanage . . . that was the first time I've really gotten to see how gracious you are. How well you can handle these really hard things. I'm blown away by you."

I don't feel gracious. I'm still numb.

The following morning is dedicated to a visit to the military hospital to meet soldiers wounded in the Russia-Ukraine conflict. I'm supposed to show them what's possible with prosthetics and medical advancements, to be a source of inspiration for these men who've come home from the war without parts of their bodies. It's also the twenty-fifth anniversary of the Americans with Disabilities Act in the United States, the civil rights law that prohibits discrimination against people with disabilities, which the US embassy is working to leverage. Among other things, the ADA required buildings and public transportation to make modifications for wheelchair and other handicapped movement. Just simple things, such as installing ramps or curb cutouts, or plowing snow from sidewalks in winter.

Ukraine has none of this. Our first night here, on the way to dinner, one of our embassy handlers took us to a bar, to illustrate what people with disabilities are up against here. It was underground, and she showed us the steep stairs to get down to it, which were basically stacked wooden planks.

"If you want to get down here in a wheelchair, this is your route." She told us this is pretty universal. The country is trying to find ways to adapt so that wounded military servicemen can still be part of society. The goal is to bring down the heartbreakingly high suicide rate among veterans here, she says. My brain shies away from my own ten-year-old brush with that word.

The military hospital is a squat yellow two-story building trimmed in white, clean and cheerful from the outside. But the inside is a different story. It makes our hospitals in the United States seem palatial. Two flights of stairs separate the ground floor from the patients' rooms. I'm here to talk to men who've had amputations, but this place has no elevators, and I don't see a single ramp. If they want to leave their rooms, they have to figure out how to scoot down the stairs. My chest tightens.

We enter a hallway. Stacked against a wall are dozens of mattresses. Foam ones, striped and plain and different colors, all of them stained, with blood and who knows what else. They're disgusting. My whole body electrifies.

They're exactly like the mattresses I slept on when I was little.

Just past the stack of moldering foam is an old rollaway bed. It's encased with a dull metal rim. Its springs are exposed. Some are broken, some are missing.

Blink.

It's so dark in here. There are no sheets on the bed. There's no blanket. I can feel the springs in my back. The door opens, ugly shoes, horrible weight, flick of a knife—

Blink.

I tear myself from the memory, struggling to breathe. The anxiety in my throat threatens to overflow. This is too much. I can't take this. I gulp air.

But I calm my face. I can't show this to the cameras that are running, always running. I know well how to hide emotion, ironically, from my training as a kid in a Ukrainian orphanage.

We step into the patients' quarters. Six to eight men are stuffed into each room, their beds separated only by curtains. The smell in here is awful. Unwashed bodies, maybe rotting flesh. The technology, or lack thereof, is so dated that it feels like we've stepped into a movie from 1870 because this can't be real. A few men are sleeping, but otherwise the quarters are empty.

We head into a cramped common room, where everyone is waiting for me. I force a smile to my face. *I'm here for them,* I remind myself, again. At least in here it's bright, with plants giving the space a little much-needed life. People are arrayed in a semicircle, less than twenty in the room. Men in wheelchairs, men with crutches, missing one leg, two, an arm gone. Legs that disappear from pants like a magic trick. Stumps wrapped in bulky bandages. Some men are big, hard looking. Some are gaunt. At least one looks years too young to be a veteran. Their wives, or maybe their sisters or mothers, are standing behind them, sitting beside them.

A few months ago, these men were fully functional, defending Ukraine in the Donbas region. Now they're here, in this dismal place, facing down a future of getting down steep steps made of wooden planks in their wheelchairs. And that's just the beginning of it.

They're all looking at me. I can't put my finger on what the feeling is in the room. So I just start talking. I tell them my story. This time, for these men, I tell them my story about learning to row, how it saved me after my second amputation, and how learning what my body can do with sports has become my bridge to loving it. Some of their faces start to change, just a little bit. They start to animate, I think.

I tell them that it's important to accept that we no longer have limbs. We must get used to our new bodies.

"Don't be afraid to try things. Even things that might hurt. The only thing that can stop the physical body from doing whatever you want— is the mind."

I sit to take off my prosthetics. I undo the straps and slide one off, and the men gasp. There are exclamations in the room. They've never seen something like this, the translator explains. *Of course they haven't,* I realize. Just look at what they're forced to deal with here. I only recently learned from Mom that a single one of my prosthetic legs costs at least $100,000 (thank God for her health insurance with the universities)—how would these men have access to prosthetics without significant help? I take off my other leg, then walk across the floor on my stumps to hand one of my legs to the man closest to me, a young guy in a camo jacket missing one leg. He takes it disbelievingly. There's a moment of total silence.

Then he just starts laughing. The whole room peals with laughter. Now the men are talking excitedly to one another as they pass my legs around, examining the hinged knee, the foot, the socket. They're shaking their heads. They had no idea these pieces of equipment existed, that these kinds of opportunities existed. I walk around on my stumps pointing things out on the prosthetics, laughing with them at the wonder of it.

The translator leans over to me. "They have hope. That's what they're saying. They have hope now."

I look around, stunned. I realize now what the heavy feeling was in the room when I walked in: bleakness. Then they saw a person without legs—missing *both* legs—moving around, walking around, taking artificial limbs off and still moving across the room on what remains. A person who looks like them—but who is happy and comfortable in an adapted normal.

It hits me that *this* is why I do this. Because it's not about me at all—even though I never thought it was until my memories slammed into me like a runaway train and I only thought about protecting myself from them.

But we *need* to share stories, I suddenly understand, even the hard ones. Especially the hard ones. Because we have no idea how it might change someone's life. If a single story is the reason why one of these men has hope now to live, and to do something with his life in his new normal, if he in turn becomes an example for someone else—that is an incredibly powerful thing. It's an enormous, bigger-than-any-of-us thing.

They pass my legs back to me eventually, and I show them how I attach them. "It's the best of both worlds," I joke. "In the morning I'm already half-dressed with my shoes and my pants on my legs. It's perfect."

They laugh with me. The men are beaming. One or two ask for my autograph as we wrap up, which feels weird.

I'm whisked away, leaving them to the impassable flights of stairs and awful quarters but maybe, now, with a little bit of desire to persist.

That night for dinner we go to the home of the general consul for the US embassy. It's a small reception for the children's welfare community, some of the more important people in the embassy, and some politicians, all of whom are working to reform laws and find solutions to make the orphanage systems around Kyiv better. I don't know anything about the city systems other than the baby house I saw yesterday; my orphanages were in a rural area hours west of here. I know, again, that this is bigger than *me*, though. They want me here because of what I represent: a success story, in a place where people are sorely in need of hope. *Here's this girl who was adopted from Ukraine, look where she is now. A professional athlete on Team USA.* I'm still processing what I've seen today at the military hospital, and I haven't even begun to process everything from the day before at the orphanage. But I'm prepared to share my story again with this small crowd of decision makers who've invited me to speak.

In the consul's home, Mom and I chat with people for a while. Most speak English, and it's a welcome break from the awkwardness of translating, my shame at not speaking Ukrainian, and the mental acrobatics of straining to understand. The ombudsman from yesterday is supposed to introduce me to speak and kick off the agenda for the evening, but he's late. I'm talking with the consul, who seems a bit annoyed with the ombudsman's delay. The consul's a big man. I wouldn't want to be on his bad side, I think idly. Mom is talking with some people across the room.

Finally, thirty minutes after the reception has started, the ombudsman walks through the door. He scans the room, then makes a beeline for the knot of people that includes me and the general consul.

"I'm sorry I'm late." The ombudsman's speaking directly to me, but loudly, as if he's making an announcement. The room quiets a bit in response. His face looks just the slightest bit smug. As if he's about to save the day. "I just got off the phone with your father. We had a good call."

I move to brush him off, return to my interrupted conversation. I don't have a father. Mom's never been married. This guy has no idea what he's talking about.

Then my whole body just . . . stops. The blood freezes in my veins. *My father.*

"Oh yeah," the ombudsman continues, as I stare at him, "and your brothers say hello."

There are no video cameras at this private event. But there are photographers. From far away, I notice flashes going off. The ombudsman's expression is triumphant, expectant: *I just reconnected you with your birth family. You're welcome.*

"What?" I whisper.

"Yes, I just had a wonderful long talk with him," the ombudsman goes on nonchalantly, obliviously. "I have pictures here on my phone that they just sent, if you want to see. They want to meet you tonight. You have two brothers, by the way."

My body takes this moment to decide to jolt back into motion. It sends all of its energy into a sob that explodes into the quiet room. I can't control it. I don't even know where it came from.

I feel so, so stupid. This roomful of people I don't even know, who likely don't even know who I am or why I'm here, are watching me cry. It's one of the things I hate most in the world: people witnessing my weakness. I feel like someone has punched me straight in the middle of the stomach. There's a spot between the belly button and ribs, right below the sternum. When you're punched there, the pain is blinding. It robs your breath. I should be used to having trouble breathing on this trip. But I feel like I'm dying right now.

The consul roars something at the ombudsman in Ukrainian, then takes me in his huge arms and whisks me down a hallway with his wife on my other side, and they settle me in their own bedroom and she tells me to take all the time I need and then they shut the door and I'm alone in there, with my tears and pain and confusion, and my body that won't stop vibrating.

Mom tries to come in, but I don't want to see her. I need to just be alone. She understands because she always does. I hear her raised voice.

She's transformed into her bear self. I can't tell what she's saying, but I can hear the consul clearly. He's telling the ombudsman in English, maybe for Mom's benefit, that this was out of line, the wrong thing to do. He asks him to leave.

I cry for a long time.

The ombudsman said he talked to my *father*. My *brothers* want to meet me. What about my mother? She must not want anything to do with me. After all this time, all this fantasizing and wondering, these hailstorms of emotion . . . she doesn't want to know me. At all.

On the other side of the door, I know that there's a room full of people who just shared the most intimate moment of my life. Total strangers who found out the thing I've been wanting to know forever—at the same time I did. Strangers who are powerful, important people who watched me fall apart. I'm a weak little girl all over again with no control. I think this is perhaps my most embarrassing moment ever.

I don't give that talk that I'm here to give. I don't share my story. When I emerge from the room, there's a lot of apologizing. The consul and his wife apologize profusely. I apologize profusely, mortified at my puffy face and red eyes. The ombudsman is still there for some reason. I apologize to him, too. I would apologize to a wall if I walked into it.

Mom doesn't apologize. She takes me back to the hotel. On the way she fumes, "That man owes *you* an apology. He violated all kinds of policies and procedures—in front of government officials! I hope he's fired. Honestly, I would have punched so many people in that room if I thought I could actually land a punch and not get beat up for it."

Mom. She makes me laugh, even right now.

———

A few hours later, a Facebook message pops up on my phone. It's from my birth brother. My *supposed* birth brother, I remind myself. He knows the ombudsman told me about my family tonight. He says that he's a real estate agent. His brother is a cop. I'm skeptical—these don't seem like typical lifestyles where I came from. My new "family" is too successful. But I'm also trying to interpret his messages through Google Translate, which is frustrating and unreliable at the best of times.

It's late already, and I know Mom is trying to sleep, so I take the phone into the bathroom. While I'm sitting on the toilet lid, my supposed brother tells me the story of how my birth family found me after all these years.

After Sochi, when Russia and Ukraine were claiming medals with me, Ukraine televised backstories on the three medalists. He says that he was watching it at home while his mom did the dishes, with the volume on high for her to hear. All of the sudden, the loud crash of a breaking dish came from the kitchen. He found her in there. She was crying.

He never knew their mother had a child before them, he tells me. She never told them she had a daughter whom she gave up. So she sat down with him, and she told him.

The doctors told her that she couldn't keep me. She was poor. She didn't have the financial resources to pay for the medical help that I would need. "You don't want her," the doctors told her. But she did want me. She tried to fight for me. She tried to fight so hard, she told her son, that the doctors eventually told her I'd died. But she could see that I was still breathing. (In the harsh light of the bathroom and even accounting for the weirdness of Google Translate and autocorrect, this story is bizarre. I don't trust it. It makes no sense. But I'm reeled in and I can't cut this off.) So the doctors tried a different tack: "We'll put her in an orphanage. She'll get what she needs there. Relinquish her."

If she couldn't keep me, she says, she wanted to give something of herself to me: her name. Her first name is Oksana. (I'm not surprised at this. I have no reaction to the revelation. It would be a pretty easy lie to come up with.)

My supposed brother tells me that he always used to dream about having a sister when he was little. He always felt like there was something missing.

Now I think this guy is playing me. This is getting too weird. I'm about to put a stop to this and head back to bed—as if I could sleep. I don't need to subject myself to more of this.

But that's when he says the one thing that could possibly convince me he knows who I am: my middle name. In Ukraine, your middle name is patronymic. It's derived from your father. I've never told anyone what my middle name is. None of the television reports would mention it. It's only on my birth certificate, locked away in some file in the middle of the country.

Your middle name, he types, *is Alexandrovna.*

It's true.

"Mom!" I can't help myself. I know she's trying to sleep; it's one in the morning. "He knows my middle name!"

"Oksana, it's late," she calls back. Ever the practical one. "We have a full day tomorrow. You can talk to him later. Go to sleep!"

It's possible the ombudsman could have told these people my middle name. But I don't know what to believe right now.

He tells me that our mother wants to meet me.

Why didn't she talk to the ombudsman, then? I ask in clunky Google translation.

Because, he says, *this is a man's society. Man-to-man. She had no say in the matter.*

Under the harsh bathroom light, I feel like I don't know myself. Everything I knew, I'm starting to believe, I didn't know. Like there's an entire world, an entire *life*, I've never lived. There are people I don't even know who know a whole lot about *me*, who hold this history that I've always wanted to hold. And it could all be fake. This guy could be making all of this up. They think I'm famous and I have money. Yeah, right.

Can we come meet you? he types.

No, I reply. *We have a full agenda tomorrow and the next day. And then we're leaving.*

He persists. I evade. I'm still trying to handle everything I've seen, and now this entire night. I'm not mentally ready for this. It's too much too fast. I click out of the conversation and turn off the bathroom light.

The following day I meet with high school students, parents, and teachers; accompany my mom to a panel she's sitting on about parenting children with disabilities; and give three separate interviews for radio, a newspaper, and a foundation that videotapes our conversation. They all want me to share my story, they all want to broadcast "my message" to the people of Ukraine. (It's still so much pressure, so hard, to always have a message to share—with an entire country. I never know what to say or if I'm saying the right thing.) It's hard for me to stay present and focused. I can't stop worrying that my birth family will just show up. At each new engagement Mom and I are ushered to, I imagine an older couple with two sons, who tell me what reality is supposed to be and bulldoze their way into mine.

Our last full day in Kyiv, Mom takes charge. She makes sure our embassy handlers and translators have the photo of my birth family that the ombudsman had obtained. I still haven't seen it, refuse to look at it even if it's in my hands. At our last event in Kyiv, which is an informal audience at America House, the embassy officials screen people at the door using the photo, pledge to keep my birth family out if they do show up.

I tell myself that this isn't my real birth family so that I can get through the last of my time in Ukraine. It's easier for me to cope if they're lying. The same way it's easier to cope if you simply hate someone rather than wade through understanding and empathy. The same way it's always been easier for me to forget things by burying them in anger.

On the flight home, my emotions battle for control. They're like little people orbiting me: the anxious person, the angry person, the excited one, the sad one. They're all chattering, all hitting me at once. I analyze with Mom every detail of my possible birth family: *What if this is real? My birth family is alive, they're actually* alive. *No, it can't be them. It was* them. *I had the opportunity to meet them. I passed it up. But I have the ability to meet them now. Oh my God, I have brothers.*

I can't do anything about this hurricane of emotions. I'm mentally and physically drained, entirely wrung out. I finally let Mom sleep, and I watch a movie—I don't even know which one—and fall asleep, too.

When I wake up on this endless flight, I pay for the Wi-Fi on the plane to finish my conversation with my maybe brother.

He tells me he's disappointed the family couldn't meet me before I left Ukraine. He explains that, on the first day of this visit, they waited for me at the baby house I was sent to as a baby. They thought the embassy would take us there for the orphanage visit on our itinerary. But the embassy took us to the media-friendly baby house in Kyiv instead. *A narrow miss,* I think. *If he's telling the truth.*

He says his mother regretted what she did by relinquishing me. She used to go constantly to the baby house that the doctors told her the authorities had taken me to. She wanted to try to recover me. But the caretakers would never let her in, she says, and finally, like the doctors, they told her I'd died. Stop coming, they said.

My body goes hot in the plane seat. *The blond woman.* Holy shit. I can't conjure her face. The memories are so faded, but I know a blond woman visited the orphanage a few times. I think she came to see *me.* Was she my birth mom? That whole time? Coming to try to save me?

This time, my supposed brother tells me, she believed the people who told her I'd died. She grieved for me. Until that night when the news on the television revealed that, *no, here is the child, she is very much alive.*

He keeps saying "our mom." I don't associate this woman as *my* mom. My mother is sitting right beside me on this plane. Maybe that sounds horrible. I don't know. I've never had a child. I don't know how it feels to lose one, to have your daughter ripped out of your hands—if that's what happened. To have that decision made for you.

Back at home, I message a few times more with this man who says he's my brother. I look desperately for similarities, grasping at anything that makes sense. We get on the subject of cats somehow, and he tells me he just rescued another one. Is he an animal lover, too, then? Is that a family trait? I finally allow myself to check his Facebook photos. They're limited. But he and his brother look nothing like me.

Eventually, I just stop engaging. This has become too real. And *not* real, at the same time.

Every day of my life, I fantasize about my birth family. I zone out randomly and find myself in a dream scenario. I go through every iteration. I'm sitting on a couch in a home—theirs, mine, Mom's. My birth father and mother walk in. I hug them. I don't hug them. I cry. I don't cry. I alternate in my head who starts talking first. I put myself in each situation, to desensitize myself, so that when the real moment comes, I'm not experiencing it for the first time, unprepared and unaware. I know this isn't a healthy exercise, but I often practice those moments to make sure the real moment will hurt less.

Some things are always the same in every scenario, though: I take off my legs almost immediately—maybe as a comfort thing, maybe as an authenticity thing, maybe so they can see exactly who I am and why.

One thing is always the same: my mom is there by my side. Gay, who is and will always be my real mom.

I worry, now that I've shared parts of my story with the world, that my birth family might *hate* me. I don't get to choose the words when a reporter says "*abandoned* by her birth mother." I hold on to some hope now that I wasn't just dropped off on a doorstep. Someone who names her child after her isn't *abandoning* her daughter. What if she doesn't want to meet me? But I do know, from what this man who is supposed to be my brother has told me, that my birth family most certainly doesn't hate Mom. In their eyes, she's the one who saved me, my brother says, and they want to meet her.

I always dream that I'll be mentally ready for an encounter sometime at the end of my sporting career—when the reality of meeting these figures from my past can no longer affect my presence and control in a race. But I also know that if I want this dream to come true, it has to be somewhat soon; my birth parents are aging. They won't live forever.

chapter

nineteen

"Maybe we should look into getting you an agent," Mom says to me one morning over coffee. "It could help you financially—with finding sponsors."

I had moved back in with Mom after Winter Park. While the US Olympic Committee awards money for medals won at the Games, Paralympians still get far less (Olympians receive $37,500 per gold while Paralympians receive $7,500). Which is to say that my Sochi medals have reduced somewhat what it's costing Mom to support me, but my winnings haven't been enough to live on and definitely aren't enough to start paying back my debt.

"I'm not Jane," I say. Testily. I haven't finished my first cup of coffee yet.

Mom ignores me. "An agent could make it easier to chase your dreams."

I think about it. Jane, after all, wasn't sleeping out of her car before Sochi. She had sponsors *paying* her to train.

I won bronze in the 2015 World Championships for cycling, surprising everyone, including me—a familiar story by now. The road to Rio looks real. It would be incredible to have the resources to train properly, not to have to borrow from Mom. And I have an even more ambitious goal: to be able to pay Mom back someday.

Thinking about Jane, I realize that a lot of sponsors were attracted to her story. Who's going to want to sponsor what *my* past represents?

I stare at the card on the table. I've been staring at it for ten minutes. I can't believe I didn't lose it. I lose everything; it seems like a miracle that I still have this.

Brant Feldman, agent.

I look up his website. It doesn't seem like he represents any other para athletes. But I don't know much about agents, so I'm not certain what information is important. I do know that I have nothing to lose here.

I open my laptop and type:

Hey, I don't know if you remember me. I met you with your athlete Steve a while back, and you gave me your card. I'm really interested. I've never done anything like this before, I don't know how it works or how the process goes. But if you're looking for athletes, would you be up for a chat?

I write a few more sentences about myself, add a link to my Team USA profile, and read it over a couple times, editing, debating. I finally hit Send.

He replies pretty quickly.

There are too many girls on Team USA with my same story line, he says. He names two, in different sports from me, who were adopted from outside the country with serious disabilities, and now they're Paralympic athletes.

I don't see how you're going to be different, he says.

I read that line again. And again. An old anger rises up. People think that every adopted person is the same. Every disability is the same. Different? How about the difference between being adopted at nine months old versus seven *years* in a corrupt system? Or the difference between being a below-the-knee amputee on one leg and . . . me?

I can't help myself. I write him back. *Yes, in broad strokes, we're all adopted. But that doesn't mean the same thing. My story is different. I'm different.*

A few days of radio silence ensue. His response, when it comes: *Do you have time to get on a call and talk?*

My armpits are already sweating when my phone rings at the designated time. I tell myself to act cool.

"I put your name out to some contacts, did some research on you," he says. "You did the ESPN Body Issue? Who got you that?"

I'm not sure what he means. "Um, they approached US Rowing to find me." I hope that's the right answer.

"Huh. And you were in *Sports Illustrated*. Who got you that interview?"

"Someone from the magazine just called me and asked me."

"You're getting all of these things with no one representing you?"

I don't know how to respond. I've already told him I don't know what I'm doing.

"Okay." He blows out some air into the receiver. "We can do this thing for one year and see how it goes. I can't promise you anything for Rio, though."

"What? Really? I mean, okay."

Okay.

———————

What do you think about this place? Can you check it out for me? It's so cheap, it's amazing!

Yeah, cuz that's in the ghetto, Aaron's text comes back. *Please don't live there.*

I frown, disappointed. Beth and I are looking for places in Champaign. We're moving out there together to get serious about training for cycling. Beth still isn't sure she even likes the sport, but she's game to pursue it with me for a little while longer. Champaign *is* flat, after all, and Louisville is too crowded to find open roadways, and Rio is six months away, and the 2016 World Championships are coming up, which will be a way to secure spots on Team USA.

Even though Aaron and I don't say it out loud to each other—we don't need to, not even in the notebook—I'm moving to get serious about him.

Well, what about this place? It costs more, but it looks good.

I watch the three dots of Aaron's reply in progress, wondering how many more apartments I'll have to hunt down before something works. I'm sick of researching, it's definitely not my strength.

Oh my God, he texts.

I blow out a breath in frustration, watching the three dots blinking and dreading what he'll say next. It's full of mold. It's party central. No one sane lives there.

It's right where I live. You'd be literally across the way.

Oh. Well, then.

I guess I should finally tell Mom I'm moving.

———

Brant calls. He tells me he found me a sponsor. Even though I didn't podium in the 2016 World Championships, I did well enough to secure my place on Team USA. This will be my first—and only—sponsor going into Rio.

"Have you heard of KT Tape?"

"Are you serious?" I nearly scream. "I use it all the time!" Holy shit. I can't believe it. But then I come down hard from the high. "Wait. Did you tell them I'm not likely to medal? I'm so new to the sport." I want them to know exactly who they're supporting. I don't want to set them up for disappointment.

"It's not about that. It's not about that at all."

I have a hard time believing him.

In Rio de Janeiro, I'm walking out of Aaron's accommodations with the track team on my way back to my own hotel. I'm trying to calm my nerves about *his* upcoming race in the marathon. I know by now to wear black to cover my anxiety sweat, to put my hair up to keep it from soaking my neck. It's starting to mean more to me that he's happy with his race when he crosses the finish line than how *my* races turn out. For his previous events, if we're together, I get up with him at four in the morning and make his coffee for him. When we're not together—if he's racing in New York or London or somewhere else in a different time zone—I'll get up in the middle of the night just to monitor the live tracker of the event (since these races are rarely televised). I'm turning into my mother.

I'm jolted out of my thoughts by the US rowing team walking by. I know who they are because I still follow rowing religiously, and I wave like a total dork. In turning to watch them walk away from me, I realize the depth of devastation I still harbor over losing my first love.

It doesn't help that even though I'm on the cycling team, I've never felt more unwanted on a team in my life.

From the outside, it looks like we're a team. When we do course recons, we roll deep—twenty-hand cyclists, upright cyclists, and coaches all wearing the USA kit—a cohesive unit.

On the inside, though, it's a different story. From the beginning, I've overheard jabs from other women on the team—ones I think I'm meant to hear.

"She's not even a real cyclist. She's just jumping from one sport to the other."

There's so much I still don't understand about cycling. I've never needed tactics before. Or had to know about lines: how to cut a course to take a faster line, how to take a turn to maximize speed, when to draft off another racer, when to break and push hard—the latter called attacking or surging.

"She took a spot from this other rider who deserved it more."

But I love this sport. I love that I can push myself physically, accepting only the limitation that sometimes the equipment on the bike will fail. I love that cycling also requires me to know how to fix my bike, that I'm dirty and covered in bike grease and feel so *accomplished* for being capable.

"She's just doing it for publicity."

I'm burning to prove to them that I *can* do this. And not just to "do a sport." I *will* make it onto that podium in Rio.

I set the bar unrealistically high. Which I'm all too aware of because I'm a realistic racer. I have so much respect for all my competitors' years of training; they've dialed in their equipment and know the sport and how to race. That's something I won't take away from even my biggest rival: respect. And that's one of the things that drives me: going against those who are the best in the sport right now.

So I have no expectations—yet, at the same time, I have a shit ton of expectations. It makes no sense. As usual.

———

I'm staring across the tiny pathways that separate the tents where athletes are warming up. I know Germany's tent is close, but I'm not sure where. I close my eyes, try to focus on my own warm-up. I know the German woman is most likely to win because that's what my coach told me.

"Whatever she does, you stay on her. Just sit behind her," he says now. "If people peel off, you just stay there. She doesn't chase, you don't chase. And don't lead. You're inexperienced, you have no business pulling a race. Use this race to learn."

He knows I have a hard time *not* chasing people in races, so this is a good strategy for me. The time trial the other day was good for me in a different way, since it's raced individually. But that was about the only thing that was good about it. I didn't know I could practice on the start ramp before that race. No one told me. So I thought the course was straight, and I gunned it hot off the ramp. And ran right into a fence on the very first turn. I was so mortified, it made me glad I was racing alone so that none of the other cyclists watched it in real time.

Now, we line up at the start line for the road race. I'm terrified. On top of the usual nerves, my directional anxiety is kicking into high gear. What if the course isn't blocked off? I don't have it memorized. What if I get lost?

The beep goes off.

We're all massed together in a pod. I'm trying to find the German woman's back wheel and hang there. The course veers off to one side. *I had no idea it went this way.* My armpits start sweating, pins and needles prick my skin. Not a good sign: I'm flustered and nervous. It feels like knives are piercing my body from the inside out. But I find the German rider, and I stay there.

She doesn't like it, though. Suddenly, she drops back a little and pushes me, hard, off the course and into the grass.

Whoa, this girl's aggressive.

My hand fell off the pedal in the push, interrupting my flow, but I recover well and get back on her wheel. She does it again though, dropping back for a bit, hitting me, and sprinting around. And again. She's seen that my hand falls off every time she does it. I hear her shout something in German to the Dutch athlete who's also been hanging in the lead pack. That woman starts hitting me, too. Soon they're working together to exploit my weakness to drop me, trying to kill my speed, knock my hand off, and sprint around me.

I'm *pissed.* This feels like dirty racing. I want to beat someone in their best race on their best day, not because I disadvantaged someone. Otherwise I'll never trust the win, never trust that I earned it.

But I'm also psyched. I'm keeping up with these women, who would have dropped me like a bad habit only a couple months ago. Every time they surge, I'm there with them. They keep looking over their shoulders, as if I'm an annoying gnat that won't leave them alone.

Finally, we come into the last five hundred meters. My muscles are burning at the same time my body is vibrating with energy. We hit the last corner, the one that's a hundred meters out from the finish, the one that I know I want to round in at least third place—because that will mean the podium. I'm right there, right behind the Dutch and German women in the lead. They each have a teammate behind them now, too, crowding me over. I'm worried one will attack, take my spot in third place. I've been so patient this entire last lap, just waiting, not making a move, following the advice of my coach.

But I'm done sitting behind now. I want this. I'm so close. I can achieve it, achieve this impossible goal of medaling in cycling at Rio after rowing was taken from me. I pull out next to the Dutch and German leaders, and we scream three abreast around the corner.

It's a mistake. I can almost feel the other two women beside me smile smugly. They surge, and they pull their teammates behind them in their slipstream. The second Dutch athlete, in her teammate's wake, comes in third, a mere hundredth of a second before me.

I'm watching the flower ceremony, but I'm far from present—I'm busy beating myself up. Even as I crossed the finish line, I knew what I should have done in that moment instead of what I did, and I replay it over and over in my mind.

It's not the strongest and the fastest person who's going to win a road race. It's the one who goes about it the smartest way. I might be a slow learner. But once I learn something, I don't forget it.

That I didn't achieve this goal for myself doesn't mean I'm going to quit. I don't think I knew how badly I wanted that podium until I missed out on it. I'm not just cycling to "do a sport." I'm going to prove to those women that I *am* a cyclist.

And I'm going to prove it to myself.

But the thing is, I probably lost my first and only sponsor. I butchered this Games and failed KT Tape. I'll be back to square one in trying to support this dream on nothing.

———

The morning after the 2017 Para Nordic World Championships races have concluded in Finsterau, Germany, I'm packing my things in my hotel room to go back home to the United States. The last thing I do before heading down to the lobby to meet the team is stack the medals I just won in Nordic and biathlon behind the TV. I can't bring myself to throw them in the trash; that feels like the ultimate disrespect. I drape a towel over them to secure their hiding place and, satisfied, walk down to meet the rest of the team to head out for the airport.

For some people, that medal means everything. I wish I felt that way. For me, it's quite the opposite. I didn't get into sports to win everything I could; it was therapy. I loved sports from the beginning as a way to become healthier, and to see strength in myself that I didn't know I could possess after my legs were gone.

My weird relationship with winning has only become more complicated over the last years. Most of the time I still don't feel as though I've earned the win. Someone else had a bad race. Another, more formidable racer didn't show. Chalk up my win to this. Chalk it up to that. I spend hours after every race in a self-critical tunnel, reviewing what I could have done better.

Once you win a medal, people expect you to do it again. There's so much anxiety associated with it. Like with KT Tape. To my shock, they renewed their support of me through the winter. It's amazing. I'm so grateful. But I feel the pressure not to let them down again.

I never once consider that I make all these excuses so that I don't let *myself* down.

There's a delay in leaving the hotel. The team is lounging in the lobby, milling around and talking. The elevator doors ping open, and one of the women on the cleaning team walks into the center of our knot of people.

"Did someone leave these?" she says in beautifully accented, perfect English. She's holding up my medals. All five. Four gold, one bronze. *Oh my God.* My face flushes bright red. It's obvious they're mine. My whole team is going to think I'm crazy. Or ridiculously arrogant. This looks so bad.

"Ohhhh," I say lamely. "I forgot about those."

"They were behind the TV." She's thrilled to help.

Everyone's staring.

"Did you leave this, too?" She holds up the stuffed octopus all the medalists received as a gift.

"Oh my gosh, *yes!*" I snatch it with enthusiasm. "I can't believe I forgot that!"

Now people start laughing. Of course I want the stuffed animal more than the fistful of medals. Typical.

I stuff the medals into my luggage, even though I don't need them as a keepsake. The point for me isn't the prize. These are just hardware. The point is the striving—pushing that limit to see how far I can go. I'm still chasing that perfect race.

In my bones I feel that the perfect race will be when I can finally win a Paralympic gold. World Championships are incredible to win. But there's no greater pinnacle for an athlete than the Olympics, the Paralympics. *That's* the gold medal I want to give to Mom. I still haven't kept that promise to her. I still haven't been able to give back to her for everything she's done for me—a level of support she's added to exponentially over the last seven years of my trying.

All of my goals live now in the 2018 Winter Games in Pyeongchang.

chapter

twenty

My phone buzzes with a call from Brant.

"I'm just going to take this, you guys," I say to Aaron and our other two teammates, Andy and Kendall. We're all sharing a house in Bozeman, Montana, where we've come to train for the winter leading into Pyeongchang. We work out together, cook in the same kitchen, travel to the World Championships together, return together. It's a *lot* of time together. I can't say that any of us are the kind of people who'd normally live in such a situation, but we've made it work. Luckily, this house is massive.

I head into the room I share with Aaron, shut the door, and sit down on the bed.

"I got you another sponsor," Brant says. "Are you sitting down?"

"Um, yes."

"Visa wants you on their team for Pyeongchang."

I almost choke. When I can get words out, all that comes is *"What?"*

"They'll be using you for some content pieces." He explains I'll be in a commercial. Alongside Olympians. Badass, sexy ones, such as snowboarder Chloe Kim, freeskier David Wise, alpine racer Mikaela Shiffrin. Gold medalists who will dominate.

Then there's me. A Nordic biathlete amputee who doesn't even have a Paralympic gold.

When I hang up with Brant a few minutes later, I just sit there on the bed. Visa is a massive, iconic global brand. I never thought I'd be the kind of athlete who'd have a sponsor like this. I'm *not* the kind of athlete that would have a sponsor like this.

Holy shit, I think. *I can't believe this is happening to me.*

When I pull Aaron aside and tell him, his face lights up like a thousand-watt bulb. He pulls me into his arms and holds me there, laughing and shouting, and now it feels like maybe it's all real.

The sports psychologist walks slowly up and down the practice range. The US Paralympics Nordic program brought him in ahead of Pyeongchang to give us tips specifically for biathlon, which is—just as Eileen promised five years ago—an intensely mental sport.

He's mostly just watching and absorbing this training session, since it's his first time with us. But he does lean down and offer some tricks to athletes here and there. I only catch a little, but it mostly seems to be about how to believe in their abilities.

On the mat, I miss another shot. "Goddamn, shit!" I let out, followed by three or four more words that are even worse. It's my usual routine—I've already missed several shots today and have probably let fly with at least thirty swear words. Aaron, on a mat next to me, isn't even fazed.

The psychologist stops behind me. He leans down. "Oksana, right?"

I smile and nod sheepishly.

"Maybe next time, instead of saying five swear words, you only say three."

He moves on, and Aaron bursts out laughing.

"What's so funny?" I say indignantly.

"He set the bar so low for you," Aaron gasps out. "He knew he couldn't tell you to stop swearing altogether, so he put the cap on three cuss words." Aaron rolls over on his back to try to collect himself, still laughing.

"Well, I wear my emotions on my sleeve. I'm passionate. It's a good thing."

I look at him lying there, a mix of annoyance and affection and a strong surge of *love* making my whole body warm right there on the snow, and I have a sudden realization, completely out of place on the shooting range.

In the years before this, I don't think I knew who I was. So I became the person the men in my life wanted me to be, and when those relationships ended, I knew even less of who I was. It's a scary place to be. In the years before this, there was so much to untangle. All those liaisons that I thought were relationships, that I thought were love—they were distractions. I thought I knew everything. I thought I knew myself.

While I'm allowing Aaron to love me, while I'm falling in love with him, I'm learning to love myself. My authentic, real, actual self. Swear words and all.

———————

"We got a Nike deal," Brant says over the phone this time.

"Nike?" I scream. "Are you sure? Do they know I don't do track and field, or basketball, or soccer? Do they know my sports are cross-country skiing and biathlon?" I can't stop babbling. I sound like an idiot.

This is so huge I can't make myself believe this. When you get a sponsorship from Nike, you've made it as an athlete.

I've *made* it.

Over the next days though, underneath the euphoria and pride (an emotion that still doesn't come easily), other things start to stir.

Nervousness. Doubt.

———————

"I can see that you're very determined," the sports psychologist says. We're in our first one-on-one session. I've met a lot of psychologists, but I've never been to a sports-specific one.

"I have a lot of passion."

"When you say 'passion,' though, what do you think that means? What do you actually feel when you're pushing through a training session? What are you drawing on when you're deep into a race?"

I think about that for a moment. It's not really passion, even though I always call it that. "It's more like anger."

He nods. "Which is good. It's good in the sense that it's giving you so much power. But. You're not going to be able to sustain that power if you want to continue doing this at a high level."

I don't say anything. What else is there to draw on besides white-hot focus from red anger? I don't know anything else. I have so much of it, I'm confident I can sustain it forever.

"I have an exercise for you."

I sigh inwardly. I've gone through countless "exercises" with so many therapists. *Here we go again.*

"Hold your hands out. I'm going to push down on them, and you think about what makes you mad. What you use to fuel you, what you think about that motivates you. Keep that thought in your mind and resist me trying to push down."

He pushes down on my outstretched arms. I grit my teeth, and I think about the places I always go to push through. The upstairs room. Waking up to an above-the-knee amputation. The punishments in the orphanage. I think about my hands, which don't work well. And there are the things I don't envision, but I know they're there and I only brush by them: a tiny hand across a dark floor. An unexplainable, tangled ball of emotion around my birth mother.

I can't resist the push anymore. My chest caves in and my hands drop down under the pressure.

"Okay. We'll do the same thing again. But this time, think of something that makes you feel warm and happy inside."

It's all I can do not to roll my eyes. I hate this stuff. Whenever I *try* to think of something happy, my body has a pissed-off physiological response. My stomach turns inside out, my heart hurts, my skin gets hot. My body doesn't like being forced from the comfortable space of anger. But I do it anyway. I close my eyes. He pushes down.

I think of Laney in a field of enormous sunflowers. She holds a strawberry in one hand, a flower crown in the other. She's laughing. Happy.

I think of Mom. She kneels down beside my bed when I'm seven years old, holding out an elephant.

And I think of Aaron. His smile. The safe space of his arms.

I resist the push for twice the time.

When I open my eyes, the psychologist is smiling.

"When you're happy, your muscles are more relaxed. When you're angry, your muscles are tense, and they're overworking. Your body is so much more powerful when you're filled with love and light."

After, I go skiing alone, letting my thoughts mill around as I consider the psychologist's words.

I thought that sport was my therapy. It was—is—my coping mechanism. It's been a way to usher back into the darkness the terrible shadows of my past and, for the most part, stay in the light.

But what I thought was my secret power has probably been the same thing holding me back from a gold medal.

Anger is only a piece of healing. For *true* healing there has to be sadness. It's so much harder to go there than toward the anger.

My thoughts keep returning to Aaron. He's the specific key to the right door. In falling in love with him, I've realized how incomplete I still was. From the moment he and I finally got together, I began thriving as an athlete. And as a human.

With Aaron, I'm complete.

"Procter & Gamble wants you to be part of their Thank You Mom campaign."

Brant keeps pulling these out of thin air. He also got me on Team Toyota last week. In a few months, I've gone from having next to nothing to having some of the biggest brands in the world behind me.

But this one. This one puts me highest on cloud nine.

If I can't win a gold, being a part of this campaign—where Procter & Gamble recognizes the impact that athletes' moms have on them—is the biggest thank-you I could give to my mother. *She's* the one who needs to be recognized and celebrated. Every parent makes sacrifices. But Mom's gifts to me have been of a whole different magnitude. Now everyone in the world can know just how incredible she is.

But . . . maybe I can *also* win that gold.

For the first time in my life, I'm starting to believe in myself. I'm undefeated this entire season in Nordic skiing. I'm an active part of growing the sport; for a long time, few people were on social media telling stories around it. Through my sponsors and my own platforms, I'm part of showing what the sport *is*.

But there's a small problem with winning: once you've won once, people expect you to keep doing it. Now threading through my training and the rest of my waking days are thoughts of how many people I might let down and how awful it will be if I fail. I'm used to being the underdog. I don't know how to lead the pack.

I feel like something is about to happen. This road is too smooth. In my life story, if something feels too good to be true, it's usually because it *is* too good to be true. Nothing lasts.

————————

"What is that tattoo on your wrist?"

I'm at a casual photo shoot for Players' Tribune, a media platform that allows athletes to connect with people in their own words. A photographer named Taylor is getting shots of me to go with a letter that Mom's written ahead of the Games for me. I haven't read the letter yet—I'm sure it will make me break down in tears.

I tell Taylor the story of my first tattoo, how I wanted it to help remind me of my identities. She's easy to talk to; even though we just met, we have that kind of chemistry of people who've known each other their entire lives.

"I actually have a lot of tattoos. They're all related to certain stories. They're just in places no one can see because they're meant for just me."

Taylor lights up. "If you ever want to talk about them, I'd love to hear it. That's what I love most—telling the stories of athletes and their tattoos, why they got them, what they mean."

"Maybe," I say politely, hiding my horror at the idea of explaining those stories. I'm not ready.

I might never be.

————————

Our team house in Bozeman is buzzing. The 2018 Games are less than a month away.

A month and a half ago in January, right before US Nationals, I came down with a nasty mutation of a flu that made me so sick I can't remember ever being more ill. I vomited for four days straight. I lost an astonishing amount of weight. And I had to miss Nationals. I absolutely hate missing races. I recovered, got healthy, and started training again. Hard.

But I should have known then. That was the universe trying to tell me:

Your world's about to crumble.

Since Nationals, another US teammate, Shawn, has been staying in Bozeman, sleeping on our couch to train with us. He thinks everything in life is both amazing and hilarious. I could tell him that the sky is blue, and he'd start laughing—an incredible belly laugh that builds until we're both laughing at something that's not even funny. He adds a great dynamic to our house. We've turned into a family. So when he's set to leave, I decide all of us need to go to brunch together to spend one last meal as a household. I might also have a bit of side motivation: Jam! on Main Street, my favorite brunch spot, makes a killer mimosa.

I gather the troops (no small task; getting Aaron and Shawn out of the house is like herding cats), and we finally get in the car together, Aaron driving. The roads are slick; it had snowed, melted, and frozen overnight, leaving the pavement glazed in black ice. I breathe a little easier when we turn into a parking spot in downtown Bozeman near Jam!

I'm a few steps from the car when I pause. "Aaron, do you have the keys?"

Aaron often leaves the keys in the car. He's so damn trusting. I, on the other hand, am a skeptic. I don't trust anyone. I always take the keys and lock the car and double-check that it's locked.

I pivot to return to the car to grab the keys that he's no doubt left in there for anyone to take. As I turn, I register a patch of ice a split second before my foot hits it. I slip and fall backward, except it happens too fast to even have those conscious thoughts.

Me and the ground, we dance a lot. Or I should say we wrestle and collide, since *dance* implies grace, which I've never had. All the floors in every house I've lived in are scuffed and dented from my encounters with them. So I know how to fall, I'm something of an expert at it.

But this time, I fall horribly. I extend my right hand to catch myself on the icy, oil-stained pavement. But my arm doesn't catch me at all. Instead there's a white-hot bolt through the length of it, and I slam through it.

From the cold ground, I notice the sun is out. Even though it's the middle of winter, I notice that I don't feel cold. I'm not even wearing a jacket. As an amputee, I run hot. The more limbs you're missing, I've learned, the longer it takes the body to regulate temperature. So transitioning from inside to outside might take my body thirty minutes to adjust, which means I can be a hot, uncute, sweaty mess in the meantime.

Finally I notice that I haven't been able to move my arm. I can't even feel it. Then the pain seeps in.

It's everywhere. My wrist, my forearm, my triceps. It's so pervasive and horrific I can't tell what's happened or what I've injured. I still can't move my arm. I roll clumsily to sitting, then I use my left hand to move my injured right arm.

I *scream.*

Everyone is huddled around me now where I'm hunched on the pavement. "Are you okay?" someone says—I don't know who in my haze. I don't know if I'm okay, but after that scream, I'm silent now, rocking on the ground, holding the agony inside like I was trained to do since I was little.

I look up into the backlit silhouettes of my teammates and finally say, "It's fine. I'm fine. I just pulled some weird muscle or something. I just need to give it time to pass. You guys can go ahead."

"Oksana, we're in zero rush," Aaron says. "We'll wait for you."

I move to rise, then realize I have no idea how to get up. I can't bear any weight on my elbow—it just collapses. Without my own ankles or knees, getting up from the floor is dicey at the best of times. My usual routine is to roll onto my belly, put one leg behind me, lock it out, put the other leg behind me, lock it out. Then I walk myself backward with my hands one by one, until they're in front of my toes. Then I hold on to my stomach and push up on it to stand. This maneuver might be most people's idea of a workout sequence, but it's my everyday reality.

"Aaron, can I use your chair to get up?"

He rolls his wheelchair closer and locks his brakes, and I use my left arm to push up on his leg. Everyone is awkwardly quiet. I can't stand that. I fall all the time, and I can't handle it when people are embarrassed for me.

I take slow steps toward the café, holding on to my right arm. Something's definitely not right. It feels like someone is blowing up a balloon in my elbow. It's so tight.

In the entryway of the restaurant, Shawn turns to me. "Do you want to leave? We don't have to be here, we're fine going home if you want to take care of that."

"No, no, no," I say quickly. I don't want to ruin breakfast. "This is going to pass. It's just a pulled muscle."

We sit down. I'm on the cushioned bench by the window, leaning heavily against the wall on my left side. The upside, if you can call it that, of going through what I did in Ukraine and experiencing various injuries—to skin, bone, and muscle—is my ability to identify different kinds of pain and gauge how long it will take to process it and heal from it. I've been through amputations. I've suffered from intense nausea and vomiting. I've had teeth pulled, been cut with a knife, hit, worse.

But I've never experienced *this* brand of pain.

Everyone has ordered. They're all drinking coffee. They've gotten refills. I've taken two sips of mine. Me. It's not a good sign, and Shawn notices.

"Oksana," he says gently. "It seems like this is beyond the point that it's going to pass. I think you should get it x-rayed. If it ends up being nothing, that's great. But it's worth checking out."

Aaron's nodding, eyeing me with concern.

"I can't, it's too expensive," I say through gritted teeth. "I can't afford a hospital bill right now."

But by the time our food comes, my arm has gone totally straight and stiff. I'm feeling a whole different kind of hurt than I've ever before felt—which terrifies me.

"I'm just going to go call Eileen." I ease myself out of the booth to head outside. Aaron tries to come, but I wave him off.

Outside, I hesitate over her number. This is her only day off for the next month, and it's the first one she's had in three months. She was just joking the other day that her only goal was to not get out of sweatpants. But I don't know what else to do.

Eileen picks up her phone immediately. "What's up?"

"I fell." I can feel the tears start to come. My chin is quivering, my throat is closing. I know this is really bad. *How could you do this to yourself?* I try to swallow the tears, push them down, keep it together. "Something serious is wrong with my arm, maybe my elbow. I think I need an X-ray. But I'm at Jam! with the whole team. Is there any way you can come get me and drop me off at the hospital?"

After I hang up, I think how nice it would be to call Eileen one day just to say, "Hey, how are you?" Instead of "Hey, I'm falling apart again, can you help put me back together?"

Eileen pulls in a few minutes later—she must have been speeding— and as soon as I see her face through the windshield, I start sobbing. This is not going away.

As she drives toward the hospital, Eileen tries to reassure me. "We don't know what it is. Let's just wait and see what the doctors say."

I think maybe Eileen doesn't want to believe this is happening either. Our team has three medals from Sochi, and I'm on track to sweep gold in my cross-country events in Pyeongchang, and to at least podium in biathlon. Our entire team is a force. But now I might just have shorted them all. Including Eileen.

I should never have pushed us to go to brunch. I just wanted a damn mimosa (that I didn't even end up drinking) with everyone together. When we're supposed to be training and taking care of our bodies. *I'm so selfish.*

At the hospital, Eileen helps me fill out my paperwork. She writes that I was born in 1983.

"Nineteen eighty-nine!" I correct her. "I'm not *that* old."

She smiles. "Clearly you're not in that much pain," she says wryly, crossing it out and fixing it. "Actually, in all seriousness, that's one of the things that's amazing about you, Oksana: you're so good at keeping it light in stressful situations."

I don't feel light. I feel like a tornado dropped the weight of a whole town right on top of me. We go straight to X-ray, and as we sit in the ER waiting for a doctor to come in and read the results, I can't stop berating myself.

How stupid I was to believe I could have a gold medal. Life gets me so close and then takes it away. I got a taste with that bronze in rowing, and it was taken away. I was told I could keep my knee. My first-ever home in Buffalo. The dance team. All of it.

The doctor finally walks into the room, head down over the X-rays. "Basically, what you did is dislocate your elbow. In the process, the radial head fractured and the bones broke off at the connection points. That's partially why you can't bend your elbow. Bone particles are caught in the joint. A significant amount of blood has also pooled around the elbow, which is causing the tightness."

I don't breathe while he talks. This is the worst-case scenario.

Eileen just nods briskly. "Okay, so what does the recovery look like? We're leaving in two weeks for the Paralympic Games, and she's favored to win almost every event. She's a priority. What do we need to do to get her ready?"

He shakes his head. "Oh, no. There's no way. She can't race on that."

My face crumples.

Eileen purses her lips. "Okay. I hear you."

It drives me crazy when she does this to me. You can give her an answer, but if it's not the outcome she knows you're capable of, she's already moving on to how to achieve the outcome she's certain is possible. I can see the doctor's annoyed, too, but he has plenty of other patients to move on to.

"Okay, that's just the first step," Eileen says half an hour later as I walk, thankfully drugged now, back to her car. "We're going to the orthopedic surgeon in town. I already called him while you were in the bathroom."

I text an update to Aaron. It takes forever one-handed. He's incredulous. None of the rest of them can believe it either, he says—I was sitting there so quietly, how could that be what was going on inside my arm? He texts me that he's here for me and to keep him posted.

I text Mom next.

Hey. I can't talk now. But I need to talk to you once I get back from the hospital. I'm okay. But the future is very unclear.

Her response is immediate: *OMG. Yes, call me whenever you can.*

"This would be a four-to-eight-month recovery. For a *normal* person." The orthopedic surgeon looks at me pointedly, somehow encompassing my entire fraught medical history in a single instant. "She can't race."

I start crying again, amazed there are even any tears left in there. *I'm not going to the Games.* Eileen's still stone-faced, though—she's not convinced there's nothing else to do. She's not doing this for the team, I know. She's doing it for me. Because she knows the depths of what my first gold medal means to me.

Seeing Eileen's resolve, the surgeon finally turns to address me: the last resort, apparently.

"It's not possible. If you race on that elbow, you will tear it apart. You'll never be able to use it again."

All my hard work, sweat, dedication. All the times I missed Christmas and Thanksgiving for the last four years so I could train and go to qualifying races. And the sponsors. I finally get sponsors, and this is what I have to tell them. I'll have to go back to living in my car.

The doctor says gently:

"This is where your road stops."

I close my eyes.

I'll never get that gold medal for Mom.

———————

I slip quietly back into the house after Eileen drops me off. Aaron finds me crying on the bed. *Still* crying, twenty-plus years of pent-up tears all gushing out in one day. The pillowcase is soaked with them. I have to pee, but I don't know how to get up by myself with my shattered elbow. I'm scared to leave the bed.

Actually, I'm not scared. I'm terrified. Sport keeps the demons in my head at bay. But it's more than that, too. It's my career. My life. My identity.

Who am I if I can't do this anymore?

Aaron touches my shoulder. It takes me a while to look at him.

"I lost everything," I rasp out. "My dream is over."

He gets out of his chair and lies down next to me, carefully pulling me into a half embrace.

"This isn't fair. It's crushing. I know." And he does know. I overheard him talking to Travis on the phone last week. "She's just been *dominating*," he said proudly. "There's no doubt in my mind she'll win every race."

He holds on to me while the tears keep coming. Then I feel a tear that's not mine high on my cheekbone. His.

"The doctor said four to eight *months*! How am I supposed to put my legs on? Or get around at all?" I flash back to my hospital bed at Shriners and the tree outside my window. *Until then—when my abnormal body betrays me—I will move.* I sob harder.

"I'll help you," Aaron says simply.

———

Finally, I call Mom.

"Basically, I fell." I'm still sniffling, amazingly, even though I'm sure I've cried out all the fluids in my entire body by now. "I have multiple fractures in my arm and bone fragments floating around."

"You hurt yourself falling? You fall all the time!"

I smile through my tears. "I might need you to come out." I don't want to put so much pressure on Aaron to take care of me. And right now, I have to admit, I just want my mom.

"If you need me, just tell me. I'll come."

———

This is stupid. All I'm going to hear is the word no *again.*

Eileen and I are walking down an eerily empty hallway in the Steadman Clinic in Vail, Colorado. It's part of the National Medical Network, which provides care to eligible Team USA athletes. Eileen must have sent a hundred emails yesterday to get one of the surgeons to see me and get my X-rays sent at light speed. Our appointment is after his normal workday. After *everyone's* normal workday, it seems—half the lights are off, and no one's around. My arm throbbed sharply from the plane's takeoff in Bozeman to our landing in Denver. Eileen rented a car to drive us up to Vail, and we talked about everything except the injury, as if we were just normal friends on a normal road trip.

Dr. Viola meets us in an exam room. He specializes in elbows and works with the Denver Broncos and the US Snowboard team. He looks like an athlete himself. He sits down at the desk, turns to face me sitting in the chair next to it. Eileen leans against the door.

"All right, here's what I can do for you," he says directly to me.

I snap to attention from my resigned slump. *Oh my God. There's a chance.*

"First, I just want to understand. You want to compete in two weeks. And you want to race in six events?"

"Yes," I say emphatically. If I go, I'm not going to go to race in just one. Or two. I want to race in every event that I qualified for.

"Okay." He nods. "This is going to take a lot of work on your end, and you have to follow this process I'm going to give you. To. The. T. If you do this, I believe I can get you to where you can at least be there and race." He holds up his hand when he sees my expression. "I'm not telling you that you're going to win or even medal. I'm telling you there's a chance you'll be able to ski."

It's all I need to hear. I nod again.

"You need to know that if you choose to do this, you may jeopardize your elbow." He spends some time laying out all the risks. What I'll do to the joint. What it means for my life where I need two functioning arms to put my legs on, or even to push a wheelchair, should it ever come to that. He gives me all the information I need to make the decision for myself.

It doesn't take me long. "If you're saying it's possible, I'll choose to do it."

Dr. Viola pulls a pen from his pocket, clicks it open, and begins writing out a master plan.

Before we leave, Dr. Viola says, "We're going to have to extract the blood from your elbow. Go ahead and get comfortable on the exam table. I'm not going to lie to you. This is going to hurt."

"What?" I panic as he pulls an enormous needle from the tray he'd had his nurse (who was also kindly staying late for us) bring in. "I didn't know we were going to do that today. I . . . I'm not ready." I can't get enough air. I force myself onto the table—on my back—and my body instantly slides into an anxiety attack. I start hyperventilating. Maybe I can't do this after all.

Eileen's beside me in a heartbeat. "I'm right here. I'm going to give you my hand. You can squeeze it as hard as you want."

"I have a horrible grip, you know I can't squeeze that hard," I get out between shallow breaths.

"Then you can bite it. Whatever you need."

Dr. Viola slides the needle in.

"Oh my God," I scream. I'm soaking wet. The new paper under me is dissolving in my sweat. I try to get my breath under control. "Was that it? Are we done?" I gasp.

"That was just the numbing medication," Dr. Viola says while attaching an IV to the needle that *stays in my arm.* "We haven't started yet."

"Here, let's watch this race," Eileen says quickly, pulling out her phone with her free hand. The Olympics are happening right now, and Eileen pulls up a live feed. It's the women's cross-country team sprint. Kikkan Randall and Jessie Diggins. The sprint is an electrifying event, both frantic and focused, and this course in Pyeongchang is brutal with hills.

Right off the bat, the US team is in the lead pack. They're bouncing back and forth between second and third, vying with Sweden and Norway, who always dominate this sport. The US women's cross-country team has never won a gold medal. In any event. This could be huge. I forget about the needle.

Randall, in third place, hands it off to Diggins for the last leg. "Here we gooooo," shout the announcers in tinny voices over the phone speaker.

Diggins pushes to second. Goose bumps rise on my skin. All of a sudden, she surges: she's got her poles up, she's skating her ass off. She's right next to the Swedish skier, leaving the Norwegian behind.

"It's Sweden and the United States!" shouts the announcer.

Diggins pushes with everything she has. She pulls ahead. She slides her ski over the finish line an instant before the Swedish skier.

It's the first-ever gold medal for the US women's cross-country team.

Diggins falls to the ground. Randall falls on top of her, the two of them shouting and crying and hugging.

Tears are running down my cheeks as I watch them. They put everything on the line, and they just reached their goal. They lived their dream. What a pure, genuine moment. How incredible to get to watch something like that. I don't know if there's anything more powerful to witness.

I'll never experience that, I think, as thirty ccs of blood drain from my broken joint. I might be able to ski in the Games. But there's no way I'm winning *any* event. *I'll never be able to achieve that now. I can't. I can't.*

But behind that loud denial in my mind, another smaller, quieter thought peeks out. I might not even have noticed it if I weren't immobilized.

But what if you can?

When have I ever done something the easy way?

"Taaaaake . . . this broken wing . . . and learn to fly again," Aaron croons off-key while he helps me hook up the ice-fed compression brace I have to wear anytime I'm sitting still, including sleeping.

I don't want to smile. I'm sitting here getting slower while my teammates are out training, getting stronger and faster and peaking as athletes. But I can't help it. I burst out laughing. He laughs, too, triumphant.

Aaron's been doing everything for me. He puts my legs on. He pulls my pants up (all the way to my waist, like a grandma, which he thinks is hilarious)—he even learned to braid my hair. When I have to pee, he puts me on his lap and wheels me into the bathroom. I showered by myself the other day—painfully, but it was worth it—and when I pulled back the curtain, I saw that Aaron had written on the mirror with a pen, *Oksana, you're the strongest person I know.*

He's my rock. But I feel so horribly guilty. He should be sleeping well heading into these races, not listening to this damn ice machine on my arm at night. He should be recovering from training hard with everyone else, not cooking for me. I'm dragging him down with me.

I told Mom she didn't need to come out after all, but I feel bad about it. She says she trusts Eileen to take care of me and help me make smart decisions. And she trusts Aaron.

"I'm just worried about what harm you might be doing to your arm, honey," she said over the phone yesterday.

"But I'm going to lose all my sponsors. Everyone's going to be mad at me. All these media stories say I'm favored to win and I'm *not* going to win."

"All you can do is what you always do. You give an honest effort and your best effort. You race clean and be fair and compassionate whether you win or lose. That's all anyone cares about."

Mom doesn't argue any more about harming my arm. She knows that self-doubt is my biggest issue. But put me on the starting line, and I'll do everything I can. Even if it kills me.

I told Mom I'll see her in South Korea. But that was before Eileen let me try skiing for the first time today, two days before we're supposed to leave for Pyeongchang.

It hurt like *hell*. It was almost unbearable, even with the brace and the complicated compression tape from wrist to biceps. I didn't even go that far.

"I don't think I should go," I grit through my teeth to her.

"You're going. Even if you don't race. You're going."

I've gone from fighting for gold to fighting just to be on the start line.

Which isn't what sponsors want to hear, but Brant has to tell them, per our contract, what's going on with me. They've all been supportive so far, which is shocking. But they're the only ones we've told. I've kept this injury quiet, on social media, in interviews.

They'll believe they've beaten you, whether they did or not. Katy's voice.

And Bobby's: *When they know you're weak, they've gotten to you mentally. They will pounce.*

You've got this. You're strong.

twenty-one

Y ou know what you're risking if you do this," the head Olympics doctor said as he prepped the steroid shot for my elbow. It was my first task in Pyeongchang according to Dr. Viola's master plan. This shot, at this stage, was the only way I'd be able to manage the pain. "Steroids stunt the recovery process. It could cause permanent nerve damage. Ten years from now, if you want to use your arm—"

"Yes, I'm committed," I cut him off, as politely as possible.

"Okay, then. This won't hurt. And it will take the pain away."

The doctor lied about the first part. It hurt like a bitch. (Eileen let me hold her hand again. She challenged me to try to break her fingers this time. Good thing my grip still sucks, or I might have.) Right now, two days later, at the start of the Games in my first event, the biathlon sprint, my arm hurts so bad that it's clear the doctor was also incorrect about the second part.

I hit the ground for my first round of shooting, having no idea what to expect—I'm teaching myself, in the middle of a race, how to shoot with this brace on my shooting arm. Pain already radiates everywhere from the climbing sections on the first lap. Now I can feel every cell in my elbow, every torn ligament, every bone fragment pulsing in agony. The elbow feels like it's *moving*. It's totally unstable. I try to find my focus through the fog of pain.

I hit all of my targets.

Holy shit.

I get back on the course. John is there on one of the corners. "Masters, you're in second!"

WHAT?!

I cross the finish line. I win silver.

I'm in a daze. It feels impossible. I went from not even knowing if I would be on the start line last night to getting a medal. I hear a commotion and look over to see people surrounding my teammate Kendall. I glance up at the board. She won gold. It's her first Paralympic gold medal, in her first Games.

Oh my God, US went one and two. This is amazing. What an incredible way to kick things off.

Then my thoughts nose-dive. Kendall only *just* started skiing. She's never known failure. She's never known what it's like to get so close and fall short. Success happened so instantly for her. Her road was so smooth and effortless. Instead of being happy for her, as I should be, I can only focus on what a bitter pill it is to swallow.

This is my *fourth* Paralympic Games. I've been on my quest for ten *years*, on a road twisted in U-turns and blocked by angry mudslides.

Maybe I'm meant to always be only second or third.

Day two of the Games is the cross-country long. This is my favorite event. It's the event that won me my first silver medal, in Sochi. After debriefing with Aaron last night (by *debriefing*, I mean venting irrationally about how much I hate this and don't want to do it anymore), he helped me realize *I won silver* on day one. I could still potentially fight for a gold. Just one. I only want one gold medal. And I could do it in this event, *my* event.

I put on the brace and the tape, winding it extratight. Too tight. It cuts off the circulation as I'm racing. I can't climb without pain so intense that I don't even have words for it—me, who's so good at describing pain. Climbing, usually my strength, becomes my weakness. And it's clear that in the three weeks I've taken off, I've lost my fitness. I disappear into the pain cave and just do what I can to finish. Only finish, that's all I ask.

Then there's John's voice on the last stretch cutting through.

"You're in third! Dig, Masters, dig! You didn't come this far for fourth place!"

I look around and there's the Russian athlete, right on my tail, that I've been dimly aware I've been neck and neck with for some time. John points her out. He knows I need the competition. "Beat her, beat her!" he shouts.

I struggle across the finish line, coming in third by only two or three seconds.

Kendall wins. Again.

I'm so demoralized. I feel broken. Physically and mentally. I can't go on anymore.

I can't do this.

"Oksana!" A reporter catches me as I'm leaving the course. I force a smile. "How do you feel about your teammate winning back-to-back gold? The first golds in cross-country and biathlon for the US in the Paralympics. I know you were favored to win. Can you tell me how that feels?"

I'm speechless for a minute. How it feels? It hurts. *Deeply.* Knowing everything I put into the last years to be the one to achieve that, and someone else just walked in and got it. But it's also so exciting that Kendall—my teammate, my friend—is the one who achieved it. That Team USA achieved it. It's historic. On the podium, all the anger turns to pride.

Most people still don't even know why I'm wearing a brace. I don't want my injury to get even more into my head than it already is. Or into anyone else's head. To anyone who's asked why I'm wearing it, I just reply, "Oh, I'm working through some things."

But that's all too much to articulate right now to this reporter. And so all I say is "It's great. She's having an incredible debut."

I pole away on my ravaged arm.

Today: biathlon middle distance. It's five ski laps with four shooting stages. I had a day off after the cross-country long, and I used it to talk myself into being present for this race.

I can tell my fitness is coming back. I'm skiing well. My shooting's not the best, but at least I'm skiing. I've been bouncing between third and fourth position.

I'm coming into the curved downhill on my fourth lap, heading into the range for my last shooting stage. It's warm on this sunny afternoon, and at least half of the snow here is fake, so it's slushy and sticky, like syrupy sugar. My sit ski slips out.

As I'm falling, my instinct is to stick out my right hand.

My arm shocks like a thunderbolt. I wipe out completely and roll, lost in the agony of it. I push myself up with my left hand and have to start the uphill from scratch, with zero momentum.

My elbow's moving. It won't stick together. I come into the range and set up to shoot. But I can't bear any weight on the elbow. The pain is from another universe. I take forever to shoot because I can't set the rifle down. The salt from my tears, from the pain, mixes with snot on my lip. I can't focus; the only thing in my brain is the burn in my elbow intensifying with every second.

I miss four shots. Four penalty loops.

I'm far out of medal potential now, but all that matters is crossing the finish line. It's all over. I'll never ski again. I'll probably never cycle again.

I've done what all the doctors warned me about: my arm is permanently destroyed.

But I'll finish this last race.

Eileen's out on the lap course. Over her radio, she hears from our range coach: "Oksana missed four shots."

"Was it the wind?" Eileen asks. The wind has been variable today. It was brisk a minute ago.

"Honestly, I think she just couldn't see the targets through her tears."

Eileen tenses. "Can you get over to the penalty loop? Tell her she needs to stop. She's super-tough, if she's crying, there's a serious reason for it. Tell her to stop."

The range coach yells at me on my second penalty lap. "Do you want to stop?"

"No!" I gasp out. "There's just something wrong with my elbow."

I don't care if I'm dead last. I won't have a DNF next to my name. Not now.

"She won't stop," he says over the radio.

Eileen's post is on the far side of the course from the penalty loop. She starts running.

On my next lap, Eileen is there. "Stop, stop," she shouts. "Think about the next race!"

I don't stop. I ski past her. Eileen sprints after me. She plants herself in front of me and puts her hands out.

"You're done, you're done," she says to me gently.

I break down. I'm sobbing.

"We got this. It's going to be okay. Get on my back."

I try to extricate myself one-handed from my sit ski. We do this all the time. But a camera crew is right behind Eileen, and they zero in on what looks like a dramatic scene. She plants herself squarely in front of them, blocking me from their view.

She reaches back to help me. "Just put your sunglasses on, put your head down on my shoulder." She knows I don't want anyone to see me cry. She starts jogging with me on her back off the course, heading straight for the team doctor.

It's the longest ride of my life.

So many people are in the Sports Med room in the village. Eileen, my coach. John, our performance director. Amber, our team doctor. Another Olympics doctor whose name I didn't even catch. Essentially, they say, the joint subluxated: it popped out and then popped back in again. The ligaments are beyond stretched.

"I'm sorry to say," the nameless doctor says, "but unfortunately, it's over."

I don't know how many times I have to hear this before I believe it. But this time, it's like someone's snapped a plastic bag over my face. My body flashes hot and sweaty.

It feels like it's been hours of them talking over my head and examining me. It's only been forty-five minutes. But that's been enough time for me to process things in my head. I didn't do any new damage, other than further stretching the ligaments.

The next race is the cross-country sprint. I want vindication in this race. In Sochi, Jane intentionally impeded me; she skied over my skis, bringing me to a dead stop. We never protested it because she was my own teammate.

"I want to race the sprint." Amber and the doctor exchange a look. "Tomorrow's an off day. I'll do everything I can."

"You don't understand," the doctor says. "You have to think past this two weeks of racing, about the longevity of your arm. You're already going to need surgery. There's likely already permanent nerve damage. As a double above-the-knee amputee, you can't risk the quality of your arm any further."

"Exactly. I already need surgery. It's already broken. So how do we support it for the sprint? What's possible here?"

From my room after the marathon medical session, I call Mom's hotel. She was at the race, but wasn't in a spot to be able to see what happened. She spent the afternoon trying not to worry herself sick until Eileen called and updated her.

"They told me I'm done." I hear Mom take a breath to comfort me and I cut her off. "I told them I'm not. I'm going to race."

Mom is quiet for a minute. "Is it smart?" she finally asks.

"Probably not. But I'm going to try anyway."

The morning of the sprint, Amber spends fifteen minutes taping my arm. We experimented yesterday, settling on a mix of rigid and low elasticity to mimic ligaments. Now, as I sit on the bench in the team room watching her work, I can't stop second-guessing myself.

The sprint is short. But this is a long day. If I make it through the qualifier and the heat into the finals, I'll end up racing three times.

Amber adds another piece of tape on top of the web that's become my arm.

I'm not known for making the smartest choices—as Mom already knows. Is this the right one? Eileen's told me over and over that if I'm risking my body, I better know why. I better be okay with it.

All over the room are the banners of my sponsors, who turned out, to a one, to support me unconditionally. Toyota's slogan for the Games looks back at me from the wall: *Start your impossible.*

My very first partner, KT Tape: *Finish stronger.*

And the P&G words that jolt my heart every time: *Thank you, Mom.*

Amber finishes with the last piece of tape.

Here's what I do know: the pain of regret—the what-ifs, the failure—will outlast the pain of surgery. It will run deeper than the permanent nerve damage that will affect every day of the rest of my life.

I can't think of worse pain than that of regret.

I end up with the fastest qualifying time in my first heat of the cross-country sprint. In the middle of it all, when I knew I was racing well, everything just . . . *switched* for me. I knew in my body this was the right decision.

I want to see what's possible.

I'm the only American in the final. As the women find their places on the start line, I try to focus on anything but my elbow, which is throbbing and radiating a searing sensation all the way up to my fingertips. It feels fat and powerless, despite our intricate tape job.

I close my eyes. I think of Mom out there in the stands. I think of Aaron, everything he's been to me over the last three weeks even while trying to focus on his own races.

Then the announcers start shouting over the loudspeakers. The men's sprint final is coming down the last leg, finishing just before the women start. I look up and over. All the men are streaming down the last hill. My teammate Andy is in the back. This is his last Games, he's said. He won't compete anymore after this.

But right now, he looks like he's flying. He's picking people off, racer by racer, closer and closer to the finish line. The announcers are screaming. The crowd, my coaches, my teammates, me—we're all screaming together. My competitors remain calm on the start line, staring at me in my explosion of emotion.

Andy comes in first, only just barely beating out the athlete from Belarus. It's Andy's first gold medal. The stands go wild. He raises his arms to the sky.

The beep goes off, and it's like Andy handed me his momentum. I'm so pumped.

But I go nowhere.

I'm third off the line, with no power in my elbow. On the first corner, the Russian athlete cuts ahead of me. The snow is much softer now in the afternoon than when we started this morning, and every pole push is killing me.

What if I gave away everything in the qualifier and the heat, and I have nothing left now in the final? *This can't be happening.*

I can feel the anger at my situation rising.

I use it. I attack every hill. It hurts so much, but I know the minute I get over each hump, I'll have an instant of rest for my elbow on the down. I pass the Russian girl. I can't catch the German girl at all, though, until finally I pass her on the last climb. But then there's a right turn. On my right elbow. I hit the pole, and the pain is so blinding I freeze.

I hear the German coach screaming. Her athlete is right on my ski tips.

I don't think so.

Everything comes down to this moment.

I pull out everything I have left. I shut out the insane pain that's getting worse. I can feel the girl's breath. She's right behind me, even with everything I've got. I don't want to look back, I won't show that I'm worried and exhausted and *I'm so mad* that I'm in this position at all and all I want is to stop.

Then I feel the push. Someone propels me forward.

It pushes me through the misery and into a second wind. When I finally look back over my shoulder, the German athlete is nowhere near me. I'm out front.

I cross the finish line.

I slide to a stop, cradling my elbow. I can't comprehend anything right now.

Eileen runs up. She kneels down and pulls my forehead to hers. "I am. So. Proud. Of you."

"What just happened?" It still doesn't register. I haven't fully emerged from the cave yet.

"You did it." She chokes up. "You're a gold medalist."

The wave of emotion hits its crest, breaks over me. I'm smiling, sobbing. I can't speak for a minute. When finally I can, all I can say is "I never thought I would actually do it."

She smiles through her own tears. "I always thought you could."

Aaron appears out of nowhere. He hugs me from behind. He's laughing and shouting and then we're both crying together there on the snow, wrapped in each other's arms.

"You think I can get away with not wearing this brace?" I ask Eileen. My first gold medal ceremony, and the brace will be memorialized in pictures for a lifetime. I don't want it in pictures. I don't want this memory at all.

"No, you wear that. You just did this on a broken elbow. You wear that proud." Then she gets serious, Eileen-style. "Also, you have another race. We discussed that you would follow doctor directions to the letter."

I try to fit the brace under the Team USA jacket, but the sleeve is too tight. *Fine. Just don't cry on the podium,* I tell myself. *It's overrated. Just hold yourself together.*

Ours is the last award ceremony for the day. It's late in the evening when we walk out onto the podium: the Russian athlete in third, the German athlete in second, and me. In first. The official hangs the gold medal around my neck. Then she hands me a stuffed black bear, the mascot of the 2018 Winter Paralympic Games.

It represents courage and a strong will to prevail.

I look down at it. I flash back to a little girl and a white bear in a different part of South Korea, four years ago. One dream was dying on the water as my back gave out, just as the fire for another dream was lit on snow. Life sometimes has the most imperfect, chaotic way of working out. It delivered me here, but I had to untangle the knots to arrive in this place, pulling at all the snarls to get to the end.

The American flag starts rising. The anthem begins, and I put my hand over my heart. The key tattoo pulses beside it.

I look down to my coaches in the crowd: John, Eileen. Amber's there, too. Most of my teammates are there: Andy, Kendall. Aaron. They're why I'm standing here at all. There are always those who doubt you—there were so many along the way. And then there are those who believe in you. I wish I could put them all on the podium with me—everyone here and not here, such as Randy and Bobby. I understand suddenly that *this* is what I was chasing: this experience of standing in the middle of the podium and looking into the eyes of the people who got me here.

Then I find Mom in the crowd. Tears stream down her face. I stop trying to hold myself together.

To anyone seeing this now, I'm at the peak moment of a peak race at the peak of my life. Social media, reporters, my sponsors—all are just now tuning in and highlighting my success. It looks like my path was effortless. The media love to show airbrushed, buttoned-up versions of the people we put on pedestals. What they often fail to capture is the rough road barricaded in setbacks along the way—the hard parts—that can drive a will to succeed.

The anthem ends, and I bring my gold medal to my lips.

After time in the media room (mostly quiet this late) . . . after John ambushes me with his iPhone camera and excitedly calls out questions ("Oksana, what just happened? How do you feel? Who are you right now?" and I barely respond that I'm a gold medalist) . . . after a mold is made of my handprint, which will be added to those of other gold medalists to form a celebratory mural (I've never been so proud to see the mark of my ugly hand) . . . I finally find Mom.

This moment is happening so much later than I ever wanted it to. It took me so long to earn this physical symbol for her. Everything I've just done was rooted in fulfilling this promise.

I never imagined it would be so hard.

The arena is mostly empty. It's not the picture-perfect scene I had in my mind with a bright and colorful backdrop of celebration. Lights are being turned off, things are shutting down, and people are leaving.

It's a perfect fit for the story of our life.

I put my hands on Mom's shoulders and look at her. Then I take the medal from my neck, and I hang it around hers.

As its weight settles on her, she smiles. The same smile from the passport photo, that shines from the inside out. It doesn't matter that it's dark in the arena. Right then, she is all the light I need.

epilogue

et's start with the flower-to-birds tattoo. What did that come from?"
Taylor is filming me. This time, she approached Katie, my publicist, whom I started working with just before Pyeongchang. "I really want to work with Oksana on this project about her tattoos," Taylor had said to Katie, outlining a video/photograph series of my body art with me telling the stories behind them.

It's been two years since Pyeongchang. (The first thing I did when I got home was pay off my debts, so I was no longer getting collection calls. I'd never felt so free in my life.) I'm more used to giving interviews now, even though I still don't talk much about my past. But I thought I was good enough now at sharing the parts people want to hear that I could finally make this video project happen for Taylor. So I accepted.

"Do I show it?" I ask. I'm wearing a beige sports bra and boy shorts for the shoot. We're at my house, in my living room, where Taylor has draped gray curtains and set up lights. I banished Aaron to our bedroom for this, and I try to pretend he's not here at all.

"Yeah, for sure."

I peel the shorts down a little to expose my hip bone. When I was nineteen, I got a tattoo of a dead flower with its seeds blowing in the wind to become birds.

"Um. This one was kind of . . . I don't know. I consider myself a very free-spirited person." I stall to gather my thoughts, looking down at the

315

tattoo. "I think it came from me rowing, and the release I got from it in not needing to verbalize everything that I'd held in so much." I seem to hit my stride a bit, so I keep going. "I woke up one morning with this vision: I had this flower, and it was being blown away into birds and just letting go. I was listening to Frou Frou, and her song 'Let Go,' that says, 'Jump in, Oh well, whatcha waiting for?' It's kind of . . . I guess . . . the metamorphosis of me starting to love myself as I got into sports. Loving who I am, accepting my uniqueness. The fact that I don't have my full body and I was different, but . . . Just let go, you never know what life's going to bring you."

I come to a stop, embarrassed. My tattoos have been a way of facing my past. For me, though. It never occurred to me to use them as a way to tell my story publicly, and I'm not nearly as prepared for this as I thought I was.

"So, sort of like freedom?" Taylor nudges.

"Freedom, and just letting go of . . ." I shake my head, trying to figure out the right words. "Of a lot that . . . has happened, of uncontrollable things that I think, for such a long time . . . I tried to control my thoughts of . . . not the most comforting thoughts from things I experienced—back in my early years . . ." I trail off, uncomfortable, swinging my arms slightly to shake it off. I cough into my arm—I'm getting over pneumonia, and I hate that I look so pale for this shoot.

Taylor tells me not to worry, we'll go slow, talk about whatever I want. Taylor says, "Let's move on to the key."

I tell her the safe stuff: how I have a memory of looking through a keyhole at a TV, how I love old doors.

Then I stall out. "I don't know how to . . . how to talk about my friend there . . . in a way . . ."

Taylor's there to catch me. "It's okay to say that some things are just for you, and you don't have to talk about them. But sometimes it's good to talk through those things, so you can understand why it's just for you. And we can edit out and cut anything you don't want in there."

I nod. After a moment, I start talking about Laney. For the first time since I left the orphanage, I talk about her. Hugs, sunflowers, love. But I skirt the dark things and end up on subjects far away from her.

Taylor redirects me to the stories on my body. She asks me about the rose tattoo.

The same thing happens—I start, tell some things, come up against the wall of how I got the slash that it covers—and I say for the third or fourth time in twenty minutes:

"I don't . . . I don't know how to say it."

I can't talk about one thing in my past without talking about the things it refers to. I can't talk about Laney saving my life and expect someone to understand it without also talking about how she saved it. I can't talk about surviving without talking about what it was I was struggling so desperately to survive.

You can love the whole of yourself—which I think I do now, finally—but hate the marring and imperfection that is part of the whole. It's like loving a house: you can hate the cracks in the walls but love the potential it shows on the outside.

Helplessly, I ask Taylor, without really expecting a response:

"How do you say the hard parts of your story out loud?"

Taylor turns the camera off and says, "If this was your best friend, and she's telling you this story right now—you're the one who's listening— what would you be thinking? Would you be encouraging her to share this? Or telling her to stop because she doesn't want to make other people uncomfortable?"

What if it were Laney sharing her story? Or another little girl, or boy, who's dealing with all these things and just feels so misunderstood because they have all these parts of their story that make it hard for people to understand where they're coming from? Maybe they just need to know that others have similar stories. Maybe they need someone they can connect to and bond with because that person understands exactly what they went through.

But I don't say any of that. Taylor reminds me that tomorrow we'll do a full interview (with my clothes on, thankfully), so I have plenty of time to process today. She tells me I don't have to say anything I don't want to say. She suggests I take some time tonight to think. Just to see what comes up.

I pour a glass of red wine. Aaron is out with some friends. I settle myself on the couch, and I just think.

I worry what will happen if I tell people about my past. How will they view me? How will the average person whom I've never even met, but who hears my story, perceive me? Would their strongest emotion be pity? It's just like with my prosthetics. When people look at me, I don't want them to just see my limitations.

My sponsors. What will *they* think? They're my lifeline right now. Why would they support someone like me, once they know?

Mom. She still doesn't know so many of these things: how Laney died, how I got that scar. Hasn't my mom been through enough without having to deal with this, too?

And Aaron.

If I told this story, why would he—why would anyone—ever choose to love me?

I can't fathom why I would do this to myself. To them.

I think about all the dreams I haven't yet achieved. I dream about the day I finally have the resources to take care of my mother. I dream about having my own children. I'd teach them to be strong and independent, to have their own voices. Because for the longest time I didn't know how to see power in myself or how to think, *I am strong.*

I find myself wanting to say to *any* girl or boy, no matter what age, if you look different or think you look different, *never* let society determine what you see when you look in the mirror. *Never* accept the limited views of others regarding what you can achieve, who you can be.

I remember Eileen's question from all those years ago: "What would you say to your eight-year-old self?" Now I know. I'd tell her, *Don't change a thing. Keep on fighting.*

This is not your forever.

There are so many layers to all of us. Nearly every person has some kind of hard experience or trauma, emotional or physical—some worse than others. Often we replace that pain with some other pain: cutting, drinking (I've done plenty of that, too), whatever pain makes us feel like we're in control. We think we're helping ourselves but we're doing the opposite.

I was lucky enough to find an outlet that was healthy, rowing, and I learned to use my past as fuel—instead of living in that trauma nonstop. That was thanks to Mom. She opened the doors of sports and waited for me until I was ready to walk through. But not everyone has a mom like mine to open those doors for them. Maybe they need a different kind of door.

I think about how at first glance people might think I'm a superhero. But it's so important that they understand *life is messy.* It's okay not to come from beautiful experiences. And it's okay to talk about them and share them and use them as the engine to get where you want to go.

After hours of thinking, I keep coming back to the other women out there, and other children, who've been through what I have—and how meaningful my story might be to them. I keep thinking how important it might be for them to see me, not just unbroken, but alive and well. Not as some object of pity, but as an example of strength. As a woman who's gained power on the other side of her trauma, and who deserves to be known not as the sum of her experiences but as the sum of her actions.

The next morning, we're back in my living room. I'm sitting on the floor.

Taylor has the camera turned on. "Are you ready?"

An image of Laney flashes into my mind: she puts her hands on my shoulders, looks into my face, then pulls me in for a long hug.

I hope that she's happy with how I've chosen to live my life—that instead of getting lost in the dark, I've chosen to celebrate life and all it has to offer.

The image of Mom comes next, when she knelt down next to my bed in that darkness and saved me from it.

There are some things I won't ever express. They're only for me. But I can share my story of failures and successes and everything in between—those things that make *all* of us human. Everything that prepared me for what I needed to step onto the start line and reach the finish.

I take a deep breath.

And I begin.

To the people of Ukraine: my thoughts are with you as you endure your own hard parts. Fortunately, as I've learned, on the other side of darkness there is light. Слава Україні

acknowledgments

F irst and foremost: Mom, I'd like to thank you for all the sacrifices you made for me (the ones I know of and ones I don't). Without you, I wouldn't even be here to live, race, dream, and, most important, thrive. Thanks for choosing me. Without you, there'd be no story to tell.

Cassidy Randall, my creative partner, you worked tirelessly and helped give my story a voice. You truly listened to me and brought my story to life. You took the vulnerable and raw parts and helped make them whole.

Thanks to the team at Scribner, especially Rick Horgan, my editor, and Nan Graham, my publisher, for listening to me and believing that there was a story to tell. Thanks for giving me the opportunity to write this book, and for your continued faith in my story.

Many other Scribner staffers worked countless hours on *The Hard Parts,* including, in marketing, Brianna Yamashita and Zoe Coe; in publicity, Clare Maurer; and, in the art department, Jaya Miceli. They were all early readers and champions of the book. Thanks for all your efforts in support of *The Hard Parts.*

Thanks also to my book agents at Aevitas Creative, Michael Signorelli and Max Edward, for being there from the beginning. You helped light the spark within me to tell my story and you gave me the confidence to share it with the world.

Bobby, Randy, Rob, Eileen, Amber, and the Louisville Adaptive Rowing Club—you've all been instrumental in my life. Thank you.

Thanks to Brant and Katie for your guidance and support—you're the best.

Titka Sherry, you traveled at your own expense to Ukraine with my mom. You taught me how to make a blanket for my first doll, took turns with my mom when I stayed in the bathtub for hours, and swam in the pool with me at our magnificent hotel in Warsaw as we began our journey to my new home. Your sense of adventure gave my mom badly needed comfort as she embarked on the difficult adoption process. Thanks for taking this journey with us.

My grandma and grandpa loved me fiercely in the few years we had together. My grandma convinced grandpa to help my mom financially so she could adopt me. My grandpa wanted to write a check so that I'd have a new boat and could travel to the World Cup for my Paralympic dream when US Rowing wasn't willing to take a chance on me. He did this from his deathbed. That support helped propel me to my first bronze medal at the 2012 Games. I know he was with me in the boat.

Aaron, it wasn't until you came into my life that I truly started to live. You make me laugh when I want to cry. You help me see the bright side in the middle of the darkest moments. I never knew a love like this could ever exist—that I could ever feel this way. Your passion and how you love *all* parts of me helped me learn how to truly love myself.

I also can't forget to thank Laney. You were my friend from the orphanage and someone I claim as my sister. You protected me then— to the death. You are a part of all my sporting accomplishments as much as you were my family during the hard parts. I feel you in that unexpected puff of wind at my back that seems to push my boat, ski, or bike, and I feel you in the strength that flows into my exhausted arms and burning lungs. You will always be my "why."